THE SHADOW
IN THE EAST

THE SHADOW IN THE EAST

Vladimir Putin and the
New Baltic Front

Aliide Naylor

I.B.TAURIS
LONDON • NEW YORK • OXFORD • NEW DELHI • SYDNEY

I.B. TAURIS
Bloomsbury Publishing Plc
50 Bedford Square, London, WC1B 3DP, UK
1385 Broadway, New York, NY 10018, USA

BLOOMSBURY, I.B. TAURIS and the I.B. Tauris logo are trademarks of
Bloomsbury Publishing Plc

First published in Great Britain 2020

Copyright © Aliide Naylor, 2020

Aliide Naylor has asserted her right under the Copyright, Designs and Patents
Act, 1988, to be identified as Author of this work.

For legal purposes the Acknowledgements on p. vi constitute an extension
of this copyright page.

Cover design by Adriana Brioso
Cover image: Winter in Tallinn, Estonia. (© e_rasmus/Getty Images)

A catalogue record for this book is available from the British Library.

A catalogue record for this book is available from the Library of Congress.

ISBN: HB: 978-1-7883-1252-3
        ePDF: 978-1-7867-3644-4
        eBook: 978-1-7867-2638-4

Typeset by RefineCatch Limited, Bungay, Suffolk
Printed and bound in Great Britain

To find out more about our authors and books visit www.bloomsbury.com
and sign up for our newsletters.

CONTENTS

ACKNOWLEDGEMENTS

First and foremost, I would like to thank Thomas Stottor, who saw the potential in the article that led to this book, had continued confidence in it, and whose constructive advice has made it exponentially better. I would also like to thank Tomasz Hoskins who took over as my editor after Thomas left and brought the book over the finish line. Both of you have been very patient and encouraging, and you are not only great editors, but lovely people too.

I am indebted to Marc Bennetts and David Patrikarakos. I sought professional advice from both of you, and you have given me a great deal of your time and engaged in several hilarious and informative conversations. Marc, you read my early chapters and encouraged me with your positive feedback, while injecting everything with your dry humour. David, you connected me with people looking for regional expertise and have been championing my writing. You're a constant source of motivation and I am very grateful for that. I hope this work lives up to both of your high standards.

My heartfelt thanks go to the numerous people who facilitated my research over the course of writing this book. Primarily, my interviewees who gave me their time and multitude of varied perspectives. As I travelled, several people hosted me for free. It is impossible to name them all. However, I am particularly thankful to Ieva (and family) for allowing me to stay at the Ventspils apartment without being there herself, having never previously met me. Eugenijus too, for basically saving the project by selling me a ten-year-old laptop for €40 in Vilnius after mine unexpectedly broke. I am grateful to Rees and countless others on the ground who gave me vital assistance, and the two anonymous reviewers who provided insightful and extraordinarily helpful feedback on the manuscript. This book could not have existed without any of you.

One of the pitfalls of having lived abroad for so long means losing touch with old friends, and emerging with new friends scattered across the globe. I am thankful for the depths of the connections that have survived despite long periods of physical distance. I am particularly grateful to Ian Helmke, who has been a seemingly inexhaustible supply of support, love, and patience. You have motivated and sympathized, brought me coffee and sashimi, and keep tolerating me even on days when it must be quite difficult to. Thank you, for everything. Hazel McMichael and Ben Conroy, you are dear, unfailingly reliable friends, and I love you both deeply. Delphine d'Amora, for several insightful, empathetic conversations even if only via Skype. Solange Masher, Noah Woodman, Helen R. Lewis, Doug Wills, the TW Forum crowd. I would be lost without all of you. Zhenya Pavlovna, Simone Peek, William Echols for so much hilarity, creativity and such meaningful relationships while abroad, and the lovely game group (Jen, Angela, Robin, Maria, Elisa, Luca, Shobhan, Tom, He Xiang) upon my return to the UK. I am also thankful for various tutors and academics over the years, who have both inspired and helped me. At undergrad, Emmett Sullivan, for making me believe in myself, and Holocaust historian Dan Stone, who ran an absorbing comparative course on genocide, as well as staff and faculty in the 2011–12 MA cohort at the European University at St Petersburg for imparting their vast knowledge in such a difficult academic climate. I would love to list scores of twentieth-century (and particularly late-imperial/Soviet) historians but I again fear running out of space.

Equally importantly, I would like to extend my thanks to the editors and staff at *The Moscow Times*, who helped me hone my writing skills in the early stages of my career and and who gave me the opportunity to do my first 'serious' reporting. I am similarly grateful to various editors at the list of publications mentioned in my biography, in particular Anoosh Chakelian at *New Statesman* and Jessica Leber during her period with *Vocativ*, both of whom have been as meticulous as they are kind and communicative. My gratitude also goes to Gordana Andric and Siri Sollie, with whom I worked closely as an editor myself.

Last (but not least), to my family. My mother Linda, father Robert, Alari, Elvine, Paige (and Nick!), as well as the various branches in Canada, Scotland, New Zealand and Estonia.

INTRODUCTION

In the centre of the Lithuanian capital Vilnius, close to the ebbs and flows of the Baltic city's main train and bus stations, US President Donald Trump, with his infamous wisp of orange and blonde, is exhaling a jet of vapour through pursed lips into the expectant mouth of a heavy-lidded Vladimir Putin. Trump cradles the Russian president's head in his left hand, a lit cannabis joint resting between his fingers, dense smoke spiralling upwards.

This street art is pasted on the wall of café Keule Ruke. The name loosely translates as 'The Pig Smoked', using a parochial dialect and a play on words to suggest that the pig is either smoking a cigarette, or that the meat sold inside could be of the smoked variety. The image originally depicted Trump and Putin locked in an even tighter embrace when it appeared in the first half of 2016; an homage to Soviet leader Leonid Brezhnev and German Democratic Republic (GDR) leader Erich Hönecker who were snapped kissing by photographer Régis Bossu in 1979, and immortalized on the Berlin Wall in 1990 by Russian artist Dmitri Vrubel in a painting titled *My God, Help Me to Survive This Deadly Love*.

In present-day Lithuania, sandwiched between Latvia, Belarus, Poland and Russia, the image touches several nerves. Both Trump and Putin are wearing identical black track jackets, suggesting a superficial similarity in political identity, and the closeness of two modern world leaders acting in agreement with little regard for any external background entities. Supremely wealthy, yet both attired in streetwear. The appropriation of an image from the now-defunct Berlin wall evokes a definitive pivot towards Europe, especially when combined with the visibility of suggested drug usage and homosexuality – both of which in Russia would be touted as symbols of 'western decadence'. There, the promotion of 'homosexual behaviour among minors' is against the law. To the left of the picture, English-language text reads 'make everything great again'.

Trump and Putin are both easily recognizable figures in Lithuania, and indeed the other two Baltic states, Latvia and Estonia. However, it seems unlikely that the average American could pick out any presidents of Estonia, Latvia or Lithuania from a line-up. In October 2018, the US president himself reportedly managed to confuse the Baltics and the Balkans, blaming the Baltics for the war in the former Yugoslavia, despite being married to a woman from Slovenia, which was itself part of the war-torn region until independent Slovenia was recognized in late 1991–early 1992.[1]

The Baltic countries are smaller than most US states: Estonia's population is 1.3 million – about the same as New Hampshire or Maine. London has seven times the number. Latvia has just under 2 million, and Lithuania is approximately 2.9 million. They are hardly global heavyweights. Yet somehow, these minuscule nations have managed to collectively resist one of the largest superpowers of the twentieth century, the Soviet Union. The countries were the first outlying Soviet republics to start rebelling, demanding their freedom from Moscow. Nationalist movements in each country were adept at forging alliances with pro-independence movements in every region, and soon after republics such as Ukraine, Georgia, Armenia and Moldova started seeking independence too. Without the momentum of the Baltic nationalist movement, preceded and facilitated by the last Soviet leader Mikhail Gorbachev's liberalization policies, the Soviet Union may not have collapsed in 1991.

While Russia's domestic politics have since undergone dramatic periods of transition (which will be covered later in the book), including Putin's first stint as president in the year 2000, the geopolitical arena has changed significantly in the past decade or so, especially in Russia's near-abroad. In 2008, Georgia (the country) started a war with Russia after months of Russian provocations, which ultimately allowed Russia to recognize parts of Georgia's territory in the north, Abkhazia and South Ossetia, as independent states (the majority of other countries recognize Abkhazia and South Ossetia as Georgian territory under Russian occupation).

In 2014, a revolution in the Ukrainian capital, Kyiv (or a coup, as Russia reasonably terms it), ultimately saw Russia annexing the Crimean peninsula from Ukraine in March 2014. Russia-backed separatists in eastern Ukraine attempted to form further self-proclaimed breakaway 'people's republics': the Donetskaya Narodnaya Respublika (DNR) – recognized only by South Ossetia – and Luganskaya Narodnaya Respublika (LNR). There was an almost immediate wave of news stories declaring that the Baltic states were growing increasingly nervous about their own fates in the wake of Russian aggression in the near-abroad, specifically with regards to former Soviet republics. While the Baltic countries are small nations, Crimea's population is also fewer than 2 million people. The annexation issue still garnered a stupendous amount of coverage on a global scale. Along the Europe-Russia border, the local is the geopolitical, and the affairs of smaller states have repercussions worldwide.

Historically torn between east and west, the Baltic states have in recent years faced the question of whether they are better off under potentially friendly relations between Trump and Putin or mired in the haze of a 'new Cold War'. Trump's ascension to the US presidency at the beginning of 2017 after soaring to a surprise victory in the 2016 elections brought with it a host of questions in both Russia and each of the Baltic states alike, amid rumours of 'collusion' – that Russia had actively intervened in the US elections to secure a Trump-fronted executive. Over the course of Trump's campaign, Putin paid Trump compliments saying Russia would welcome good relations with him at the helm of the nation, and as the pair shared their first official phone call at the end of January 2017, the Baltics warily watched to see what this would mean for their security, that of Europe, and their place in the world order. A perceived shift towards 'great power' politics and right-wing populism signposted a possible step away from cross-border cooperation and the 'rules-based international order', as lauded by its proponents, who in many cases were key in shaping it.[2] The UK's Brexit vote also threw notions of a united Europe into question, inspiring both similar movements and blowback on the continent. I will be exploring this further in Chapter 6.

In 2004, the Baltic states joined the North Atlantic Treaty Organization (NATO) – a US-led military alliance which today consists of twenty-nine states. The following year, in 2005, Putin called the dissolution of the Soviet Union 'the greatest geopolitical disaster of the twenty-first century'. In historian Neil Taylor's book about the history of Estonia, he recounts an anecdote in which Putin listened to the president of a freshly independent Estonia giving a speech in Hamburg in the 1990s. Lennart Meri denounced the Soviet occupation of the Baltics, reportedly prompting Putin to exit the room in outrage.[3] Since he assumed Russia's presidency, various pundits have suggested that Putin, a former KGB officer, seeks to restore the territory of the former Soviet Union.

Location-wise, the Baltic states are the most vulnerable of all NATO states, nestled in north-eastern Europe underneath Finland, each one sharing some form of border with Russia. The alliance's Article 5 ('an armed attack against one or more of them in Europe or North America shall be considered an attack against them all') asserts that all NATO members are united in a pact of collective self-defence, and are required to aid one another militarily in the face of any external threats.[4] This means that any armed incursion from Russia into one or more of the Baltics should in theory result in the article's invocation, and subsequently other NATO member countries would dispatch their armed forces. Around 3,200 foreign troops are already stationed in the region: a UK-led battalion of 800 in Estonia, a Canada-led battalion of 1,200 in Latvia, and a Germany-led battalion consisting of 1,200 troops in Lithuania. Poland is home to a further 4,000 US-led troops.[5] These troops may be a paper tiger or a tripwire, unable to resist Russia's military might in the event of a full-scale invasion – but thus far they have served as an effective deterrent, and the Baltics are encouragingly optimistic about the likelihood of continued peace, in one sense at least.

But even if there is no direct military threat from their much larger eastern neighbour, Russia still conducts acts of aggression in the region, and the new global developments that have been taking place in the twenty-first century call into question the specific kinds of attacks that could fall under the remit of Article 5. While it explicitly states that the attack must be armed, new battlegrounds have started to emerge since it was established in 1949. Social media usage has exploded worldwide, the term 'information war' has fallen into the vernacular, and cyberattacks on media or government websites, banks or even electricity grids are part of the new normality. Humanitarian movements, governments and western society in general is starting to take psychological harm into account more seriously, too (at least on a surface level). The world is rapidly changing, as are the natures of international power relationships and struggles within it.

Russia has rolled out a variety of operations globally that fall into these categories. In March 2018, the US released a report outlining a Russian government attempt to target 'government entities and multiple US critical infrastructure sectors, including the energy, nuclear, commercial facilities, water, aviation, and critical manufacturing sectors'.[6] The 'Lisa case' in Germany in 2016 saw a fake story about a Russian-German girl raped by Arab migrants whip up a media storm. The now-infamous Internet Research Agency (IRA), or 'Russian troll farm' as it is colloquially known, has been accused of various low and high-level feats, from rewriting news stories with a pro-Russia slant for fake websites, to posting on Facebook and Reddit, as well as comments on Russian political sites. In late 2018, Twitter released data that indicated that Russia had mobilized some 3,800 accounts on the day of the UK's Brexit vote, making comments in favour of the country leaving the bloc.[7] The overwhelming impact of Russia's activity is likely vastly overstated (the UK invariably has enough of its own domestic issues to arrive at Brexit independently), and often Russian entities can use western reactions as 'evidence' that the country is playing a pivotal role in foreign affairs. But intent is important, and through trial and error Russia can poke holes in and undermine existing western institutions to significant effect.

The Baltics are uniquely equipped to deal with the challenges posed by modern Russia. Having experienced the Soviet occupation, in Putin's Russia they have also been a 'testing ground' of sorts for methods that are later deployed further afield, albeit testing grounds with their own very specific sets of domestic issues that can be exploited. Their proximity, history and heightened exposure to the language and tactics of their eastern neighbours mean that they have a degree of expertise which the rest of the world could stand to benefit from in the present climate. Yet, they must also have to contend with being consistently defined as 'post-Soviet' – seen solely through the prism of their former occupying force.

Estonia, Latvia and Lithuania's paths to absolute independence were convoluted, violent and arduous, but also very heartfelt. On 23 August 1989, some 2 million people – pro-independence residents of Estonia, Latvia and Lithuania – united against Soviet occupation. They stood in a seamless line stretching for more than 400 kilometres. The non-violent protest, an expression of international solidarity, was timed to mark the fiftieth anniversary of a secret agreement between the Soviet Union and Nazi Germany which divided Europe into spheres of influence – the Molotov-Ribbentrop pact. In the wake of the Second World War, the US, UK and other western countries never recognized the subsequent occupation of the north-eastern European states as legitimate. But nonetheless, they remained under Soviet control for several decades. In December 1989, the People's Deputies Congress of the USSR finally declared the German-Soviet pact and its 'secret protocols' legally null and void. Lithuania was the first to declare independence, on 11 March 1990.[8]

The Soviet government imposed economic sanctions on Lithuania after March 1990, and less than a year later, in January 1991, fourteen people were killed and more than 500 wounded as Kremlin troops crashed into the capital, Vilnius, to break up crowds of thousands who gathered to protect media outposts from direct Soviet influence, as well as the parliamentary building.[9] A similar situation took place at the Tallinn TV tower in August 1991, just one day after the Supreme Council of the Republic of Estonia declared the country independent: Soviet troops made an attempt to seize the structure but ultimately failed. In Latvia, crowds made barricades across Riga to preserve resources essential for the fast transfer of information, such as the international telephone exchange. Even back then, the 'information war' was at the centre of the confrontation, with each side recognizing the value of holding the tools through which they could impart their narrative to the wider populace, and the world. The call to the barricades was broadcast via radio. 'Communication was everything,' recalls Latvian state media.[10]

Nowadays, Soviet troops are long gone, and Vilnius' Cathedral Square sits serenely in a valley of craft beer pubs, baroque buildings, accordion players and teenagers Instagramming pictures in the sunshine or snow. Tallinn's TV tower is a major tourist site with panoramic views over the medieval city skyline. The vast Riga barricades (not unlike those of Kyiv's Maidan in 2014) that sat in the channels between the city's art nouveau buildings have been reduced to a small pyramid monument outside the centrally located St James's Cathedral, while crowds light fires in Riga's old town every January in commemoration of the collective Latvian effort and the seven participants who died (six resulting from attacks by Soviet special forces, one accidental).[11] Younger generations often look towards other capitals such as London or Berlin for cultural connections and travel, rather than towards one another or Moscow (although in recent years this does appear to be changing). However, this isn't the case with all residents, and the Baltic states are home to some significant social currents, very specific to the region alone. Just under 30 per cent of Estonia's population are ethnic Russians, with a similar percentage in Latvia (although the split in Riga is much more equal – Riga speaks more Russian than Latvian).[12] The proportion is much lower in Lithuania, with only 5.8 per cent of the country being ethnic Russians; there are actually more Poles – 6.6 per cent.[13] Lithuania was the only country of the three Baltic nations to automatically grant full citizenship rights to all local Russians after the Soviet collapse: both Latvia and Lithuania imposed citizenship restrictions on the native Russians, and nowadays there is still a sizeable 'resident alien' population in each country. In Lithuania, the politics of the domestic Russian-speaking community is a comparatively minor issue, but one that the Russian state is willing to exploit in all three.

In a general sense, this book seeks to outline these modern internal currents in the Baltic states and Russia's presence there, in the context of wider geopolitical issues and the tumultuous history of the twentieth century, in particular looking at how the past informs the present (whether that be a mythologized or a factual understanding of the past) and how that framing of the past has influenced the social and political forces at play in the present day – including attitudes towards the necessity of continuity. In particular, I will be looking at relations with Russia and the future of Europe, but I also seek to present the Baltic states as vastly different entities from one another (despite the collective grouping) in addition to some significant similarities. Each Baltic state has oddly specific stereotypes of the others. Estonians are perceived as slow and reserved, Latvians are said to have six toes and the country is considered 'the worst' for Russians out of the three. Lithuanians are basketball fanatics with more of a 'large nation' mentality than the other two countries; as an old European power it occupied its surrounding regions in the fifteenth century. The village of Purnuskes, Lithuania (according to Lithuanians) is officially the geographic centre of Europe, and it honours the location with Europos Parkas or 'Europe Park'. In 2018, Lithuania even released a new campaign to encourage visitors to Vilnius, terming it the 'G-spot of Europe' to widespread international coverage, accompanied by an image of a woman's hand gripping a sheet bearing the image of a map at the point at which Lithuania is located. Lithuanian and Latvian share some linguistic commonalities – both have Indo-European roots (although they are far from mutually intelligible), and Lithuanian has been repeatedly linked to Sanskrit. However, Estonia's language is Finno-Ugric (related to both Finnish and Hungarian). It is often mocked for having 'no sex and no future' – genderless and devoid of a future tense. The country regards itself as more 'Scandinavian' than its two Baltic siblings.

The region is characterized by acres of dense forests, lakes and swamps, home to wildlife including wolves, wild boar, and the occasional bear, providing a certain sense of rural simplicity and fairytale-like mystery. One Estonian proverb says 'mets on vaese mehe kasukas' – 'the forest is a poor man's coat' and the topography has played a significant role in twentieth-century history too, providing vital cover for the Baltic guerrilla movements against the Soviets; the partisans who waged covert war during the occupation were known in each country as the 'Forest

Brothers' and have attained an almost mythological status. The Baltic states remained pagan until the fourteenth century (making them the last pagan states in Europe) and there is still a present and pervasive sense of this nature-rooted spirituality in each country – even today the woods are scattered with sacred groves, sacrificial stones and magical sites steeped in ancient lore. But the forests also serve to bolster the local economy; for example, the timber industry makes up one-tenth of Estonia's exports and 22 per cent of its industrial GDP, and mass deforestation is becoming a strong political issue among conservationists and proponents of old pagan spirituality alike.[14]

This spirituality can be over-romanticized too, and the countries are often used as a marker of backwardness. 'Even Latvia', 'even Estonia', 'even Lithuania' are frequently used as comparative examples when western Europe falls behind, suggesting a lack of progress in the region. Yet these countries' prior instability has produced the perfect climate for flexibility, practicality and innovation. Freedom House's flagship 2019 report saw the US falling below 'Greece, Latvia and Mauritius', the implication in several subsequent news stories being that the US should be embarrassed about a lack of progress relative to 'eastern Europe'. The countries have made leaps and bounds in terms of technological progress, for example Skype and TransferWise both originated in Estonia, and Starship Technologies' delivery robots have 'even' been deployed in Silicon Valley.

Politically, since the early 1990s, Estonia, Latvia and Lithuania have all had to deal with the consequences of totalitarianism, as well as mixed governmental, international and physical results from active similar efforts to 'decommunize'. There have been several common features across the Baltic states: the removal or relocation of Soviet-era monuments, the need for concerted nation-building efforts, and various lustration processes. Even the celebrations of anniversaries have some commonalities; in 2018, the Baltics celebrated 100 years since independence – not from the Soviet Union but rather the Tsarist era, from which the Baltics freed themselves in 1918. The Russian Empire absorbed the Estonian and Livonian areas in the eighteenth century after the Great Northern War, which at that point had both been Swedish dominions. At the end of the eighteenth century, the Austrian Empire, the Russian Empire and Prussia ultimately managed to divide the Polish–Lithuanian Commonwealth during the First, Second and Third Partitions of Poland, with Imperial Russia annexing territory that spanned parts of today's Ukraine, Minsk, Vilnius and the coastal city of Liepaja in today's Latvia. After the Russian Revolution in 1917, the

Bolshevik party ultimately recognized the independence of the Baltic nations – much to the displeasure of the Latvian and Estonian communists attracted to the movement (in northern Latvia, not including Riga, the Bolsheviks attained 72 per cent of the vote in Russian Constituent Assembly elections in November 1917).[15]

The Baltic nations had to rally around points of commonality in order to secure their second independence in 1991. Estonian scholar Vello Pettai identifies five different commonalities present in the struggle for independence from the Soviet Union: environmental mobilization, calendar demonstrations, intellectuals' leadership, organized movements and personnel changes. The marking of anniversaries was of prime importance – regular people would gather to observe a particular political anniversary. 'Given considerable overlaps in the history of the Baltic states during the 20th century, it was not surprising that the three nations would quickly find common or analogous historical dates around which to recognize moments of national suffering or triumph,' Pettai wrote.[16] In Latvia, dissident opposition group Helsinki-86 organized its first public meeting on 14 June 1987 to commemorate the mass deportation of Balts by Stalin in 1941. Estonian dissident, Tiit Madisson, happened to be in attendance and took the idea back to Estonia and began an underground effort to organize a similar demonstration on 23 August, the anniversary of the Molotov-Ribbentrop Pact. The idea spread to Lithuania, too, and a broad selection of anniversary dates started to be marked. That the Baltic states mark their centenary of independence in 2018 is a direct result of this Soviet-era drive to establish common timestamps.

De-russification has also seen stringent language policies adopted, to ensure that national languages are used instead of Russian. Estonia and Latvia had more direct and stable political paths than Lithuania as parliamentary democracies and have devoted considerable resources to restitution to ensure property is returned to former owners who lost out under Soviet nationalization policies. Lithuania developed as a presidential democracy and was generally more decentralized. Following the Soviet collapse, it was widely acknowledged that former communists could not be allocated the task of undertaking democratic reforms, and Estonia's Communist Party elites 'proved incapable of reconsolidating their power in the new republican legislature'.[17] In Estonia and Latvia the lustration laws implemented in 1995 allowed for the screening and 'prosecuting' of former communist leaders, candidates for office, and selected public employees.[18] The process in Lithuania was slightly different because of the automatic granting of citizenship to the comparatively low Russian population – 'there was no legislation restricting those who had connections to the KGB from holding state office, which resulted in a chaotic search for the KGB informants among the political leaders of the new country, even incriminating such well-known independence fighters as Prime Minister Kazimiera Prunskiene,' wrote Dr Ieva Zake.[19] Lithuania's Law of Lustration was only passed in the year 2000. In each Baltic state these processes happened in a climate of some uncertainty; the Soviet collapse saw systematic file destruction and loss, so records of KGB activity and complete lists of inactive agents were difficult to piece together, despite a concerted effort to vet public officials and whether or not they may have aided or collaborated with the Soviet apparatus.

Nowadays the words 'socialism' and 'communism' have assumed an ugly shapelessness in the formerly occupied Baltics. The Soviet collapse and the equation of Stalinism and the Soviet era with socialism or communism means that the humanistic and pluralistic ideals buttressing the ideologies buckled, subsumed by the cacophony of occupation. Inequality actually grew in the Baltic region following the Soviet collapse – quite rapidly in its immediate aftermath as the market economy emerged, but it has since lessened; there was no unemployment and gender, age and nationality had little bearing on wage discrepancies in the Soviet Union.[20] Women's wages are lower (approximately 70 per cent of those of men by some accounts) – there have been no major interventions aimed at achieving gender equality. On top of that, older people who do not have a strong grasp of the local languages can have a hard time fitting into the labour force. Youth unemployment remains an issue, especially now there is no centrally governed system aimed at engaging youngsters in labour market activities.[21] Soviet factory closures have also contributed to high unemployment levels, especially in areas which developed around specific industries. Outward migration is the highest in the European Union, and there are concerns of a brain drain as skilled workers such as medics can often find higher pay abroad.

Russia, as well as the Baltics, has also had to cope with the hangover from the Soviet collapse. There is still sweeping nostalgia for the USSR and vastly exaggerated, but widespread, declining, support for Russian President Vladimir Putin inside Russia (and vastly understated support outside). The population has had to compartmentalize the Soviet and Russian Federation periods and register the ideological separation, but must also simultaneously, unconsciously integrate them both, especially the older generations. To many people, the Soviet Union symbolized morality and justice, and the population was community-spirited – this is strongly felt among those even in the Baltics who remember the Soviet Union. 'I have read many stories, watched many films where the role model was a young pioneer who is helping elderly people, is brave and honest, etc.,' says historian Ieva Gundare, who now helps edit a Latvian literary monthly *Rīgas Laiks*. 'I am absolutely sure that there is an impact of Soviet ideology on my mindset. Of course, it is very mixed with all kinds of other ideas (many of them contradictory, [and] gained when I was in high-school during the perestroika period: nationalistic ideas from our history teacher, general humanist ideas from our Russian literature teacher. In my family we did not talk of values like this,' she adds.[22]

One of Nobel Prize-winner Svetlana Alexievich's Russian interviewees, a former Communist Party secretary, nostalgically observed: 'socialism isn't just labour camps, informants and the Iron Curtain, it's also a bright, just world: Everything is shared, the weak are pitied, and compassion rules. Instead of grabbing everything you can, you feel for others.'[23] However, she added that 'They weren't building themselves yachts with Champagne showers,' suggesting part of this nostalgia is tied to Russia's present situation under Putin – ostensibly a kleptocratic petrostate with a gaping divide between rich and poor.[24]

But Putin is not only popular inside Russia. He is also something of a symbol of rebellion internationally, and even enjoys a degree of popularity inside the Baltic states. Putin's disregard for international protocol, the 'rules-based international order' and partial reliance on informal power networks, which operate both inside Russia and abroad, combined with his strength and dismissiveness of others, have earned him some respect among those unfamiliar with Russia's domestic situation first-hand. Elements of class war are still at play, and a certain veneration of Russia as a haven for the socioeconomically deprived or disenfranchised lingers. In the Baltics, many of those people are native Russians. One major theme I try to explore in this text is the idea of 'Russophobia' in the Baltic states combined with its manifestation – how native nationality relates to present-day socioeconomic position and perceived victimization, how much this is attributable to language policies as opposed to xenophobia (and where that overlap might occur), and to what extent the original occupation is still perceived as 'class warfare' – whether Estonia, Latvia and Lithuania still symbolize the bourgeoisie in the twenty-first-century shadow of Russia's 1917 revolution. Several complicated currents are at play.

My personal interest stems in part from a combination of my own lived experiences and lineage. As a journalist, the obvious narrative to espouse is that the black hole in my family history led me to seek my Baltic roots. But in truth, I do not know to what extent this had an impact. I was born with two somewhat archaic Estonian names – my own maternal grandmother, 'Grandma Meeri', escaped Estonia on the roof of a train during the Soviet occupation, and other relatives by boat to Sweden. But I have never considered myself anything but British. My primary fields of interest were originally contemporary Russian politics, late-imperial literature and twentieth-century art history; I first moved to St Petersburg in 2011 to study these subjects for my MA and ended up leaving Moscow in 2015.

In that time, I worked both inside a Kremlin-backed news organization and in independent media. I witnessed first-hand the slow erosion of civil and personal freedoms in all directions, and the pervasive political apathy, opportunism, incompetence, fear, and sense of disempowerment that this generated, but which itself helped to facilitate this erosion. I observed both the patriotic pageantry of World War Two in public memory and impassioned personal responses rooted in loss, as well as both regret and relief at the Soviet collapse. I also saw the vast differences in living standards between Moscow and almost everywhere else that I travelled to in the country. As the geopolitical situation escalated when Russia-backed troops entered eastern Ukraine (to use the wilfully blind terminology for 'Russia invaded'), and flight MH17 was tragically shot down in 2014, I started wondering more what further escalation in eastern Europe could mean for the Baltic region – aided by speculation on that very topic. But it was a real concern. What would happen to the countries I grew up knowing to be free, as an impassioned supporter of that freedom on account of my own personal history?

I became more sensitive to the stream of propaganda being pumped out by internal Russian news outlets relating to the Baltic states, namely that they are NATO puppets, full of Nazi sympathizers, and subjugate their Russian-speaking populations. Just as I went to Russia to explore its present-day realities first-hand, I was compelled to understand the position of the Baltics between east and west first-hand, armed with this new experience from 'the Russian side'.

In each country (Russia, Lithuania, Latvia, Estonia) I undertook great efforts to explore all layers of society. My work on Russia is largely based on a combination of well-documented cumulative experience, used and unused 'potential article' material I collected over my years there, and long-distance web-based interviews. However, I conducted formal in-person interviews across the Baltic states specifically for the book, totalling somewhere between 120 and 150. I gathered personal stories from skinheads, religious fundamentalists, 'non-citizen' aliens (those who never took new citizenship after the Soviet collapse) and local Russians, as well as information from high-level politicians, academics, and the creative artists and curators who help shape public memory and culture. Through all of these I hope that I developed a strong understanding of the relationships between domestic politics, geopolitics, socioeconomic problems, past and present, and different generations' responses to family histories that penetrate each culture.

I relied predominantly upon qualitative social research, rather than quantitative, although I have consulted a variety of statistics portals and academic journals across my studies to bolster my sense of perspective. Interviews were conducted in English and Russian; there was a generational divide and I could speak to older people in Russian, and younger people in English. I also leaned on the occasional interpreter. I do not speak Latvian or Lithuanian, and I consider myself a beginner in Estonian. I only know the songs or phrases that I have absorbed through basic study, several trips over the years, and fragments passed down via my mother.

Parts of my own family history are still something of a mystery; it seems common that the generation forced to leave under the Soviets do not want to discuss the events of their departure in great detail, and many people left loved ones behind with little or no knowledge of what might have happened to them, or vice versa. Some may have collaborated with either Soviets or Nazis, and survived with a burden of guilt. I am only alive because my grandmother was one of the 'fortunate' ones who managed to escape. While in the past five years it is academically fashionable to explore emotional histories, individual and collective trauma, mental health, and its interaction with society, relationships and politics, it is only in recent years – in my generation – that the stigma surrounding trauma has started to fade.

Interviewing some older members of society was very difficult at times for both the interviewee and myself. I am particularly grateful to those who were able to speak so candidly about their experiences, some of whom I have not done full justice to, but who still remain imprinted on my memory.

1 THE SHADOW OF THE PAST

'Trust me: if you scratch any Estonian, Latvian and Lithuanian of my generation, and you ask them who was worse – the Soviets or the Nazis? – the Soviets were way, way worse,' says Felicia, an eighty-year-old woman via Skype from southern California. She has a halo of thick white hair, eyes nearly as round as her glasses, and is surprisingly glib about an illness which she believes will kill her. When the Soviets occupied Lithuania in the 1940s as part of Joseph Stalin's plan to annexe the Baltic states, she was bundled out of the country as a refugee to spend a chunk of her childhood in displaced person camps in Germany. She was only eight or nine when she left. 'It was kind of an exciting trip,' she says. 'For my sister it was sheer misery. And my parents, the poor things.'

Her bleak history is almost hard to believe; she is merry to the point of being ethereal and now owns the vast collection of dolls she once longed for as a child. Her twinkle is perhaps indicative of her youthful lack of awareness in the 1940s, blind to the full harshness of wartime Europe. But her story, and that of her family, is one of many similar tales that shape the modern consciousness of Baltic residents and refugees alike – however mythologized or imagined they might be.

There were two Soviet occupations of the Baltic states: the first in 1940–1, and the second from June 1944 which lasted until the collapse of the Soviet Union in 1991. In 1941, the Nazis broke the Molotov-Ribbentrop pact overnight – the secret nonaggression agreement between Hitler and Stalin (which saw Lithuania initially fall on the German side before a revision in September 1939).[1] 'All of a sudden ... we hear these artillery shells and shots going on, and it turns out the Germans just had their blitzkrieg,' Felicia recalls, adding that they thought 'thank God' when the stormtroopers arrived. They were 'very polite and they were very nice, and they were kind, and they were clean. And they were all the things that the Soviets were not.'

Felicia pauses, realizing the gravity of what she is saying. She takes a moment to emphasize that she is only speaking on behalf of the 'ethnic' populations, rather than the Jews. She mentions 'barbaric' thievery and rape.

The memory of the Second World War and beyond is still deeply etched into the fabric of modern society in every single Baltic state – in public space, education and art (to name just a few). The brutality of accounts from the era is horrifying, and undoubtedly helps sculpt present-day Baltic attitudes to contemporary Russia. They provide a dominant narrative of Baltic residents being cornered into self-defence after victimization at the hands of two militarily superior invading forces. It's hardly surprising they take on this tone; conservative estimates suggest that, in total, Soviet mass deportations saw at least 200,000 people forcibly removed from Estonia, Latvia and Lithuania and taken to Siberia and Kazakhstan.[2] Higher estimates put the figure closer to 371,000–400,000.[3]

In the Museum of Occupations in the Estonian capital, Tallinn, people of around the same age as Felicia recollect similarly dismal experiences of having been displaced after fleeing the Baltics. Others who stayed in the country during and after the war recount the grim events to which they bore witness. Magnus Kald from the largest Estonian island, Saaremaa, died in 2014, but every twenty-five minutes or so, his voice still echoes through the glass-walled building on loop. 'Soviets tortured people at the castle – the hands of most of the women were tied behind their backs with barbed wire, breasts amputated.' As his voice circles, a steady rotation of tourists take the three seats in front. He says that pins were pushed into their noses and under their nails, and that in another building, orchestras played to drown out the sounds of screaming.

The personal and inherited memories of violence from the era unsurprisingly spill over into the literary canon. In Finnish-Estonian author Sofi Oksanen's 2008 novel *Purge*, both a guarded elderly woman and one of her younger relatives are subjected to sex crimes at the hands of Russians. The book describes the elderly woman's attempts to isolate herself from society while simultaneously managing to silently identify fellow survivors. 'From every trembling hand, she could tell – there's another one. From every flinch at the sound of a Russian soldier's shout and every lurch at the tramp of boots. Her, too?' The semi-autobiographical *A Woman in Amber: Healing the Trauma of War and Exile* by Latvian author Agate Nesaule also details similar, graphic experiences of acts of sexual violence committed against Latvian women at the hands of the Soviet soldiers during the Second World War, and how she learned as a young child that women easily become prey during conflict.[4] In the book, Nesaule's own mother encouraged her to move to the front of a queue to be shot so she could avoid witnessing others being tortured.

Of course, both texts illustrate problematic boundaries between history and fiction. It is impossible to quantify how widespread gender-based violence was, and the topic is so ephemeral too because of lack of documentation and stigma. One man of Latvian émigré parentage, when I brought up the subject, said it was 'an interesting topic that I have not heard about'. Even documentary accounts are sometimes left implicit or tackled in an evasive manner. In Imbi Paju's 2005 documentary *Memories Denied*, despite focusing on the female experience, she never directly confronts the subject of sexual violence with her interviewees who were incarcerated at Tallinn's Patarei prison.[5]

'I wish my sister were still alive,' Felicia clarifies. 'She was terrified of falling into Soviet hands when they returned in 1944.' She relays unverifiable, but unnervingly specific stories passed though the teenage girl rumour mills, that her sister later passed on to her. 'Rape for the ordinary Russian peasant-soldier was a group game, showing off who could do it longer-shorter-wilder ... her opinion [of Nazis] was that for them it was more a single person act of anger, expression of power or resentment,' she said. 'Germans prided themselves on being "cultured".' The absence of written accounts provides very strong grounds for denial, and along with the dearth of proof, such accounts rely on an understanding of individuals or groups as representations of the whole (e.g. in terms of their nationality).

In the event that a case was reported, there could be serious negative consequences for the accuser. Lithuanian Elena Spirgevičienė filed a complaint with the Soviet Union's Central Committee of the Communist Party on 10 June 1959 alleging that a Soviet partisan (there were both Soviet and Lithuanian partisans), Alfonsas Čeponis, was part of a group who raped her, murdered her sister and attempted to rape then killed her daughter. Čeponis, along with two other Soviet partisans with distinctly Lithuanian names, had been posthumously granted the title Hero of the Soviet Union in 1958 as part of a Soviet attempt to suggest Lithuanian origins to the Soviet partisan movement. Spirgevičienė portrayed herself as pro-Soviet and termed Čeponis a bandit, therefore presenting the violence 'in the language of ordinary criminality, as if disregarding the wartime context' and stepping outside the constraints of nationality.[6] However, it was Spirgevičienė who was discredited as a 'class enemy' and her allegations erased as the committee focused on the food taken by the partisans ('if they took things they needed them') and politicized the affair into one couched in German collaborationist sentiment and anti-Soviet leanings.[7]

Memoirs occasionally describe events from the occupations in lurid detail. One Estonian woman named Hilja Lill, born in 1905, describes how 'the Reds' had 'torn about everywhere, demolishing and ransacking houses, looting storage buildings and slaughtering animals' and how 'the furniture and the walls were smeared with excrement.'[8] In Lill's case she was sure to ascribe responsibility to the nation, not the 'bandits' or 'criminals' within it. The Red Army soldiers' reputation persists to this day. The generations that survived this period retained serious and often tragic memories of trauma, perceived through the polarized ideas of nationality and ethnicity that pervaded wartime Europe. Some members of younger generations in the Baltics – even those born after the Soviet occupation ended – assume a gormless expression, make gorilla noises, or tap their temples to indicate stupidity when referring to the forces from the east. 'They murdered our intelligentsia!' is a common indignant outburst.

The shadow of history similarly hangs over the refugee population and their descendants, many of whom, having been forced to leave, retained a close attachment to their homeland. But instead of living out their time under Soviet rule, they attained fresh experiences abroad on the understanding that returning to the geographical homeland as they knew it was not an option, nor did they know when – or if – it would be. In this uncertainty, they possessed a certain determination to preserve memories of their country as they nostalgically remembered it, maintaining the language and traditions, with a sense of the homeland as utopia. 'Don't talk badly about Latvia!' a child reprimands her parents in biographical novel *Five Fingers*, having grown up in Siberia hearing how 'beautiful' and precious' the country is.[9] When independence eventually returned to the region in 1991, after the Soviet collapse, many Baltic refugees or their descendants went back to their countries of origin, leading members of the younger generations who stayed to refer to them a little sarcastically as 'wise old elves' who obtained an education in the 'freeland' to later impart their knowledge to the 'peasants' who stayed.[10] While the older generations replete with either raw memories of the occupation or displaced personhood are incrementally dying out, lingering undercurrents of elitism and inverse elitism both remain embedded in the populace. Those who fled are simultaneously revered and resented, even today. After the war, official Soviet histories of the three former republics were required to outline how the local proletariat threw off the 'bourgeois yoke' to establish socialism.[11] This conflict is embodied well in a quote from former Estonian President Toomas Hendrik Ilves, who was born in Sweden and grew up in New Jersey – he was one of these returnees. He once said, 'the Soviet period was like a Crazy Eddie's commercial in the middle of a Mozart Concerto', itself suggesting a certain "class" divide between the populace that experienced the Soviet era and those who left.[12]

This disconnect was also evident in Lithuania, when former Communist Party head Algirdas Brazauskas became its new post-independence president from 1993 after winning against the independent Stasys Lozoraitis, who was born, educated, and involved in diplomatic service outside of Soviet Lithuania, and popular in Washington DC. Lozoraitis had 'carried the torch' for Lithuania during the occupation, and he had the support of Vytautas Landsbergis – ostensibly the leader of the independence movement, who had a reputation of being more 'professorial' than charismatic. Yet Brazauskas was perceived as more down-to-earth, and a strong orator.[13] The understandings that developed during the war and in its aftermath remained deeply present in the rhetoric, experiences and politics of all that followed.

After the Baltics were successfully annexed to the Soviet Union in August 1940, the subsequent Sovietization process saw private industries nationalized and the suppression of dissenters. Residents met the incorporation with mixed reactions. One Lithuanian political scientist, Aleksandras Shtromas, who lived through both Soviet and Nazi periods, said there was 'almost total dismay but very little, if any, outward resistance.'[14] USSR People's Commissar of State Security Vsevolod Nikolayevich Merkulov ordered deportations on 19 May 1941, which started on the night of 13–14 June 1941. Nearly 60,000 people were removed from the Baltics over the course of the week.[15]

As part of the more-than-200,000 deportations from the Baltics, in the space of just four days, Operation *Priboi* ('Coastal Surf') in March 1949 saw 90,000 deported alone. Over 70 per cent of them were women and children; in Estonia at the very least, men hid in the woods and joined the guerilla forces.[16] A high enough number of people died in the process to the point that the European Court of Human Rights has officially termed it a crime against humanity.[17] Even more serious (albeit more contentious) accusations have been put forward. 'The swath cut by deportation was so wide that the issue of genocide ought to be considered,' renowned political scientist Rein Taagepera stated in relation to the Estonian deportations.[18] A deportation the previous year, in May 1948, Operation *Vesna* ('Spring') affected only Lithuania. In memoirs written by women taken to Siberia in this deportation there are records of Soviet officers demanding women 'pay' them in sexual favours, amid hints or suggestions of sexual assault, such as in the writings of Lithuanians Jūratė Bičiūnaitė-Masiulien and Paulina Motiečienė.[19]

In the personal accounts from the Baltics, 'whitewashing' the past is at play. There was a 'flowering of memoir-writing in the postwar years', write Tiina Kirss and Juri Kivimae, who collected life stories from twenty-five Estonians who lived through the occupation era.[20] 'Thick silences surrounded certain facts, such as serving in the German army during World War II, facts that were not looked on favourably by the countries where the refugees settled.'[21] The Baltics were home to several concentration camps. But many served with guns to their heads, says Felicia. 'To this day I read in some Jewish articles how Lithuanians shot the Jews, how the Nazis exterminated the Jews. Well if the Nazi troops are standing behind you with rifles and saying "go shoot, or we'll shoot you" – what do you do?'

This narrative is also prevalent in Latvia. Chairman of the Board at the Occupation Museum Association of Latvia, Valters Nollendorfs, expresses incredulity at the idea volunteers could be 'drafted' into an army. 'How can you be drafted as a volunteer?' he asks.[22] Jewish survivors and Russian state actors have both expressed distaste and even outrage at this argument. The Soviets suffered staggering numbers of fatalities in the battle against Nazism, losing as many as 11 million soldiers in their victory over Hitler.[23] Numerous scholars have identified a 'tendency to minimise Baltic collaboration and come to the defense of accused Baltic war criminals', among Baltic émigrés to the West.[24] The Jewish population across the Baltics was decimated – in Lithuania, approximately 94 per cent of the nation's Jews died in the Holocaust, and nearly all of Latvia's 70,000 Jews were murdered.[25] Every year, some 1,500–3,000 men participate in a Latvian Waffen SS veterans' march in Riga, just 22 kilometres from a former camp at Salaspils and even closer to the area that once housed the Kaiserwald concentration camp. 'The Germans related to us more humanely,' a former Russian prisoner of war (and march participant), Aivars Ozols, said in 2010 (while adding that he and his compatriots had 'no choice' in the matter of going to war).[26]

In the 1970s and 1980s, Latvian immigrant communities in the US fell under scrutiny, with some members charged with having concealed their participation in war crimes during the Second World War.[27] It grew to be a huge scandal. From the Baltic states 'at least 85 naturalized American citizens and resident aliens, including some most ardently praised by their neighbors, are suspected of having concealed participation in World War II atrocities in order to enter the United States after the war', states a *New York Times* report from 1976.[28] But the émigrés often hit back – 'individual Latvians were co-opted to participate in the killings, which were oftentimes manipulated to look like they were carried out without German participation', reads a 2004 statement from the Latvian Ministry of Foreign Affairs, prepared in part by Nollendorfs.[29] The mental 'western' geolocation of the Holocaust in Auschwitz serves to bolster the dominant narrative of victimhood in the Baltic region. 'If you're in Belarus, Ukraine, Lithuania, Poland or Russia, if the history of the Holocaust is understood to be synonymous with Auschwitz, then there is no particular reason for a national conversation about collaboration,' write historian Timothy Snyder and policy analyst Simas Čelutka. 'It wasn't the Holocaust because the Holocaust is located in Auschwitz. In a strange way nationalist self-exculpation works together with the common Western simplification of the Holocaust.'[30] While the Salaspils camp is commemorated by a vast monument, Kaiserwald's existence is marked only by a small memorial, and some former sites are completely invisible to the public. The Baltic states' neat narrative can stir unease through these attempts to whitewash the past. While a real and justifiable sense of victimhood remains, the idea that there was no culpability on the part of the 'native' Balts stirs a sense of injustice among descendants of the former Jewish populations.

'They had a national narrative that Lithuanians were blameless,' says Grant Gochin, a man of Lithuanian Jewish heritage, and like Felicia also based in southern California, as we speak via an online video connection. Despite their close geographical proximity in the present day and familial ties to the same obscure Baltic nation, his perspective is worlds apart from hers. Born in South Africa, Grant was involved in the liberation struggle which got him into 'trouble' before he moved as a result. Even when he was based there some thirty-five years ago, he had a deep-seated interest in genealogy. 'Every branch of the family tree until 1941, except for my grandfather – everybody was murdered,' he says. He identifies more than one hundred relatives who were killed in just one area. 'And one name kept coming up – Noreika,' he states.[31]

Jonas Noreika, or General Storm, had a commemorative plaque prominently displayed on the wall of the library of the Lithuanian Academy of Sciences in central Vilnius until 2019. A school in the northern village of Sukioniai is named after him, and there is a stone memorial next to his birthplace.[32] However, in 2018, his own granddaughter, in a wide-reaching article for *Salon* magazine, revealed her horror at discovering his brutal Nazi past after promising her dying mother she would continue working on a book about him.

'Growing up in Chicago's Marquette Park neighborhood,' Silvia Foti wrote, 'I'd heard about how my grandfather died a martyr for the cause of Lithuania's freedom at the hands of the KGB when he was just thirty-seven years old.' Family myths stipulated that he fought the Nazis and was sent to a concentration camp. Something of a national hero, former President Landsbergis and his wife both attended the funeral of Noreika's widow and daughter at Vilnius Cathedral in October 2000. But when Foti visited Sukioniai she heard the first whispers of how he had been a 'Jew-killer', prompting further investigation.[33] She hired a Holocaust guide who showed her the sites of mass graves, books on Noreika's murky past, and who ultimately suggested his was responsible for the deaths of 2,000 Jews in Plungė, western Lithuania, in an initial uprising in 1941 – an uprising that predated the January 1942 Wannsee Conference (the point at which Nazi Germany decided to make extermination state policy). She concluded her grandfather sanctioned the murders of over 14,000 Jews across the country, with her own research showing that her grandfather actually killed Gochin's relatives.[34]

The backdrop of persecution in Lithuania helped to inform the path Gochin's immediate family took. 'I asked relatives why they were so engaged in the liberation struggle [in South Africa],' he says. 'My aunt said to me, "when we were in Lithuania we weren't able to stand up for ourselves, and now we see injustice and we're standing against it". So, that experience translated into the South African liberation struggle.' Close-knit Jewish communities of Lithuanian-Litvak descent existed in both Johannesburg and Cape Town.

Gochin now wants Lithuania to 'tell the truth' about Noreika and others involved in the Holocaust in Lithuania. 'I want them to admit that one of their primary national heroes is the man that murdered my cousins,' he says. Gochin is taking the issue through the domestic courts system, pushing up against several obstacles that he deems artificial in nature.

Ultimately, he hopes to take the case to the European Court of Human Rights (ECHR) in Strasbourg. 'I'm still relatively young. I could spend the next forty years in court with the Lithuanian government. I'm not going away', he finishes.

Today, personal and collective memories of the occupation period are widely publicized in a variety of museums and commemorative sites at central city locations – at times it can seem that the Baltic capitals are almost built around their painful pasts. The Soviet era is mainly documented through tourist sites at which struggles and suffering are the sole focus. The 'dramatic and recent nature' of the period, as well as a desire to inform the public and preserve collective memory, mean that negative aspects of history are prioritized more than the impressive Tsarist or Soviet sights which have survived – for example the Academy of Sciences building in Riga, Toomas Rein's administrative building in Rapla (Estonia), or St Nicholas Naval Cathedral in Karosta (western Latvia).[35] Some of the Soviet structures are even occasionally (but not necessarily unfairly) derided in tourist literature for their instability and the ineptitude of Soviet architects or construction workers criticized – this has become part of the modern Soviet legacy. Tallinn's Olympic Village poses 'intriguing questions regarding its structural integrity' and the Soviet Union tasked the construction of the Viru hotel in Tallinn to a Finnish construction company, Repo Oy, for its comparative aptitude in the face of other Soviet options, according to Estonian tourist literature.[36]

Among present-day tourist sights preserving and commemorating the tragic aspects of the occupation eras is the aforementioned Museum of Occupations in Tallinn, established in 2003. The building was constructed specifically to house the museum, with the glass walls symbolizing openness, the silver birches outside a tribute to those sent to Siberia (where the trees are ubiquitous), and the heavy doors symbolizing the iron curtain. While a little over-reliant on documentary footage from the bygone era, it keeps its exhibits anchored in the present day, by exploring the experiences of those who have migrated to Estonia in recent years, for example from Syria, alongside those who left under the Soviets. Annually, the largest majority of visitors to Tallinn's Museum of Occupations are from English-speaking countries. In the year 2016, approximately 7 per cent of visitors to the museum were Russians.[37] Russian visitors have mixed feelings about the narrative of history it presents. 'This museum is also seen by them often as an attack,' says Managing Director at the Museum of Occupations, Merilin Piipuu. 'They sometimes come in and they say "zdravstvuytye ya okkupant" ["hello, I'm an occupant"] which is like "oookaaaay" – mostly they say it with humour, they still come in and they are still interested in what we show here but sometimes it's a bad interest.'

Piipuu's own family history contains some unusual detail despite the generalized hardship it experienced. 'My grandmother's sister was deported to Siberia and then also my grandmother's father was deported to Siberia,' she says. But her grandmother remained in the country.

'At some point she was actually hiding in the forest . . . When she was young she fell in love with a Red guy, a Soviet Estonian guy,' she recalls her grandmother's tale. This love made her a threat. 'It was the Forest Brothers at that time that were trying to kill this man as well as my grandmother, because the Forest Brothers wanted to kill everyone who was *Punane* [Red], who was collaborating with Soviet powers. She was able to actually run away and also warn her then-boyfriend to run away . . . they never saw each other again.' Piipuu's grandmother had some personal thoughts on how this impacted her future. '[She] was thinking that maybe, later on, this boy saved her from the deportations. Because later, this boy was of course in charge of different activities. In a way, this love may have saved her,' Piipuu says.[38]

Latvia's 'occupations' museum (both use the plural) is housed temporarily in the former US embassy and has a stronger focus on documents and photographs from the era than objects or modern photographs. An offshoot at the former KGB building on 61 Brīvības Street, the 'Corner House', also has a permanent exhibit. In the Lithuanian capital, a museum focusing predominantly on Soviet crimes, the Museum of Genocide Victims, existed until Lithuania agreed to rename it in September 2017 as the Museum of Occupations and Freedom Fights.[39] 'The name looked bad in the international arena, as it gave an impression that the museum assigned the concept of genocide to the Lithuanian history of the area and ignored the Holocaust,' said former prime ministerial adviser Virgis Valentinavicius at the time.[40] His comments suggest that such a move was taken to maintain the approval of other countries, even though popular memory still recognizes the Soviet era as equal or 'worse' than that of Nazism. All three museums are some of the only places in the Baltic states where it is still acceptable to present Nazi and Soviet symbols such as the hammer and sickle; in 2006, Estonia banned their display in public places (for political purposes), in 2008 Lithuania did the same, and Latvia was the last, in 2014.

In public discourse in the Baltics, people to this day continue to draw comparisons between Adolf Hitler and Joseph Stalin – which internationally, can be poorly received. 'For the Latvian people, there's no difference between the Nazi regime and Soviet totalitarianism,' former justice minister Gaidis Berzins said in 2010.[41] In all three countries, international commissions have been convened to examine 'Nazi and Soviet' era crimes, implicitly equating the two, and the museums of occupations in Estonia and Latvia lay the Soviet and Nazi periods side-by-side.[42] This has been a recurrent theme since independence. In December 2010, the European Union had to reject calls from eastern Europe to treat communist crimes 'according to the same standards' as those of the Nazis, saying there was 'no consensus' and that EU member states have 'wildly differing approaches'.[43] Foreign ministers from Lithuania, Latvia, Bulgaria, Hungary, Romania and the Czech Republic all participated in the sending of the letter – Estonia's voice was absent.[44] Repeated requests for comment from the Estonian Ministry of Foreign Affairs (MFA) as to why received the eventual response that 'documents and the content of those documents concerning the letter ... are sealed until [the] year 2020'.[45]

Old KGB surveillance equipment is also widely displayed in locations across the Baltics such as Tallinn's Hotel Viru (the top floor of which housed secret KGB observation operations). The memory of fear serves as a bridge to the past for the native population and tourists from the former Soviet world, while providing a certain sense of proximity to Russia for foreign tourists. During the Cold War era, innocuous items such as ashtrays and cufflinks were bugged; the hotel would often let its guests know they were being watched in order to propagate fear. The exhibition's curator recalls guests making a second or third visit to the Hotel Viru after having stayed there during the Soviet era: 'Very often somebody was complaining "Jesus, they even don't have toilet paper in my room", and after five minutes there was a knock on the door and the [concierge] lady was there with toilet paper,' she says. 'I remember, one Israeli diplomat told [me] they had an agreement that every morning at 9:00am, breakfast is served to the room. But one morning the lady was there already at 8:00am. So they asked "why did you come so early?" – "But you already woke up at 6:00am."' She says that the primary motivation behind the in-your-face surveillance methods seemed to be to let guests *know* they were being watched. 'Then you don't dare to do anything – just spread terror, spread fear inside people's heads and hearts. It's very easy to control them', the curator says. The Baltics are an important example of the extent to which the Soviet Union relied on fear as a method of social control, and what can be achieved if this fear is overcome.

Present-day representations of the old Soviet mechanisms of power are also highly visible in the Tsarist-era prisons used under the Soviets as similar sites of torture, imprisonment and executions. Now, they are open to the public with grisly, immersive tales of the inmates' experiences. Tallinn's Paterei Prison, the old Tsarist barracks which kept people incarcerated from 1820 to 2004 and held political prisoners and victims of Soviet oppression, was closed to the public in October 2016; until then, remnants of former inmates' lives still lingered – magazine cut-outs of western popstars, Russian-language comics and bibles, operating theatre equipment, and a chair upon which prisoners perhaps stood before they were hung from a noose – as morbid reminders of just how close visitors were passing to those pieces of history. Estonian Minister of Justice Urmas Reinsalu now envisages the prison as a potential centre for the investigation of communist crimes – some €3 million has been set aside for the centre over the coming three years.[46]

In Latvia's coastal Liepaja region, enormous concrete blocks rear their weathered heads from the windy seas, and crumbling debris peppers the shoreline. In Karosta Prison (located in an old Soviet naval district, formerly off-limits to foreigners, and described as a 'ghetto' by locals), guests from around the world can be incarcerated overnight in the graffiti-dented cells being verbally abused by guards, or forced to undergo strenuous physical endeavours amid the abundance of Soviet kitsch and prison graffiti making proclamations like 'Rose is a bitch' in Russian. They can choose from varying levels of severity and must sign a waiver. For the more faint-hearted there is an on-site escape room, which only takes an hour. In Paterei Prison, too, longer 'experiences' were offered for a brief period (at least until 2006, and not overnight) – a simulation of the transport of prisoners, official registering, consumption of prison food, and interrogation – in one case, allegedly to help visitors understand the value of freedom – but another experience ('Mass Kidnap & Banged Up in a Russian Clink') commodified imprisonment under the Soviets to the point of fetishization. It was part of 'a gruesome and bold adventure' and described as 'perfect for a group stag weekend'.[47]

However, triumphant remnants of the Soviet past, such as the monuments erected in the postwar era, are (sometimes controversially) relegated to cemeteries, or other sites further from the main Baltic city thoroughfares, as the Bronze Soldier of Tallinn was in 2007 – instigating a night of pro-Russia demonstrations which saw more than 100 injured and one killed; the man who died had a Russian name.[48] The event preceded a wave of cyberattacks – a 'digital invasion' – directed at media, banking institutions and government bodies.[49] In Lithuania, the out-of-the-way Grūtas Park houses most of Lithuania's Soviet-era statues, ensuring that the relics are all concentrated in one place, and Soviet sculptures were removed from Vilnius' Green Bridge in 2015, much to the delight of President Dalia Grybauskaitė, and the annoyance of Russia (Lithuania later offered to exchange them in return for Lithuanian items held in Russian museums).[50] While the Red Latvian Riflemen monument still stands outside the town hall in Old Riga – politics aside, it is an aesthetically impressive artwork – a monument to Soviet sailors was removed, officially for public safety reasons, in the northeastern Latvian town of Limbazi in late 2016. The remnants of the Soviet era that are permitted to remain part of the fabric of society are carefully selected, but predominantly distanced from modern life. At times it seems like a kind of compartmentalization. The occupation era is 'othered' and remains an alien presence inside the countries even as it is recalled as part of their own history.

The rise of Putin

The Ministry of National Defence in Vilnius, Lithuania has signs on the wall banning handguns. Men stroll around in military fatigues, and a painting by Lithuanian artist Vytautas Mackevičius showing an episode from the 1918 struggle for independence hangs in the lobby. Staff make joking reassurances that they will be bugging any belongings left with them.

Lithuanian Defence Minister Raimundas Karoblis is a tall, thick-set man, dark hair flecked with grey, and a dark suit to match. He possesses a remarkable aura of calm strength, despite the subject matter of the conversation, and expresses strong concern over Russia's potential designs on the Baltic states – specifically his own country. 'The Russian side, the Russian administration wants to regain influence – not only with Ukraine and other countries of CIS [Commonwealth of Independent States] but also the Baltics including Lithuania,' says Karoblis. He believes Russia is suffering from 'very serious nostalgia about the former Soviet Union'.[51]

Russia's Zapad 2017 military exercises are fast approaching when we meet – the first of their nature since 2013. Karoblis points out that this means they are taking place 'for the first time since the annexation of Crimea'. Some western estimates suggest that as many as 100,000 Russian and Belarusian troops are to be stationed close to the Lithuanian border – even though Russia has declared the official numbers to be under 13,000 (any higher and the presence of Organization for Security and Co-operation in Europe (OSCE) observers would be necessary).[52] He speaks with the air of someone who has become used to rattling off the same figures and same concerns to several journalists over the past few months – and there has certainly been a spike in interest in the region, especially since 2014.

'Some parts of society that supported Putin thought the Baltics were in a different situation [from Crimea],' he says. 'Now we see signs that Russia – not necessarily people in the administration but who are close to [the] administration … saying some territories in Lithuania should not belong to Lithuania,' he says. Karoblis mentions the capital Vilnius and the coastal city of Klaipeda as examples of areas that modern-day Russia says Stalin 'gifted' to the country under the Soviets – perhaps with the implicit suggestion they should be requisitioned. However, most of the Russian-language stories making these territorial claims appeared in the immediate aftermath of Crimea 2014 – it's difficult to locate the source of his concerns in more recent months beyond the ravings of ultranationalist politician Vladimir Zhirinovsky, who is often given airtime disproportionate to his actual political influence.

That's not to say Karoblis' comments shouldn't be taken seriously. Russia has proven to be nothing but flexible and unpredictable in recent years, with an increasingly confrontational foreign policy as Putin continued to consolidate his authority. The chaos of Boris Yeltsin's rule – Russia's wild 1990s – was characterized by radical risk-takers, oligarchs, organized crime, hedonism and political upheaval. The era is now mythologized, both by people who served their youth experiencing the beauty of new freedoms, those who suffered the fallout from gang wars, and by Putin, the subsequent ruler, who styled himself as someone committed to ensuring 'calm and order in the country' in contrast to the preceding chaos. The uncertainty of the 1990s was, in part, because few people seemed to understand what the collapse of the Soviet Union actually meant – while the Baltic states organized themselves around establishing a sense of nationhood and history separate from that of their eastern neighbour by exploring their regional roots, the new Russia had to establish itself in opposition to its own territory and decades-old ideology. 'We did just fine until capitalism arrived and they started talking about "the market" on TV. No one understood what it was exactly, and no one was explaining anything either,' another Alexievich interviewee recalled of perestroika. People returned to church and felt permitted to insult Lenin and Stalin, yet held onto their fiercely communist beliefs, unable to get jobs in their fields. Money evaporated, gangs roamed the streets, and in Moscow 'you would hear gunshots and even explosions at night. Kiosks, kiosks . . . kiosks everywhere . . .'[53]

The Putin of the late 1990s and early 2000s comes across as idealistic, and committed to building a functioning nation in comparison to Yeltsin's anarchy, but advocated severe measures: 'Not one of these tasks can be performed without imposing basic order and discipline in this country, without strengthening the vertical chain of command in the executive authorities,' he said. The 'wild 1990s' are a retrospective antitheses to the Putin era – a point of comparison from which people can measure his positive influence. Yet people do not necessarily feel 'better off' under Putin or even that he is an objectively good president, but he has eliminated all other possible opposition and any others would likely be worse anyway; there have been some positive aesthetic changes, and the comparative sense of stability is still preferable to further political upheaval after the country has already weathered so much in terms of political volatility. 'Making a change could lead to the collapse of the country,' eighteen-year-old entrepreneur Dmitry Shaburov said in early 2018. 'If we look back and see what happened in the past, it's better that everything continue as it is now.'[54]

Putin has managed a remarkably effective job at minimizing challenges to his power, which in recent years has been bolstered by the terse international climate. Despite widescale protests against Putin in 2011–12 (the biggest since the fall of the Soviet Union), domestic opposition has since been all but quashed and the media reined in. He has enjoyed a much greater degree of domestic support than is generally acknowledged in the 'west', although as of late-2018/2019, his popularity started dwindling.

'They ruined my big day, now I'm going to ruin their lives,' Putin reportedly said in 2012, on the eve of his inauguration.[55] Since that day, opposition politicians have been murdered or prevented from running against him, and critics have been forced into exile. Whether Putin was directly culpable or not, he has since yielded incredible results. The annexation of Crimea in the wake of the revolution in Ukraine in 2014 saw Putin's popularity ratings ascend to an astonishing 89 per cent in June 2015.[56] The domestic rhetoric of NATO expanding eastwards despite perestroika promises is prevalent in modern Russia, and the Ukraine crisis was presented as a coup; a Russian ally falling to 'the west' and its conspiring against Russia. From Russia's position, the nation now feels threatened by the possibility of the US-led alliance edging closer to its borders, and the Baltic states embody that sense of betrayal and potential danger, having been the first from the former republics to join the body.

Since 2014, Lithuania has beefed up its defence budget and reintroduced conscription, which was abolished in 2008. All three Baltic states – Lithuania, Latvia and Estonia – have built, or started to build fences along their Russian borders in the geopolitical climate of the past few years. It's easy to see why Karoblis harbours concerns. The annexation of Crimea was a turning point throughout the region – and politicians and the public alike were mired in uncertainty, wondering whether they would be next, and whether a fresh occupation could begin.[57] That year, after the Euromaidan protests in Ukraine saw the successful ousting of former Ukrainian President Viktor Yanukovych, 'little green men' (soldiers bearing no insignia) swarmed the Black Sea peninsula. It was 'returned' to Russia (as the country's domestic press often stated), technically non-militarily. Even more 'liberal' Russians made emotional declarations of 'Krym nash' ('Crimea is ours') over the course of the annexation. Kremlin rhetoric then, too, spoke of land which 'rightfully' belonged to Russia. For the Baltics, it was a 'shocking demonstration of how war by stealth can be used to cripple a sovereign state and achieve strategic objectives before that state realises that war has begun.'[58] Some 95.5 per cent of voters in Crimea supported joining Russia in a vote termed 'illegal and illegitimate' by the EU in March 2014, in a move that might strike people who lived in the Soviet era as oddly familiar.[59] To cement the first period of occupation, the Soviets held 'grotesque pseudo-elections with one-party lists [that] produced the desired 92 to 99 per cent majorities,' after an ultimatum was issued by Moscow calling for new loyalist governments to be instated in each country.[60] The international community has displayed ongoing concern: since Crimea's annexation, articles have been published across platforms such as the *Financial Times*, the *Independent*, *NBC News* and the BBC with headlines like 'Baltic states shiver as Russia flexes muscles' and 'Baltic states fear Putin amid escalation in Ukraine'.[61]

Estonia and Latvia have expressed similar concerns to Karoblis, with both official sources and residents identifying the annexation of Crimea as a catalyst for recent nervousness. 'In 2008 when Russia attacked Georgia, Western countries took it as an isolated incident,' Estonian President Kersti Kaljulaid said in September 2017.[62] She added that this marked the start of a likely 'push' against the international security architecture, which culminated in the annexation of Crimea. 'Suddenly we all woke up, and we realised that something much more serious is going on. But at least now we have understood, and we have gathered together', she said.[63] At the United Nations General Assembly in September 2017, Latvian President Raimonds Vējonis also expressed security concerns, saying 'we have a very unpredictable neighbor'. He added that the country also feared the implications of Zapad 2017, even though it did not necessarily regard Russia as a direct military threat at that moment.[64] He pointed to what he termed the invasions of Georgia, Crimea and eastern Ukraine as reasons for heightened concerns in the Baltic region, but added that the possibility of full-on military aggression was at that point 'very, very low'.[65]

This external confidence could, of course, mask a deeper sense of unease. Among Latvian policymakers, Russia is often perceived as the number one threat to national security.[66] Lithuania's 2017 security threat assessment is devoted almost entirely to Russia, and in its first-ever public security report in 2016, the Estonian Information Board clearly stated that 'the current policies practiced by the incumbent Russian government are likely to remain the sole external power threatening the constitutional order of the Republic of Estonia in the nearest future'.[67]

However, the Baltics are 'different' from Georgia, eastern Ukraine or Crimea. As fully fledged European Union nations, and three of the NATO's twenty-nine member states, they should, technically speaking, have few reasons to worry in terms of the international support they are entitled to in the face of outright Russian aggression or armed combat. An even bigger fear among officials is the possibility that Russia will attempt to co-opt each country's domestic native Russian minority populations – 24 per cent in Estonia, 27 per cent in Latvia and 6 per cent in Lithuania, as of June 2016 – in a similar 'war by stealth' to that which was seen in Ukraine.[68] But Donald Trump's ascension to the United States' presidency at the beginning of 2017 sowed doubts about the future of America in NATO. Even before Trump was sworn in as president of the United States, his strong statements about NATO being 'obsolete' were reaping headlines and suggested – at least to the Baltics – that there might be a shift in the direction of US foreign policy, which could indeed pave the way for a more military involvement. 'They're all deathly afraid of Putin. And what he might do. And they are clinging all their hopes based on NATO, and what NATO might do. And with the election of Trump, let me tell you, there is tremendous fear,' says Felicia of the atmosphere in her family.

The previous July, then-Republican candidate Trump suggested that he would have to examine NATO members' defence spending levels before the US decided to help defend Lithuania, Latvia or Estonia against any foreign incursions. 'Have they fulfilled their obligations to us? If they fulfill their obligations to us, the answer is yes,' Trump told the *New York Times* prior to his election.[69] In the same month, Newt Gingrich told CBS that 'Estonia is in the suburbs of St Petersburg,' instigating an outraged backlash in the country and prompting top officials to label the attitude that Russia is free to 'mess around' on its borders 'dangerous'.[70] Hillary Clinton was widely perceived as the safer candidate for the Baltic states, while Trump was perceived as having a softer stance on the Kremlin – public opinion polls across the Baltics showed 46–53 per cent support for Clinton, while support for Trump ranged between 13 and 22 per cent.[71] Brexit also exacerbated concerns in the Baltics. 'The two pillars of our security are weakened,' a Latvian MEP, Sandra Kalniete, told the *Financial Times*.[72]

Unease remained with regards to defence spending in the face of potential new demands: NATO requirements dictate that all NATO allies put forward at least 2 per cent of their gross domestic product (GDP) for defence. Just five members were meeting this commitment as of February 2017, and when the Balkan state of Montenegro joined the alliance the subsequent June, its defence spending also fell below the threshold.[73] Estonia already surpasses its obligations, and while Latvia and Lithuania did not meet them in 2017, they committed to spending 2 per cent of GDP on defence by 2018, and met the designated target.[74]

After Trump's election victory in November 2016, former Russian State Duma member Ilya Ponomarev, who was the sole politician to vote against Crimea's annexation, gave an interview to analytical website Hvylia, alleging that Putin was seeking the fragmentation of NATO. 'It is possible to ensure that NATO collapses,' he wrote, saying Putin would attempt to incite an incident in any one of the Baltic states serious enough for one of them to trigger Article 5 – NATO's mutual defence pact.[75] This statement lacks corroboration, but Russia is clearly greatly irked by NATO's enlargement eastwards – as evidenced by the Foreign Ministry's strong statements around the time of Montenegro's accession, calling it 'deeply erroneous' and broadcasting domestic television reports showcasing decay, crime and corruption in the country.[76] Putin has, in the past, sworn 'countermeasures' to NATO expansion, of which the Baltic states are a prime example.[77] Russian politicians often consider their joining NATO a manifestation of a broken promise; according to them, western leaders betrayed Gorbachev-era assurances that NATO would not enlarge eastwards. And shortly afterwards, NATO started including former Warsaw Pact countries like Poland, the Czech Republic and Hungary, and later – the Baltic states.

Whether such a pledge was ever made during the '2+4 Talks' – that is, the talks that took place in 1990 which involved the two Germanys and their four occupying powers – has been widely and repeatedly contested in recent years, spawning academic research, and heated political statements alike. The Baltics remain a point of conflict if only figuratively. Even the last Soviet leader Mikhail Gorbachev has appeared to contradict himself on the issue, stating in 2008 that 'the Americans promised that NATO wouldn't move beyond the boundaries of Germany after the Cold War'.[78] He followed this statement in 2014 with the comment 'the topic of "NATO expansion" was not discussed at all, and it wasn't brought up in those years ... not a single Eastern European country raised the issue, not even after the Warsaw Pact ceased to exist in 1991. Western leaders didn't bring it up, either.'[79] In 2009, after the recent declassification of significant archival materials, Mark Kramer, director of Cold War Studies at Harvard University's Davis Center for Russian and Eurasian Studies, finally concluded that: 'Declassified records of the negotiations, along with many thousands of pages of other relevant documents, confirm that at no point during the "2 + 4" process did Gorbachev or any other Soviet official bring up the question of NATO expansion to East European countries beyond East Germany.'[80]

Russia still treats 'the west's' promise against NATO expansion as a given truth, and this alleged broken pledge is sporadically still referenced by both Putin and Russian Foreign Minister Sergei Lavrov. Writing in *Foreign Affairs* in 2014, Alexander Lukin, then-vice-president of the Diplomatic Academy of the Russian Ministry of Foreign Affairs, was critical of how the US and its allies had tried to convince Russia that 'foreign forces newly stationed near its borders, in Estonia, Latvia,

Lithuania, Poland, and Romania, would not threaten its security', and in a later book expressed dissatisfaction that Russian leaders had been caught 'off-guard', expecting both sides to 'increase cooperation', 'remain responsive' and 'make mutually acceptable compromises'.[81] Western diplomats cautioned in 2008 that Georgian and Ukrainian membership in NATO would be a 'red line' for Russia, four years after the Baltic states joined. No such warnings were made about the Baltic states.

However, the rhetoric of NATO expansion also discards the Baltic states' own concerns and agency. Even twenty years ago, Atlantic Council's Stephen Blank wrote extensively on how Russia's approach to the stated strategic task of overcoming the negative heritage of the past and keeping the Baltic states out of the Council of Europe were inadvertently pushing them to seek security reassurances to their west – it seems there has been a degree of continuity.[82] Blank noted that Russia's 'endless harangues' of the Baltic states, including 'constant threats of invasion, demands for revised borders, economic pressure, boycotts and sanctions' were self-defeating as they incurred the distrust of local Russians, as well as pushing them to seek assurances of security elsewhere.[83] However, the Baltics still have some reservations about their western allies. Despite the Cold War era being long since over, there are residual feelings of being trapped between larger powers debating their place in the wider geopolitical sphere. 'A colleague of mine has called this Yaltaphobia', said a research fellow at the Latvian Institute of International Affairs, Diāna Potjomkina, referring to the 1945 Yalta conference, during which Winston Churchill, Franklin D. Roosevelt and Joseph Stalin decided the reorganization of postwar Europe.[84]

Fear

Baltic concerns about Trump forged the framework for a stark increase in people making contingency plans over the months of December 2016 and January 2017 (or at least western reports of people making contingency plans) in case they had to leave the country 'at short notice' – packing an extra suitcase, hoarding gasoline, buying boats, and befriending owners of private jets.[85] Volunteers in Lithuania and Estonia started training themselves in survival skills in anticipation of guerrilla war in the countries' extensive, thick forests – in Lithuania, learning to filter pondwater through sand, charcoal and cloth, and in Estonia, subduing fires, horse-riding and learning to identify herbs.[86] The fears bridge generational gaps, but are weaker among the under-thirties. Younger generations born into freedom might not necessarily appreciate it as much without the counterpoint of the Soviet regime seared into their living memory. However, it is still part of the fabric of their reality – even trainee doctors receive lectures on what to do in the event of war. And they are still scared.

'We are pretty afraid of what will happen to Lithuania. Everything started with the Crimea situation,' says twenty-six-year-old Elena Landsbergyte – the medical resident who spoke of her military doctor training. Elena is the granddaughter of Lithuanian politician Vytautas Landsbergis, who played a crucial role in Lithuania's independence movement. 'I think young people realized if they do that there, why can they not do it here? Especially when they [Russians] have a *lot* of military near the Lithuanian border.'

Like her compatriots she also has a contingency plan, and even though she and her husband would like to stick around and help in any hypothetical conflict situation, her family line would probably put her in more danger. 'Knowing my history, with my grandfather, I would just vanish like everybody else in my family . . . I think it would be safer for all of us to leave if that happens. Russians don't like my grandfather,' she says, believing they hold him personally responsible for Lithuania's bid for independence, which was an enormous catalyst for the Soviet collapse. These concerns pervade all levels of society. Members of Lithuanian nationalist skinhead group Diktatura express similar fears: 'How realistic was it to think that part of an independent country could be occupied like five years ago?' asks a twenty-eight-year-old factory worker and drummer, who says his name is Vlad (I have doubts that this is his real name). 'What happened with Crimea. [It could be the same kind of] realistic . . . now,' he adds.

Similar concerns are also felt in Latvia and Estonia. 'It's tense. The army is constantly moving throughout the country,' says twenty-year-old Egils Rekmanis, who helps run an international youth organization in the Latvian coastal city of Liepaja – nearly 500 kilometres from the Russian border. 'You have a lot of soldiers from different nations coming here for training purposes, and I feel it's for this defensive reason,' adding he really feels Russia wants to seize more of Europe. The first wave of more than 450 Canadian military personnel arrived in Latvia in June 2017. He references border agreements between Latvia and Russia in 2007 which saw the former, as well as Estonia, cede two small border areas (Pytalovo/ Arbene in Latvia and Ivangorod and Pechory in Estonia). 'They got part of Latvia not with the army – forcing it – but politically. They made their way through political maneuvers to take a small part of Latvia a couple of years ago.'

According to a cross-Baltic survey published in April 2017, more than half of all Latvians and Lithuanians fear outright war (68 per cent of Lithuanians, 62 per cent of Latvians and 45 per cent of Estonians that year).[87] In Estonia, this was down from 2015, which two years previously saw 12 per cent more residents fearing the same possibility.[88] The increased sense of security could come from temporal distance from Crimea, combined with the knowledge that the country is continuing to meet its NATO spending commitments.

Among native Russians and those based closer to the borders with Russia and Belarus, there are, surprisingly, fewer concerns about Russia as a military force. In those regions, people are used to living alongside their Russian neighbours (they include Belarusians and Ukrainians in this bracket), whom they see as being 'in the same boat' in terms of the daily challenges they all face such as lack of employment or low pensions, and see 'friendly neighbours' over the border line – even if they used to fight in the 1990s after the Cold War ended.

'The Americans and the Englishmen are like, "Russia is a big aggressive force for Estonia"; that's why we are here, that's why we are serving in the army,' says one Estonian-Russian serviceman named Vladimir, based in the Estonian border city of Narva under the terms of his conscription (eight to eleven months in Estonia). 'But I don't understand that,' he adds. 'I don't believe they think they will invade this territory. Estonia was not connected to Russia so directly as Crimea was.'

The Russian-Latvian former mayor of Riga, Nils Ušakovs, who had the support of local ethnic Russians, is also adamant that there is no physical threat posed by the country's eastern neighbour – at least 'much less than is usually shown on the BBC,' he laughs somewhat contemptuously. 'I don't believe that under any circumstances there is a possibility of a military conflict between Russia and NATO ... I believe in the rationale of the correct Russian regime.' Some even view the perceived cooperation between Trump and Putin with optimism. One *New York Times* reporter noted that in a secondary school Social Studies class in Narva, students made statements like, 'Trump wants friendship, while Hillary wants war' – 'in a war, we would be just in the way.'[89] Trump's perceived close relations with Putin were deemed favourable to Estonia's security at this point. Among young underprivileged men, there can be a sense of respect for both Trump and Putin, because of their perceived strength, power, and apparent disregard for the traditional 'rulebook'. Yet there is also a pervasive sense of pragmatism in the face of helplessness given the seriousness of the perceived threats. One eighteen-year-old Ukrainian-Belarusian woman living on the Estonian island of Saaremaa says, 'I know lots has happened in the past, some people still don't like Russians here.' She adds, 'if something happens seriously, I can't do anything.' Elena Landsbergyte is also apprehensive, yet stoic. 'If you live all the time fearing something that maybe won't happen – if it will never happen you will just be living in fear your whole life,' she says. NATO serves as a reassurance to some, while others harbour disdain. 'We have NATO; we're not scared,' says one Latvian street sweeper in Aluksne, northeastern Latvia.[90]

The fear of Russian incursions into the Baltics very much varies from person to person and can be affected by various factors, including location, lineage, exposure to information and professional role in society. But as long as the Baltics stay vigilant about what could be, there seems to be a much lower chance of what 'could be' actually coming to pass.

2 THE THREAT FROM THE EAST

Cigarettes and spies

The village of Stakai lies just past the narrowest point of the Lithuania-Belarus border. The area into which it leads is an inland peninsula of sorts, known as the Dieveniškės appendix. Old legend states that when the Soviets were drawing the region's borders, Stalin set his pipe down on the map and nobody dared move it – forcing the border to be drawn around its thin end. At its narrowest point, it is only 3 kilometres in length. Wooden crosses scatter the roadsides in the absence of churches (the area is too remote) so locals have somewhere to pray. Red and yellow and green, and red and green stumps (the colours of the Lithuanian and the Belarusian national flags respectively) lie either side of the demarcation fence. It is summertime and the warm air is heavy with white butterflies, and the long grass with cornflowers and poppies. Part of the divide cuts directly through a village, and the Soviet-era wooden houses look exactly the same on either side. It has all the dense serenity of a Monet.

A bronze bust of a man named Gintaras Žagunis is stationed outside the local border guard's base. Žagunis served at the station during perestroika. Inside, another small memorial wall is dedicated to him, and the station itself bears his name. Žagunis was the first Lithuanian border guard to die after the restoration of independence in 1991 – Soviet military forces started conducting attacks on border posts, and after Lithuanian border guards returned fire one day, a new series of attacks led to his death. He was only thirty-three or thirty-four at the time and the employees still invite his family to commemorative events.[1]

One guard named Linas Taskunas, dressed in full camo, shows me a recently recovered car. Its bumper, back and roof have been hollowed out

– the men found hundreds of contraband cigarettes in each impressively obscured orifice. This is how local cigarette smugglers operate between Lithuania and Belarus – crossing the lines as regular drivers or passengers after inventing a bizarre variety of hideaways in which the smugglers secrete the goods. People smuggling is also an issue in the country, but less common in this particular region – Vietnamese people based in Russia are the national group most likely to attempt illegal migration – and they simply walk over the border, through the thick forests, on foot. 'Vietnamese people working in Russia – they have been tricked, they have not been paid. And Russian currency devaluated so they have lost a lot of money,' says head of national border guard communications, Rokas Pukinskas. They cannot afford to pay the smugglers' fees from Vietnam to western Europe, which cost around $10,000–$15,000.[2] Vietnamese-organized crime groups are also increasingly becoming involved in smuggling Vietnamese nationals into the EU so they can be exploited for labour purposes.[3]

In what feels like a vague hangover from the Soviet period, there is a framed portrait of Lithuanian President Dalia Grybauskaitė in the chief's office in Stakai (a new president, Gitanas Nausėda, has since been sworn in). Pukinskas says there is a similar picture of her in every border office. The methods have flourished even if the images have changed. It is illegal to display Soviet insignia in Lithuania, and this means it is also illegal for cars displaying such images (of which there are many in Russia) to cross the state line. 'This guy – we had to turn him away,' Pukinskas says, showing me a picture of a car bearing a hammer-and-sickle inside a red star, which arrived in Lithuania from Belarus. Nonetheless, some other meaningful items make it through. The St George's ribbon is a widely recognized nod to the current Russian government and is associated with nationalist and separatist sentiments – it rose to prominence during Ukraine's Euromaidan protests and Ukrainian sympathizers termed the ribbons 'Colorado beetles' because of their colours. While it was originally used as the background for Second World War (or the 'Great Patriotic War' as it is known in Russia) victory medals, it has not been banned in the Baltics; symbols of victory are still ubiquitous during its commemoration in May every year.

At a nearby border post, we don't have to wait long until a black Audi is pulled over by Linas' gun-wielding colleagues. A St George's ribbon is tied conspicuously around the car's rear-view mirror, and a stocky, bald man in his late twenties or early thirties emerges from the vehicle. He's wearing a white wifebeater, two chains around his neck, cargo shorts and flip-flops. The man waves his thick arms in the air, yelling at the border guards in Russian, 'I have a family!' and 'this is bullshit!' as they search his car. The man's wife loiters nearby, and both are chain-smoking. He notices my presence – conspicuous as a plain-clothes observer – and starts to approach me. There is a tattoo of the Statue of Liberty weeping on his left arm. Bending down to my level, he grins. 'I fucking hate Lithuanian policemen.' We exchange small talk as his car is searched. He tells me that he thinks Putin is a wonderful man, but I press him further on his patriotism and he is more ambivalent about Stalin's role in the region's history. 'Here, people are Russian,' he asserts adamantly, but clarifies, 'I have a Lithuanian passport,' getting it out, excited to show someone new. His name is Lithuanian too – Tomas. Another car drives past, and Tomas energetically flags it down, protesting his innocence to the driver – 'Vlad'. The border guards say he's been caught twice before. As with any small village, everyone seems to know everyone else.

Smuggling gangs operate all along the Baltic borderline. The practice is also an open secret in the Latvian town of Alūksne (a popular Estonian tourist destination less than 40 kilometres from the Russian village of Laura), and three individuals there independently suggested that groups of people they were loosely acquainted with often crossed the border to Russia to procure contraband cigarettes. 'Many residents of the border areas are rather tolerant towards small-scale smuggling, believing that it provides a means of survival to the population with modest income,' concluded a Latvian Institute of Internal Affairs report in 2004.[4] This relaxed attitude does not seem to have died down much since. Huge quantities of cigarettes make their way to western Europe; in the UK in 2015, some 610 million illegally sold cigarettes were thought to have come from Belarus.[5]

But monitoring cross-border cigarette smuggling can be an extremely dangerous pursuit – as can engaging with the perpetrators, some of whom have links to Russian spies and organized criminal networks – which can bleed into one another. FSB border guards monitor people frequently travelling between Latvia and Russia in the sparsely populated areas, and Latvia has identified instances in which individuals have been subjected to blackmail and threats – Russian and Latvian nationals alike.[6] In September 2014, Eston Kohver, an agent with Estonia's Internal Security Service (KAPO), was kidnapped by members of Russia's state security apparatus. Estonia said the agent was grabbed from the Estonian side amid a cacophony of smoke and stun grenades. Russian prosecutors insisted that he had been over the border line when he was taken, and a Russian court later sentenced him to fifteen years in prison (some speculated the severity was to ensure the subsequent 'spy swap' that ensured Kohver's release occurred). Kohver had, according to Estonia, been involved in investigating a cross-border cigarette smuggling ring when he was seized. Three of the smugglers were later convicted of espionage in Estonia. It seemed that Kohver had interrupted a joint operation between organized crime and the FSB in the Baltic region – the Russian services would have had no reason to intervene in a smuggling operation it was not connected to, and unofficial links means the organization can reap revenue 'off the books'. The money cannot be directly linked to Moscow.[7] Border operations are targeted and personalized, yet not coordinated in any explicitly official way with the state – although the state can use or instigate them when it is in its wider interests.

A joint report between Buzzfeed and Re:Baltica showed that between 2015 and 2017, at least five men – ostensibly cigarette smugglers – had been arrested in Estonia and convicted of spying on behalf of Russia. Only one of the five did not have Estonian citizenship. The individuals had been coerced into working undercover in order to avoid lengthy prison terms inside Russia, to sweep information about border guards and military bases, to name just a couple of things. 'They are an easy target for FSB recruiters,' said Aleksander Toots, the deputy head of KAPO.[8] The men had to choose between working as FSB employees or serving a sentence in Russian prison – to those who know their reputation, the choice is obvious.[9] To those who are Putin supporters, the choice might be even easier. One of the men mentioned in the report, Pavel Romanov, had been suspected of being a smuggler for a long time. He was also experienced and well-known to the border guards, and deemed part of a criminal community 'subjected to a strict management style' in which everyone had a set 'role'.[10] The investigation noted the personal, small-scale targeted nature of operations and how they can have global implications. 'Russia is testing new methods – at first close to home, and then, inevitably, further abroad. As the world focuses on Russia's capabilities in the realm of cyberattacks and misinformation campaigns, is it missing Russia's ability to develop new methods of good old-fashioned on-the-ground spying?' it asked.

Russia certainly seems to be placing a focus on its bottom-up capacities as much as – if not more than – attempted infiltration of high-level institutions. Forty-year-old Tartu businessman Ilya Tikhanovski was found in 2017 to have served Russia's Main Intelligence Directorate (GRU) for years. 'Tikhanovski did not have access to Estonian state secrets but was tasked mainly with collecting official information or personal data,' a local media report noted.[11] A later KAPO report also described a focus on the Russian-speaking youth as well as Russia's continued use of 'agents it regards as of low importance, who the press gleefully describe as "economy class agents" . . . They are easy to recruit, force into cooperation and eventually disown if they are caught.'[12]

According to the Baltics, Russian actors have been conducting multi-pronged 'testing' of internal institutions, whether public authorities or private companies. While 'on-the-ground spying' is important, in the twenty-first century, it also involves engaging in small-scale cyberattacks. Both can attempt to foment unrest among the countries' domestic Russian populations, although this isn't their sole purpose. Russian state involvement is hard to pin down exactly – as mentioned, people connected to state actors are often involved, but asserting an 'official' link is still tenuous or left implied. Perpetrators can display knowledge of or complement Russian state movements without an apparent personal link to the state. An early example of this modus operandi was in August 2008, during the Russian invasion of Georgia, when the country's IT infrastructure was also attacked. The US Cyber Consequences Unit (US-CCU) concluded that at the time of the assault, complementary '[cyber] attacks were carried out by civilians with little or no direct involvement on the part of the Russian government or military.' However, 'the organizers of the cyber-attacks had advance notice of Russian military intentions.'[13] Ten years later, these methods are still a hot international topic. By keeping a watchful eye on espionage patterns in Russia's 'near-abroad' we can make educated guesses at methods that might be applied further afield, such as in the US.

The online threat

One evening in April 2007, the sounds of loud bangs and smashing glass, whistles and screaming could be heard on the streets of Tallinn. Hi-vis-clad riot police faced off against agitators and looters over a period of two days, culminating in the fatal stabbing of one Russian man, Dmitri Ganin, and at least 300 arrests. The cause? A Soviet war memorial. 'Bronze Night'

– as the riots came to be known – peaked when the Estonian police and Ministry of Defence made preparations to move the memorial, the Bronze Soldier, from Tönismägi in central Tallinn to a leafy, sleepy defence forces' cemetery near a motorway on the capital's outskirts. To Estonians, it represented an 'occupying statue'. To Russia, it represented Soviet victory over the Nazis. Boris Ockchin, a former Red Army cadet who fought in 1941, spoke of the removal of the monument with great distaste. 'Of course we feel very indignant about this,' he said. 'They shouldn't have done it. To remove it – that was like spitting at us veterans on our souls. That was wrong. They could have discussed it gradually, and then moved it to a different place in a decent way, not in the way the Estonians have done. It's like swearing at our military.'[14] One Estonian rumour said that it marked the site at which drunk Red Army soldiers had managed to run themselves over with a tank, and even today the statue's sturdy Soviet form bears the traces of red paint which its objectors have flung at it over the years.

A major reason for the memorial's initial construction was that it was a compulsory component of Soviet city planning, according to the Estonian Ministry of Foreign Affairs. Moscow required a Red Army memorial in a public place in the city centre and surrounded by a spacious square where it would be 'possible to carry out large-scale events on Soviet and Red Army anniversaries' – just as was required in each of the capitals of the Soviet republics.[15] In the events leading up to the 'Bronze Night', the area around the statue was cordoned off, pending its removal. Members of the NGO, 'Night Watch' were beaten by police, and groups of people began to assemble around it. Of the 300 arrests that were eventually made, some '40 per cent of those who were arrested had criminal records,' said then-Estonian President Toomas Ilves. 'So we're not talking about a representative cross-section of the Russian population living in Estonia. It . . . isn't the case that 40 per cent of Russians in Estonia have criminal records. They were hooligans,' he said.[16] Whether 'hooligans' or not, the riots came to be a pivotal moment in terms of Russian-Estonian relations.

A mere matter of days later, the country was struck by cyberattacks that temporarily crippled banking, media and government systems (including those of the foreign ministry and the justice ministry).[17] Some Estonian websites were vandalized with Russian propaganda, and the attack was generally framed as one perpetrated from the east – which certainly helped to garner valuable western media attention. After the attacks occurred, Russian presidential press secretary Dmitriy Peskov said, 'Russia can no way be involved in cyber terrorism and all claims to the contrary are an absolute lie.'[18]

However, that tenuous, yet implicit link with the Russian state still emerged. Two years later, in 2009, Konstantin Goloskokov, an activist with a fresh-faced pro-Kremlin youth group called Nashi (renowned for its erotic calendars, suspiciously expensive headquarters, and songs professing declarations of devotion to Putin), claimed responsibility. Goloskokov was also an aide to a member of parliament. He said that he coordinated a group to target Estonian websites – yet he still maintained his distance from the state. 'If anything did happen, it was the personal initiative of Konstantin Goloskokov,' said Nashi spokeswoman Kristina Potupchik.[19] A decade after the attacks initially took place, the former chief of staff of the Estonian Defence Forces (EDF) said that 'officers observing the riots at the time also reported well-trained young men giving instructions to the rioters'. Then-Prime Minister Andrus Ansip said, 'we know that the man who was supposed to document these events turned out to be an FSB agent, locked himself in the toilet and got drunk,' referring to Aleksei Dressen, a spy who, after being convicted in Estonia was later one of those exchanged for the kidnapped KAPO officer Eston Kohver.[20]

The attacks had broad-reaching consequences and in the aftermath of the Estonia case, people started to realize that an adversary does not necessarily have to have 'boots on the ground' to do widescale damage to a state, its institutions, or its people – and how in the event of this happening, it might be hard to both communicate and classify the nature of the problem. In Georgia's case in 2008, the very sites able to provide information about what was going on (including foreign media in the country) fell under attack – which also prevented the international sphere from learning about what was happening in a timely fashion.[21] Even if the Zapad 2017 military drills passed without too much ferocity at the beginning of September that same year, communications network interruptions and phone hacking took place parallel to the standard military drills, according to western officials. Lithuania also encountered widescale cyberattacks in 2008 (shortly after making the use of Soviet symbols illegal), and in 2016 (as did Latvia), to name just a few incidents.

Attacks do not necessarily have to be instantaneous and coordinated – rather, they can take an incrementally corrosive form, or can target institutions and individuals in a more piecemeal fashion. But both are acts of aggression that happen in a non-physical space, and thus, are difficult to conceptualize and address in terms of international law. 'If a member state's communications centre is attacked with a missile, you call it an act of war. So, what do you call it if the same installation is disabled with a cyber-attack?' a senior official in Brussels asked *The Economist* in the aftermath of the events in Estonia in 2007.[22] As the main battleground moves from physical terrain to cyberspace, new questions emerge. 'Would a cyber-attack on Bulgaria by unknown actors sympathetic to Russia invoke Article 5? What about a tiny insurrection in a Baltic border town, organised by locals with suspicious ties to Russian security services? Would all the countries in NATO go to war to keep Estonian electronic banking online?'[23] This low-level testing in an international 'grey area' keeps the premature invocation of NATO commitments at bay while allowing Russia to inconvenience the Baltics.

Estonia and Georgia are far from the only victims of such cyberintrusions to date. In 2008, over 300 Lithuanian websites were targeted shortly after the country made Soviet symbols such as the hammer and sickle illegal – as well as the Soviet anthem. The same year, Lithuania stood in the way of Russia and the EU forging a new agreement, by vetoing a mandate for talks with Russia on a new Partnership and Cooperation Agreement (PCA) – but it later dropped its opposition after the initial 'bold stone-throw'.[24] Lithuanian websites were subjected to distributed denial of service (DDOS) attacks and others were sabotaged with the very symbols that had just been banned.[25] Lithuania subsequently urged the UN Security Council (UNSC) to recognize cyberterrorism as an issue 'as grave' as any other form of terrorism.[26] In 2016, Lithuania was also the target of widescale cyberattacks, largely directed at state institutions, while the same Baltic nation estimated that it had been struck by around 50,000 cyberattacks in total in 2017.[27] The ministries of the interior and foreign affairs were among those that were hit in 2016, as well as airports and major media outlets. The attacks sought to 'restrict Lithuania's information space, detach and isolate the state from information availability and communication with the outside world within the global information space' using similar strategies to those which had previously been applied in both Georgia in 2008 and in Ukraine in 2014.[28]

The Baltic nations can spring back from these attacks, but they can also hinder foreign confidence in the mentioned countries by forcing them to admit they have been targets. In the UK's overseas business risk assessment for Lithuania, the Foreign and Commonwealth Office (FCO) specifically mentions cybercrime as an 'evolving and new type of fraud' in Lithuania.[29] Private companies may also be targeted but are unwilling to admit it for such reasons – confidence in them will be reduced, and investors' share prices will fall. This can prevent them from being too forthcoming about any attacks, reduce the scope for open dialogue and counteractions, and obfuscate the scale at which they may or may not be taking place. Personal security at every level is imperative, if state or technological institutions value cybersecurity at all. Geographical proximity to perpetrators is, however, increasingly irrelevant. And, if psychological or technological attacks can be considered harmful, they remain in ambiguous territory with regards to international law.

Regional energy networks have also been targeted in the past. Ukraine's power grid was hit in 2016 in an intrusion that appeared to have the deliberate intention of causing pervasive national physical damage via cybersecurity weaknesses inherent in its Operational Technology (OT) systems, using (what were at the time) very new methods.[30] Some later, similar attacks across the Baltics echoed incidents in Ukraine – an internet gateway to a Baltic electricity grid, a petrol distribution system and serial-to-ethernet converters (STEC) appeared to have all been targeted.[31] The act of attacking utilities and state institutions lacks a profit motive, so the desire to simply cause disruption and chaos on a nationwide level is logically the prime motivator for such incidents. It is a problem for state actors and such private companies alike – but the latter are more susceptible to cybercrime with a financial motive. The institutional attacks sow more confusion. 'Are they just trying to demoralise us? Or do they want western journalists to quote them, which will send a signal to the markets that we're unsafe, and thus send our investment climate plummeting?' asked Iivi Masso, former Estonian President Toomas Hendrik Ilves's security adviser in 2015 – even prior to the power grid assaults.[32]

There are suggestions that cyberattacks target individuals using assessments of social media behaviour and other (perhaps pseudo-) psychosocial assessments. Lithuania's annual national security threat assessment for 2017 stated that the activities of APT28/Sofacy (otherwise known as 'Fancy Bear') had 'increased significantly' in the country. APT28 is known for being able to exploit publicly known weak points or security problems in software or hardware, and has been credited with being part of the Russian intelligence-gathering operation responsible for obtaining allegedly compromising information on US President Donald Trump and disrupting the nation's political system in 2016 – although this is yet to be fully proven. However, the importance of Russian trolls assuming personalities inside (or even helping to create) niche political movements has since been affirmed.[33] Ukraine has even suggested that 'undetectable' computer viruses have targeted specific individuals 'in particular departments', which are personalized in that they are 'constructed based on the social understanding of social media by particular people', allegedly with the aid of scientists, psychiatrists and neurologists.[34]

Both Ukraine and the Baltic states continue to be a 'testing ground' for widescale cyber operations on a global scale, says analyst Jaan Priisalu, a NATO cyberdefence fellow and a researcher at Tallinn University of Technology – illogical and unprofitable attacks are often conducted in Estonia, apparently to test the functioning of specific banking systems.[35] There is indeed a cybercrime underground that intentionally strikes the Baltic region (although they are certainly not the primary targets on a global scale) in order to trial methods that might be used later on more significant targets. Understanding what is happening in the Baltic states as a testing ground is imperative to understanding bigger global currents in cybercrime. 'The international cybercrime language is Russian,' he says – a commonly held belief. Anton, a malware researcher at security firm SentinelOne, told the BBC that with regards to the cybercriminal underground forums, 'everyone can join as long as you speak Russian'.[36] Russian internet security experts, Irina Borogan and Andrei Soldatov said that hackers who grew up in post-Soviet Russia are reputed to be among some of the most active and dangerous 'in the world', as the changes during the 1990s in Russia saw defence industry cutbacks – 'the main employer of the Soviet technical intelligentsia'.[37] Perhaps because of this, the Baltic states are not only 'receivers' of cybercrime but some attacks also originate there. A Kapersky security bulletin in 2008 stated that Estonia, Latvia and Lithuania were among the top twenty countries globally from which attacks then originated – 'due to the close ties of cybercriminals from these countries with their "colleagues" in Russia and Ukraine'.[38] Online news sources and defence contractors can stand to benefit from cybercrime concerns too – US defence consultancy Booz Allen Hamilton landed $400 million of deals spread over twenty-two contracts in 2010 to deal with digital threats – as well as being a threat, countering them is a business too.[39]

More recent problems in the region coincided, once again, in a concerning way with military manoeuvres. In September 2017, Latvia's emergency services' 112 hotline failed for the first time in a 'very powerful' attack that was not 'aimed at Latvia, but towards Gotland, the Åland Islands', said deputy chairman of the Latvian Parliament's National Security Committee, Karlis Serzants.[40] The headline of this article was 'Russia may have tested cyber war on Latvia' – which again, recognized the region as an area suitable for Russia's experiments. At the same time, US Army Lt. Col. Christopher L'Heureux, who took over as commander of a NATO base in Poland in July 2017, found that his phone's security had been breached while he had been at shooting drills. 'It had a little Apple map, and in the center of the map was Moscow,' Col. L'Heureux told the *Wall Street Journal*. 'It said, "Somebody is trying to access your iPhone" . . . they were geolocating me, whoever it was,' he said. 'I was like, "what the heck is this?"'[41] Reactionary precautions were taken to ensure phones remained absent from exercises, such as soldiers being forced to jump in lakes – thus revealing whether any solider had one on their person. The episodes that served as precursors to these precautions again demonstrated the multipronged nature of the Russian approach – technological intrusions combined with 'good old-fashioned on-the-ground spying'.

However, again their influence and impact can be overstated. CNBC report stated that, 'the smartphone hacking campaign by Russia targeted a group of at least 4,000 NATO troops in eastern Europe' – while of course the contingent of NATO troops in the region numbers in the thousands, it wasn't 'at least 4,000' soldiers that were targeted but rather a small proportion of them – the US military officer and 'at least six' other soldiers' phones or Facebook accounts were hacked. Furthermore, 'several NATO soldiers' were 'casually approached in public locations by a Russian agent with information about their family and other personal details'.[42] One of the purposes of the attacks was clearly to make it known that the attacks had taken place, just as was once the case in the twentieth century.

Boots on the ground

There is at present a low-on-the-ground military threat posed to the Baltics by Russia, despite the indications of heightened defence spending and increased efforts towards military modernization on the part of Russia. Unlike Georgia and Ukraine, the Baltics are already NATO member states and it is simply not in Russia's practical interests to launch a head-on attack. But the country's capacity to inflict extreme damage on Latvia, Lithuania or Estonia is very high – even with NATO support it is unlikely that the Baltics would manage to successfully defend themselves. A frequently quoted 2016 RAND Corporation assessment concluded that: 'As currently postured, NATO cannot successfully defend the territory of its most exposed members. Across multiple games using a wide range of expert participants in and out of uniform playing both sides, the longest it has taken Russian forces to reach the outskirts of the Estonian and/or Latvian capitals of Tallinn and Riga, respectively, is 60 hours. Such a rapid defeat would leave NATO with a limited number of options, all bad'.[43]

NATO, the US and the Baltics have all had to cope with an increasingly adversarial Russia in recent years. Russia's successful involvement in Georgia in 2008, Ukraine in 2014 and Syria in 2015 was a wake-up call for the western dominance of the 1990s and early 2000s, which had up until that point been somewhat taken for granted. Russia achieved its goals in both Georgia and Ukraine – both countries had been edging closer to NATO membership at the points at which the conflicts took place. Furthermore, its involvement in Syria in 2015 was the first time Russia had overstepped the boundaries of the former Soviet Union since its collapse. The war in Georgia provided the impetus for Russia to overhaul its military, with the country 'adopting a flexible force structure' undertaking 'large-scale military exercises' and improving payment and communications among servicemen.[44] Since then, we have seen an ever-widening chasm between 'east' and 'west' in the world.

Concerns about a resurgent Russia were exacerbated in 2016 by Moscow military build-up near the Baltics and Poland, which was significant enough for western allies to station four battalions – some 4,000 troops – in the region in the first half of the year. 'From our perspective, we could argue this is extraordinarily provocative behavior', US Deputy Secretary of Defense Robert Work said of the preceding troop build-up on the Russian side.[45] Increasingly antagonistic feelings have been developing between east and west. On top of the capacity to inflict damage, the Baltics are also at higher risk than other European countries – they share a contiguous border with Russia and remain former Soviet states, however little they would still like to be defined as such. The same RAND Corporation assessment in 2016 assessed that the Baltic states were the 'next most likely targets' of attempted Russian coercion on account of the unevenly integrated Russian populations and shared border with Russia. General assumptions suggest that strategically, Belarus is a 'highly subordinate ally to Russia' and the Suwałki Gap that separates Belarus from Kaliningrad is a NATO Achilles' heel, but one analysis suggests that the Belarusian and Russian militaries are not particularly well-integrated militarily, Belarusian military spending lags, and the two countries have 'repeatedly clashed over natural gas subsidies and debts'.[46]

After an initial military shrinkage following the collapse of the Soviet Union (5 million down to 1 million personnel between 1988 and 1994), Russian military funding has been increasing over the past few years and is set to keep growing. Stockholm International Peace Research Institute (SIPRI) identified a 'rising trend' in military expenditure beginning in 1999, but it accelerated sharply in 2012 as Russia started to implement the 2011–20 State Armaments Programme.[47] In 2010, then Russian President Dmitry Medvedev, in a speech to the Defense Ministry Collegium, called for 70 per cent of military equipment to be modernized by 2020.[48] The year 2008 saw widespread military forums and massive increases in defence spending, upgrading the country's military from 'creaky' to something of a force to be reckoned with.[49] Russia has resurged as a global military power and a significant challenge to NATO. According to amendments submitted to the State Duma in October 2017, defence spending will continue to increase by 180 billion rubles (about £2.4 billion) to a maximum of three trillion rubles – in a move 'possibly related to the situation in Syria', said the Institute of National Strategy's Mikhail Remizov. However, the Russian state does not have endless funding for military innovation and the country is already invested in two simultaneous conflicts. Social spending and funds for education and medicine are expected to decrease by 54 billion rubles as a result.[50]

Russia still poses a danger to jets over the Baltic Sea, causing definite unease about the country's intentions. Russian jets frequently fly over the Baltic region, sometimes erratically, with their transponders turned off, which prevents them from being detected by ground radar. US European Command (EUCOM) captured an image in June 2017 that showed a Russian SU-27 getting so close to a US Air Force reconnaissance jet that its pilot could be seen – EUCOM said the incident was unsafe 'due to the high rate of closure speed and poor control of the aircraft during the intercept'.[51]

Russian warplanes have been increasingly flying over the Baltic Sea and Gulf of Finland, with the situation growing much worse from around

2013–14 – Estonia stated that 'several cases have been documented where Russian warplanes have, probably by accident, strayed dangerously close to civilian planes over the Baltic Sea'.[52] While earlier in the year Russia had offered to turn on transponders, it later materialized that its aircraft did not have transponders to switch on.[53] The Norwegian press has also more recently reported some technical difficulties affecting their airspace. In East-Finnmark, in the country's far north, around the time of Zapad 2017, 'noise' from the direction of Russia jammed aircraft GPS signals in the region.[54] Even if these are just attempts to intimidate, there are real technical risks that come with the recklessness, and even if there has not yet been any major loss of human life as a result, it remains a sincere possibility in the future.

Media wars

In February 2017, the office of the Speaker of the Seimas – Lithuania's Parliament – said that it received an anonymous email. The message alleged that a five-year-old girl in foster care in the central Lithuanian town of Jonava had been surrounded and raped by German-speaking men, shortly after a German NATO mission arrived in the country that year. Local government said that the allegations had been false. 'Initial conclusions indicate that the email was sent from a third-party country, that is, from a country outside the European Union', Darius Valkavicius, chief prosecutor of Kaunas region told Reuters.[55]

Valkavicius did not explicitly name Russia when he reported this news. However, the event manifested key patterns in suspected Russian media propaganda and involvement in propaganda, which see Baltic governments and western, NATO or EU allies become embroiled in stories that use perceivably taboo subjects such as sexual assault of young girls or other stories involving children, incompetence of authorities, the incitement of homophobia and racism, allegations of Nazism, and strong criticisms of allegedly Russophobic actions in the region. Such stories can be instrumental in fomenting internal unrest or reframing it in a different way – it was 'internal separatism' that saw eastern Ukraine enter into conflict with the central government.

These methods are frequently used in media. Various individuals who have no immediately obvious links to the Russian state aid the development of tainted or false stories. However, this does not mean there is no informal connection between said individuals and Russian state actors. The intention of these stories appears to be to stoke mistrust and incite internal disruption. However, the Baltics are pragmatically dealing with the propensity of propaganda, and its impact is limited but still effective among sectors of society that apparently feel disenchanted by the hand they have been dealt. Media outlets broadcasting in the Baltic region can calcify existing societal divisions and present economic inequalities and social issues as forms of ethnic discrimination.

The campaign in the Baltics appears at surface level to be very similar to Russia's campaigns internationally – again, an important reflection of how Russian actions in the Baltics can foreshadow or reflect wider international 'campaigns' thought to be coordinated by Russia. In eastern Europe (and later, in the US), Russia has had a similar modus operandi. In 2016, the *New York Times*' Andrew Higgins came into contact with a penniless Czech Stalinist, Ladislav Kasuka, who was offered tranches of a few hundred dollars each to buy flags for protest rallies and film them in Prague. The messages offering him the sums appeared on his screens in a mixture of Russian and 'garbled Czech'. His being contacted was part of a Moscow-financed campaign, mediated by Belarus-born writer Alexander Usovsky. In any official capacity, the 'small cog' that was Kasuka had no links to Russia.[56] However, Usovsky, in total, also received more than US $100,000 from Russia in order to finance anti-Ukrainian nationalist groups in Poland and to set Poles against Ukrainians, according to the Senate Committee on Appropriations.[57]

There have been further cases in Scandinavia: teenagers in a Swedish suburb were reportedly offered money by an unidentified Russian television station in return for on-camera 'action' which proved that 'large-scale' immigration was unsuccessful. 'They came up to us and said they wanted to see some action. They wanted to bribe us 400 krona [£36] each,' said one of the teenagers called Mohammed.[58] The Swedish Institute of International Affairs has since found that Russia has been targeting Sweden with a 'wide array of active methods' in order to influence public opinion.[59] There has also been propaganda disseminated in relation to families and children of Russian families residing abroad – cases in Norway and Finland and Germany, cases where someone got raped, or a child was taken away by social services. 'Russian propaganda is describing it as they are taking children from Russian families to give them away to gays and paedophiles,' says Ivan Lavrentjev, an Estonian communications officer, somewhat acerbically. 'This was one case with Norway three or four years ago and a couple of years ago it was the very same scenario with Finland. Similar to [the] "Lisa" case in Germany.'[60]

At the end of 2014, the Russian Children's Right Commissioner pointed the finger at Norway and Finland saying they had been 'terrorizing' Russian families living in the Scandinavian countries.[61] The 'Lisa' case in Germany was an incident in which a Russian-German girl alleged that she had been raped by Arab migrants in the country. Russian Foreign Minister Sergey Lavrov accused Berlin of a cover-up, but the girl later said she had been making it up, and had stayed the night with a friend, who was not being treated as a suspect.[62] It was a 'wake-up call' to the German political elites who started to clearly see 'links between Russian domestic and foreign media campaigns against Germany and Russian politics at the highest level.'[63] The same girl, oddly, was later involved in a child abuse case – twenty-four-year-old 'Ismet S.' was found guilty of child abuse and producing child pornography after having consensual sex with the minor and filming it.[64]

In Lithuania and Latvia, news stories have seemingly attempted to incite bad feeling against soldiers stationed in the two countries. On top of the February 2017 incident, a Russian language news site called Vesti.lv ran a story in June 2017 showcasing pictures of a disgraced Canadian colonel and convicted killer, Russell Williams dressed in women's lingerie. The article was headlined 'The Gay Battlegroup: NATO has dug into Latvia' – and Canada recognized that troops in the region should expect to be targeted. 'It happened to German troops deployed in Lithuania, British troops in Estonia, it happened to American troops deployed in Poland,' Col. Josh Major, who led the contingent of 450 soldiers, told CBC.[65] The article did not mention that Williams had been in prison since 2010.

Estonia has also experienced problems. 'We just had this scandal [mid-2017] ... when there was a child [temporarily] taken away from a family in Tallinn. The girl was eight years old, and both the parents and the girl they are Russian citizens,' says Lavrentjev, who was in charge of communications for the case. He says it spread in Estonian media thanks to local branches of Russian outlets, which suggested the parents were being discriminated against on account of their nationality.[66] Local media can pick up the stories too, even if they originate in Kremlin-backed outlets such as Sputnik, which serve as a 'trigger'. Isabella, from Mustamäe, Tallinn, was removed from her parents as a result of the family's poor living conditions, which 'constituted a threat to both a health and wellbeing of the child' and had been 'under constant review and not changed over an eight-year period'.[67] Within two days, the childcare case was widely discussed in Russian media to show that Estonian Russophobes were 'stooping' to stealing children from Russian homes.[68] 'The two parents have some kind of disabilities – both of them – this is why the family was under the control of social services – with the support of social services – from the very moment the child was born', Lavrentjev says. He calls the campaign 'sophisticated' because the family readily made concessions that they were not working, and they smoked indoors. Yet, they maintained that in general it was 'not that bad'. Lavrentjev received a memo from the social worker who made the decision.

'The child has never been to a dentist in her life. The child smells of cigarettes since they're smoking all the time inside the apartment – the smoke [was] preserved for three or four days in this children's facility despite the fact that the child was washed a couple of times a day … health is poor, the teeth is poor – although dentistry in Estonia is free for children.' The social worker who filed the report visited the apartment with police because the last time they had gone, and offered summer care to the child, 'the mother of the child attacked the social worker and locked her in the apartment'. The father went to the Russian embassy the same day the child was taken, and the Russian embassy was 'successful in working with the media' and a lawyer was sourced – Violetta Volkova – who was involved in the Pussy Riot case.[69] At the time Estonia could not respond in any official capacity because at that stage they were not permitted to release the health-related data of a child. One Estonian youth worker based in Kadrina, about 80 kilometres east of Tallinn, independently mentioned in passing how difficult it was to officially remove a child from its parents. The situation must be very poor for the child and follows a lengthy period of assessment, she stated. In Mihhailova's case, she had been under observation most of her life on account of her parents' situation, says Lavrentjev.

Fomenting discord, this 'hybrid warfare' is an old tactic. High-ranking former KGB officer Oleg Kalugin described the 'heart and soul' of Soviet intelligence as active measures to influence world events in favour of the USSR while undermining the US – 'not intelligence collection, but subversion: active measures to weaken the west, to drive wedges in the western community alliances of all sorts, particularly NATO, to sow discord among allies, to weaken the United States in the eyes of the people of Europe, Asia, Africa, Latin America, and thus to prepare ground in case the war really occurs', according to archival documents.[70]

Russian-language disinformation has a limited impact – each Baltic state is on high alert to ensure that efforts are being channelled into educating populations about the importance of critical thinking. However, the media – as well as the ongoing de facto segregation between Russians and native Baltic populations and general attitudes, which I will explore in later chapters – massage the idea that Russophobia exists in the different countries and that 'western media' is propaganda too, creating a false equivalency. An idea that isn't helped by panic over imminent invasions. 'It's not dangerous,' says twenty-four-year-old Estonian-Russian serviceman Boris Medveznikov in the Estonian border city of Narva. Just across the river is the imposing fifteenth-century Ivangorod Fortress and some beautiful riverfront dachas (summer houses) bathed in pink twilight. 'You have been misinformed about our neighbours . . . Russia is very strong. But we are European.'[71] His colleagues agree that Narva specifically is no more or less dangerous than other Estonian cities and believe the western media to have massaged the facts.[72] However, not all feel completely 'European'. Russian propaganda can also have the impact of persuading large swathes of native Russians who have never previously visited the country that life might be better for them over the border – a sentiment bolstered by social problems such as widespread unemployment in certain areas – especially towns or cities once home to Soviet industries or factories that later closed.[73]

Estonia, Latvia and Lithuania are making varying degrees of progress in addressing the tone of Russian-language media in the country. While the fact remains that some Russians do feel they are discriminated against and that there is some ingrained Russophobia in the Baltic states, the governments still feel they need to address the breadth of information the population can access and are all taking steps to educate their population. In late 2015, Estonia established a new Russian-language channel – state broadcaster ETV launched ETV+ to counteract the pro-Kremlin messages. 'We find it important because in the situation of Russia's propaganda – I call it propaganda – we need to have additional channels where the Russian-speaking population can get objective information, just facts,' then-Foreign Minister Marina Kaljurand told me.[74] However, ETV+ has since faced some issues – Estonia's Language Act demands that all programmes broadcast must be available with direct Estonian-language interpretation – an expensive feat. The annual €400,000 translation budget is largely spent on interpretation.[75]

Latvia is also somewhat hampered by internal regulations that require approximately 80 per cent of its state media to be broadcast in the Latvian language. 'We are allowed to broadcast in Latvian language only and the Russian language is just some percentage also regarded to the law . . . we cannot provide more than 20 per cent Russian language in our channels,' says Ivars Belte, Chairman of the Board at public broadcaster Latvian Television (LTV). Its building is situated on Riga's Zaķusala ('Hare Island') located in the middle of the Daugava river. From his sixteenth-floor office there is an incredible view of the old aircraft hangars of the central market and the Hanseatic peaks of the old town buildings. Belte, who was the CEO of a holding company representing Russian media in the Baltics for four years, sees his island more metaphorically. 'We are running this Russian news island within a Latvian TV channel,' he says. Because of language limitations and state funding, LTV has not managed any groundbreaking changes. 'We managed to strengthen the news and we managed to introduce three new programmes on a weekly basis and that's all that we have done,' he says.[76] Furthermore, Latvian politicians are required by the state language centre – VVC – to make statements only in Latvian (as opposed to Russian) – former Riga Mayor Nils Usakovs spoke out in February 2017 for being fined a (probably symbolic) €140 for using Russian on his official Facebook page the previous year.[77] The language laws have their disadvantages – while they are a confident assertion of the regional character, they can further enhance societal divisions and encourage people to seek media sources with which they identify or agree more strongly.

Still, the different Baltic countries are also channelling efforts into monitoring media consumption as well as production. Latvia has been conducting polls about the perception of media in the country and notes that its population is fairly adept at being able to identify the fact that 'fake news' is disseminated – with some 80 per cent of poll respondents believing they had come across it (the in/accuracy of their assessments notwithstanding).[78] Lithuania has also been taking the issue very seriously, and is encouraging specific curriculum changes. 'We will from next year [2018] on introduce information security lessons for senior pupils,' says Vytautas Bakas, chairman of the Committee on National Security and Defence.[79] 'We also need to reinforce media literacy and provide high-quality information, also to provide alternatives so people have several sources of information to compare.' The case of the anonymous report on the German soldier was a turning point for Lithuania. 'This news made us come to grips with reality and raised the information security issue to the highest political level,' Bakas says, adding that there was also 'fake news' in mid-2017 'about a Russian plane throwing an imitation explosive on a high-rise building in [the coastal Lithuanian city of] Klaipeda – all in all several times per month we get fake news.'

Native Russians in the Baltics consume a great deal of Russian television broadcast on domestic channels. Perviy Baltiyskiy Kanal (PBK) is a popular television news source, along with NTV and Ren TV – all of which are affiliated with a stance favourable to the Russian government. PBK entered the top three most-watched news channels in Latvia in 2014, while some 7.9 per cent of Estonians were found to watch it (along with 5 per cent watching NTV and 2.1 per cent watching Ren TV) in 2013. PBK held third place in Latvia in June 2016, too.[80] In 2014, PBK was fined three separate times by the Latvian government for presenting biased information, and fined €10,000 later, in 2015, for similar reasons.[81] Russian media is also deftly rising to the demands of the modern media climate via the internet. Online news portal BALTNEWS is an odd arm of Russian power. Ostensibly a financial news website, a Dutch organization revealed in 2017 that it was linked to Sputnik. The channel broadcasts footage straight from Moscow; it was hardly surprising to learn of its links. However, there is direct influence at work. Anatoly Ivanov, who is the head of the Russian website, frequently visits Moscow to coordinate the planner with Russia, and has encouraged staffers to strengthen ties with Russian mass media.[82]

The Baltic states are doing their best to monitor Russian media and provide alternative forms of media, but it is impossible to sever links with pro-Russia sources of information and propaganda completely. The countries follow up the loose threads of suspect stories and ensure that their citizens are well equipped to critique flaws and one-sidedness in information provided without resorting to outright censorship. Their openness works in their favour, in contrast to a Russia that has to orchestrate stories in a secretive fashion, cherry-picking or sponsoring people who might serve to illustrate a political point.

Over the course of summer 2017, fears were allayed in part, been diluted, by both President Trump and US Vice President Mike Pence's reiterations of the US' commitments to NATO member states, Estonia's assumption of the EU presidency, and the peaceful passage of the Zapad

2017 exercises of which Karoblis spoke so warily. Donald Trump started to draw a much-referenced line between 'candidate Trump' and President Trump in April 2017, clarifying his position. 'I said it was obsolete. It's no longer obsolete,' Trump said of NATO.[83] US Vice President Mike Pence renewed the nation's commitments more specifically to the leaders of Estonia, Latvia and Lithuania, telling a news conference in Brussels in July, alongside the three Baltic presidents, that, 'under President Donald Trump, the United States stands firmly behind our Article 5 pledge of mutual defense. An attack on one of us is an attack on us all'.[84] Relations between Trump and Putin started to be seen as more frosty. However, the year 2017 saw a spike in Russian 'strategic bombers, fighters, reconnaissance, transport and other aircraft' over the Baltic Sea, and while 'unprofessional' as opposed to overtly aggressive, 'the unexpectedly hostile relations between [Russia and] the Trump administration, the ever increasing tempo of military exercises in Europe, and the closer proximity of Russian and coalition aircraft in Syria have combined to drive the number of incidents up again,' Thomas Frear, a research fellow with the European Leadership Network, told German public broadcaster DW.[85]

The Zapad 2017 exercises ultimately did not result in a head-on conflict, and were deemed part of 'normal military business' by Deutsche Welle – although the observer on the ground was severely restricted in his movements, and had 'limited access' to soldiers despite asking for it 'several times'.[86] British think tank Chatham House said that Russia proved western commentators wrong 'by keeping the drills small, managed and contained', adding that 'the Kremlin could therefore credibly claim that the West overreacted and fell victim to scaremongering and reporting rumours that Moscow was not being transparent about the nature of the exercise and its intentions'.[87] It is clear that in terms of Russia's actual threat, the country values threat perception and reaction almost as much as its actual capabilities.

3 THE THREAT FROM THE WEST

The Great Patriotic War

Russia is the world's largest country, stretching across eleven time zones, from the European exclave of Kaliningrad to the far eastern, oil industry-steeped island of Sakhalin. A country of more than 146 million people, sharing borders with Norway, Azerbaijan and Mongolia – but a mere 80–5 kilometres from the US at its easternmost point. Orthodox, Muslim, Jewish and Buddhist religions, among others, live and practise on its territory. Russia, in short, is massive. Its mainland border with the Baltic states is only around 450 kilometres long – while Lithuania sits on the fringes of Kaliningrad, its closest eastern neighbour is Belarus.

Residents live in major metropolises, quaint wooden or pastel-coloured villages, sclerotic monotowns (old Soviet single-industry cities), homogenous suburban housing blocks, and ostentatious gated forest dachas, in temperatures ranging from –40 degrees Celsius in the depths of Siberia in winter, to the high 30s on the Caspian Sea in summer. Each time zone is a palimpsest of distinctive historical periods. The shadow of the Soviet Union hangs over the country, as well as the fabled wild anarchy of the 1990s, myriad clashing contemporary domestic currents, underpinned by a sense of political apathy, vestiges of old imperial splendour and rich literary landscapes. People are concerned with generic day-to-day issues of economic survival, family, gathering food, work and friends. The struggle to stay afloat is perhaps even greater than in most modern societies – wealth disparity is extraordinarily high; in 2013, 35 per cent of household wealth was in the hands of just 110 people, according to a Credit Suisse report – making inequality by their figures among the highest in the world.[1] However, World Bank Data from 2015 showed Russia as 37.7 in the GINI

Index (0 represents absolute equality and 100 absolute inequality), making it 'better' than several Central and South American and African countries.[2] There is great diversity between the capital and the regions; a famous saying in the country is 'Moscow is not Russia!' – the average monthly salary is nearly twice the national average for Russian city inhabitants.[3]

The Soviet Union lost some 20 million people in the Second World War according to widely accepted estimates (although the number fluctuates both higher and lower depending on the assessment). The Eastern Front spanned 1,400 kilometres from the Arctic Circle in the north, all the way down past Ukraine; the German army sought Baku's oil fields. Nazi Germany invaded with a force of over 3 million soldiers, 3,600 tanks and 2,700 aircraft, resulting in devastating civilian losses, as well as military.[4] Germany's infamous Blitzkrieg techniques annihilated the Soviets – far outstripping the damage the country did to London. In total, more than 1,700 towns and some 70,000 villages were razed to the ground by the Germans during the war, and those that clung onto existence did so in a fraction of their previous form.[5] Soviet 'human supplies' were running very low by 1943, and soldiers' preparation was brutal; dysentery, bronchitis, anaemia plagued the training regiments and according to one account, 'the only ones who felt at home were the released criminals', who allegedly bullied and stole from younger recruits – but who were still in the minority among 'fast talking Tatars from Kazan, quiet, ambitious Bashkirs . . . mysterious forest people from Siberia . . . cheerful, lively Kazakhs, adroit, friendly children from central Asia', and others.[6]

A key component of Operation Barbarossa was the occupation and destruction of what is, today, St Petersburg. The Siege of Leningrad alone saw more than 600,000 people die. The vicious Nazi blockade, beginning in September 1941 and which lasted until January 1944, completely cut food supply lines to the city. People were forced into drinking sawdust soup, eating their beloved childhood pets or resorting to cannibalism.[7] Survivors recalled great acts of kindness, too – soldiers protecting an eleven-year-old girl's soup pot from being stolen, thereby saving her father, and the extraordinary self-sacrifice of older relatives refusing to eat meagre food rations to ensure the survival of younger children. A young boy named Vavila disappeared in January 1942, on the way to the bread shop. His body was found during ice clearance in springtime, and he was still carrying bread and a makeweight. 'Looking at this makeweight, most likely each of us thought that if Vavil had eaten it, he might possibly have survived. But he couldn't allow himself to . . . even dying of starvation,' recalled nine-year-old Anatoly.[8] Between a third and a quarter of the pre-siege population starved to death.[9] St Petersburg today is given the moniker 'Hero City' (a Soviet honorary title granted for outstanding bravery) following the suffering it endured; one of the first major sights on the main thoroughfare to the city from the airport is a gargantuan memorial to the city's heroic defenders – the implication being that its victims were not passive observers, but rather played a pivotal role in its end. 'The suffering has no meaning of its own, it has to remain the background for a hero story,' writes historian Michael Menikow.[10] The concept of heroism survives today as a major point of association in memorials, museum exhibits and television to bolster the Russian state's current steadfastly militaristic and patriotic narrative – but there is real emotion, hardship and loss underpinning the simulacrum.[11]

Commemorative celebrations largely centre around Victory Day every year on 9 May. Tanks and armoured personnel carriers, howitzers and 22-metre-long Topol-M missiles roll through the streets of Moscow, while hordes of screaming crowds climb trees to glimpse the weaponry. Parades on Red Square and helicopter or aircraft flyovers are rounded off with fireworks displays across the city. Surviving veterans wear their decorated uniforms, while hundreds of thousands carry portraits of relatives who fought in the Second World War during the Immortal Regiment march. Russia remembers the Second World War not as the Second World War but rather the Great Patriotic War. In Russia's eyes, the Soviet Union saved the world from Hitler – and justifiably so. 'It was the Western Allies' extreme good fortune that the Russians, and not themselves, paid almost the entire "butcher's bill" for [defeating Nazi Germany], accepting 95 per cent of the military casualties of the three major powers of the Grand Alliance,' writes journalist and historian Max Hastings, who puts Soviet losses closer to 26 million.[12] Its occurrence under Stalin's leadership is today granted higher importance than the hundreds of thousands executed and millions placed in prisons or camps under his leadership in the 1930s; acknowledgement of Stalin in public memory has now rather become coterminous with the defeat of these Nazi invaders rather than a chilling memory of a murderous dictator. There is a sense that this somehow absolved him of the preceding decade's crimes. 'People often criticize the Soviet government for repression, but all the amazing achievements of the Soviets justified the means. It often feels like the stories about Stalinist repression are exaggerated . . . Stalin was a great leader – particularly if you consider our victory in World War II and who our enemy was. He shielded us from the ultimate evil,' said nineteen-year-old Ira Smirnova in the far eastern port city of Vladivostok.[13] Positive views of Stalin reached a sixteen-year high among Russians in 2016, according to Levada polling that February; 46 per cent said they felt 'respect', 'sympathy' or 'admiration' for him. At the same time, negative attitudes declined. In April 2001, 43 per cent of poll respondents personally related to Stalin with either 'distaste', 'annoyance', 'fear' or 'disgust, hatred'. By 2016, this number had fallen to 17 per cent.[14] By April 2018, 57 per cent of Levada respondents deemed Stalin 'a wise leader who led the Soviet Union to might and prosperity'.[15]

The town of Rzhev lies 400 kilometres from the Latvian border. The crumbling redbrick walls of roofless buildings are still noticeable in the quiet, wide streets – dimples in the verdant green vegetation, beautiful pink skies and discernibly cleaner (and more mosquito-ridden) air than Moscow. It's astonishing how many ruins of the Second World War are still prevalent in villages close to Russia's western border. In Rzhev, *babushky* (old women) bring their home-grown herbs, potatoes, saplings and flowers to a local street market to sell for paltry amounts, and it is still difficult to locate staple, perhaps traditionally 'western' comforts, such as 'official' taxis, cafés that open before 1:00 pm and a decent WiFi connection. I am one of only two guests staying at the old Soviet low-rise hotel (as far as I can tell by the number of windows lit up from the outside at night). The music in the adjacent bar is so loud, and lights so disorienting that it feels like it is deliberately trying to deter people, and ten yards away from the exit to the darker, blissfully dulled noises of the parking lot is a freshly built Church of New Martyrs in what locals call the 'pseudo-Russian' style – a negatively loaded reference to national architectural stereotypes which have inspired structures built in the modern era. This one vaguely resembles one of the Kremlin's towers. Hotel staff talk inanely about how in Peking they treat bookshops like libraries and stand and read in them, but never buy the books.

Rzhev is the site of one of the Great Patriotic War's most violent battles. The bloody Rzhev Meat Grinder saw one million people die in the region alone, according to official estimates. According to unofficial estimates, the figure was twice that. Rzhev was occupied by German troops on 24 October 1941. 'We flooded them with rivers of blood and piled up mountains of corpses', says a well-known verse from Soviet writer Viktor Astafiev of the region. The town was a key flashpoint in Nazi Germany's attempts to reach Moscow. Locals are still exhuming and identifying corpses; relatives still seek the fates of their lost war dead. 'Everywhere there are unburied bodies, unresolved issues, and unresolved grievances about unidentified grandfathers. There is [still] a war,' wrote Elena Radcheva and Viktoria Odissonova from independent newspaper *Novaya Gazeta* in 2017.[16] Between 2016 and 2017, the remains of 1,067 soldiers were found. 'The year before last, we buried 1,598 dead,' Sergei Petukhov, the leader of a local search movement told reporters.[17] There are Holocaust sites across 'western' Russia too, with an estimated 27,000 Jews having been executed in Rostov-on-Don. No signs mark the mass graves, with just a monument emphasizing 'communal suffering'. A request for a plaque commemorating individual names has been denied by the city administration as the list has not been verified by the state archives – which allegedly does not have a list of victims.[18]

Rzhev is also home to a military memorial cemetery where German and Soviet soldiers lie in adjacent plots, as well as a school providing rigorous training for cadets. They hold the honour of marking memorial days through marches and wreath laying. But the biggest draw is a small, bright blue wooden hut in a village, four or five kilometres from the town. The village, Khoroshevo, is tiny – walking through it, one gets the impression it is only around 100 metres long. It is surrounded by rolling green fields and the air holds a distinct smell of honeysuckle. A small river called the Rakitnya (a tributary of the Volga, which flows through Rzhev) marks the boundary at its far end, just beyond the bright blue hut. The building in question is a museum honouring Stalin, which opened in mid-2015. On the night of 4 August 1943, Stalin stayed in this bright hut on the closest trip he ever took to the front line. A joint project of the Russian Military-Historical Society (led by Minister of Culture Vladimir Medinsky), the Communist Party of Russia (KPRF), and the local administrative district, it aims to depict 'Stalin's contribution to victory'.[19] 'When we read the plan for the museum, we were very upset,' said Sergei Gluzhkov, a member of the Tver branch of NGO Memorial, dedicated to commemorating the victims of Stalin's Terror. 'We decided that such a museum now is absolutely inappropriate and impossible, a museum distorting history and celebrating evil.'[20]

However, locals of all generations seem to disagree. Director Lidia Kozlova is a stereotypically patriotic St George's ribbon-wearing supporter of 'Novorossiya' (the collective Russian name for the self-proclaimed republics in eastern Ukraine that Russia has been trying to imagine into existence), and shares and likes videos of military choirs singing on her social media page. But non-hardliners support the museum too. One woman named Natalia, who lived nearby, emphasized its importance, saying that 'before the war, 5,000 people lived here – after the war – 300'.[21] Even a twelve-year-old boy believes the plan for the museum was a positive occurrence. 'It's a mark of victory – a lot of people died,' he says seriously.[22] According to Kozlova, one poll indicated that more than 80 per cent of the district's residents did not oppose the museum.[23] This is an entirely believable statistic, and a telling microcosm of the direction in which Russia is shifting, yet it feels bizarre that word of this tiny blue hut in a village of fewer than 1,000 residents has spread worldwide via articles published in Israel, Canada and beyond.

On the day the Stalin museum opened, Medinsky penned a column in government-affiliated newspaper *Izvestia*, headlined: 'We must stop blaming Stalin for all our problems.' Several branches of Memorial (which documents Stalinist purges and human rights abuses) have been listed as 'foreign agents' (among other movements) in a presumed attempt to dampen their commitment to publicly commemorating the dictator's victims. But there is still prevalent solid criticism for his rehabilitation in educated, more socially liberal circles who recognize that a cohesive national identity is being constructed through imposing icons of state power, celebrating a personality cult and the apotheosis of war, rather than by making a nation of the constituent people. 'The rehabilitation and preservation of Soviet symbols is a deliberate policy choice of Putin's regime,' writes Russian opposition politician Vladimir Kara Murza.[24] The Russian Culture Ministry will gladly provide funding for the glorification of military victories in the Second World War, but has barred state support for films that 'defile' Russian culture (a decision made in the wake of Andrey Zvyagintsev's bleak 2014 film *Leviathan* that painted local officials in a very unfavourable light).[25] While the Baltics are more than happy to consign the Soviet era and events of the Second World War to some almost alien past, in Russia, its presence is pervasive, and intentionally so, in the fabric and culture of a society which is simultaneously distinguishing itself as modern.

Vladimir Vladimirovich Putin had an interesting rise to power. Born in Leningrad (now St Petersburg) in the final years of Stalin's iron grip on power in the early 1950s, he worked as a KGB operative during the Cold War, before entering politics in 1991. He served his first official presidency in the year 2000, and stayed in power until 2008, taking a four-year break as prime minister while his usual prime minister Dmitriy Medvedev kept his seat warm as president (it is illegal for a Russian president to serve more than two consecutive terms). He was reelected to serve a third term in 2012 and another term in 2018 – the chances of anyone else surpassing him in the polls were laughably slim.

Putin carefully cultivates an image of being strong and active, authoritative and firm, highly perceptive yet austere and enigmatic. But one incident some ten years ago perhaps stands out as a strong reflection of Putin's deeper personality: German Chancellor Angela Merkel is scared of dogs, according to an aide. She was attacked by one as a child, sustaining a nasty bite and has since steered clear of the animals.[26] At Putin's Sochi residence in 2007, Merkel and Putin had a meeting – to which he brought his burly black Labrador Koni. Merkel, clearly tense, says in Russian, '[the dog] doesn't eat journalists, after all'. Putin sits back, legs apart, relaxed, gleefully eyeing Merkel and his dog with a seeming sense of expectation, barely suppressing a smirk. He denied all malicious intent a decade later, but this is a Putin who at least appears to pride himself on being hyperaware of the background of anyone he meets, and when ignorant of it, it often seems intended as an insult, to insinuate somebody may not be important or interesting enough to research. He is a pragmatist, often inflexible, and when convenient he uses the room for manoeuvre he carefully constructs; a combination of secrecy and informal power networks allow for a degree of plausible deniability. 'Putin plays by different rules; indeed, for him, there are no inviolable rules, nor universal values, nor even cast-iron facts (such as who shot down flight MH17). There are only interests,' *The Economist* observed in 2015.[27] When Putin first assumed the presidency, he appeared a humble yet comfortably self-assured, soft-spoken man of few words, with a good sense of humour, eager to take the reins of the country. But he was far from naïve. 'It needs to be understood. Well, actually it is evident, that there is harsh competition taking place not only in the market place but also between governments on the international arena,' he said in video footage from his first night inside the Kremlin as president. 'I'm very sorry to say, as it is very worrying, because we are not within the ranks of leaders in this competition.'[28] Between 2000 and 2007, his character clearly evolved quite dramatically – but his aim to restore Russia to a place of international prestige has remained consistent.

Putin's popularity ratings are extraordinarily high – in part precipitated by conflict with the increasingly cleaved-off 'west' (Russia has repeatedly promoted the calcification of 'west' and 'east' as separate entities) through conflicts in Ukraine and Syria, and the perceived threat of US influence among Russia's long-term allies, as well as increasing, carefully orchestrated control over the media. In March 2016, Putin had a staggering 83 per cent approval rating.[29] In October 2017, 60 per cent of people across the country said they would likely support him in forthcoming elections, according to independent Russian pollster the Levada Centre.[30] Conversely, opposition politician Alexei Navalny – well-known in the west (a basic Google news search yields some 103,000 results at the time of writing) – would only receive 1 per cent of the vote, despite his comparatively high media profile abroad.[31]

Putin's popularity is in part also attributable to the perceived absence of any other option. Navalny was prevented from running, Boris Nemtsov was assassinated in 2015. Putin does not participate in televised debates which see other candidates heatedly sparring; Ksenia Sobchak throwing water at a shouting Vladimir Zhirinovsky makes Putin seem like the only sane option. Ilya Klyuchnik, a nineteen-year-old factory worker from the 'golden ring' monastery city of Sergiev Posad, some 75 kilometres northeast of Moscow, despite regarding himself as fairly apolitical, plans to vote for Putin. 'He and the officials who work for him are the only ones capable of getting things done at the moment; there aren't really any other candidates,' he said. 'The regions beyond the capital are developing thanks to what he's done.' The drip-down effect of television's messages is also evident in his views. 'Everything that the Ukrainians are doing is just stupid. They are fighting each other; they've made a mountain out of a molehill,' he believes.[32] Domestic perceptions of the security services are also becoming increasingly appreciative: 22 per cent of respondents considered the KGB in a positive light in 2000 – this rose to 41 per cent at the beginning of 2018. Sociologist Denis Volkov attributed this both to Syria and Crimea, as well as the absence of criticism on television and positive depictions of secret agents.[33]

But in 2012, Putin's ratings were surprisingly subdued by today's standards – a different Levada Centre study documented his presidential rating as 37 per cent that year, while VTsIOM (the state pollster) recorded it as 52 per cent.[34] And his latest premiership has not gone unchallenged: 2011 saw the largest-scale protests since the collapse of the USSR, and up to 50,000 people took to Moscow's streets to rally against the government and forthcoming elections.[35] Both February and September 2012 saw tens of thousands protesting in the capital, while thousands participated in a 'March for Peace' in September 2014 against Russia's role in the conflict in Ukraine. City authorities granted their approval for a rally of 50,000 to take place on 1 March 2015 after opposition politician Boris Nemtsov (Putin's only real potential challenger) was murdered on 27 February that same year. On the first anniversary of his death in 2016, march attendee number estimates ranged from 7,500 to 100,000. There have been pockets of consecutive protests in farther-flung areas, but they have failed to comprise more than 3,000 participants and in many cases mere hundreds have rallied alongside Moscow.[36] Putin has made concerted efforts to reassert his hold over the country in the face of these movements.

It is impossible to accurately assess Putin's exact degree of popularity among Russians. Russia has two main polling agencies – the aforementioned state pollster known as the All-Union Center for the Study of Public Opinion (VTsIOM), and the Levada Centre, which was originally a breakaway institute from VTsIOM. But the Levada Centre was declared a 'foreign agent' towards the end of 2016 – a disparaging term which hints at a predilection towards espionage for the 'west' – after reporting an 8 per cent drop in approval ratings for the ruling party, United Russia. Its inclusion meant there were, by that point, a total of 141 'foreign agents' since the law entered into force in 2012 (well-timed to complement Putin's re-assumption of power) in what critics termed part of further restrictions on independent civil society.[37] Electoral fraud is rampant in the country – one educated estimate by a Russian analyst reached using Central Election Commission data suggested that falsification in favour of United Russia in the 2016 elections amounted to approximately 12 million votes.[38] Reuters reporters found 'inflated turnout figures, ballot-stuffing and people voting more than once at three polling stations' in two regions that year – while issues at these stations alone would have not impacted the result, this was only a 'narrow snapshot' of what was occurring.[39] On top of that, voter turnout can be inflated through a variety of methods – for example intimidation.[40] Employers or others in positions of power can also be vote-brokers, coercing their staff or underlings into voting. Students were 'required' to attend a March 2018 rally in support of Putin (and at St Petersburg State Polytechnic University, students were informed their efforts to collect signatures for Putin's nomination would 'ostensibly play an important role in end-of-the-year exams').[41] Crowds were also paid to attend the rally through a web forum (massovki.net), which promised 500 rubles to each person attending.[42] To encourage youth turnout in 2017 gubernatorial elections, gifts such as headphones and concert or cinema tickets were provided at polling stations.[43]

Putin's popularity is clearly high enough in Russia that he would win with or without electoral fraud. However, he would not win by the same margin, and would have less power than apparently legitimized by these higher levels of voter turnout and electoral fraud – for example, in 2008, that same analysis suggested that United Russia should have been given 277 seats as opposed to 315, which allowed the party to surpass the number required for a constitutional majority.[44] A University of Chicago study concluded that in 2011 the actual share of votes for the incumbent United Russia party should have been at least 11 percentage points lower than the official count (36 per cent instead of 47 per cent).[45] The 2018 elections, as expected, saw Putin be elected into power for another six years, but the real issue for him was ensuring a decent turnout for a result that already seemed so certain. The ultimate aim was a win of 70 per cent of the vote with a turnout of 70 per cent in a political climate that basically regards voting to be pointless.

In 2005 Putin famously declared that 'the collapse of the Soviet Union was the greatest geopolitical disaster of the [twentieth] century,' adding that 'for the Russian people, it became a genuine tragedy. Tens of millions of our fellow citizens and countrymen found themselves beyond the fringes of Russian territory.'[46] In 2018 he reiterated that if he could change any event in the nation's history it would be 'the collapse of the Soviet Union.'[47]

In addition to Estonia, Latvia and Lithuania, the end of the USSR saw Armenia, Azerbaijan, Belarus, Georgia, Kazakhstan, Kyrgyzstan, Moldova, Tajikistan, Turkmenistan, Ukraine and Uzbekistan become separate national entities from Russia – the country lost roughly a third of the Soviet Union's land mass. The year prior to Putin's comments saw US-led military alliance, NATO acquire seven new members: Bulgaria, Estonia, Latvia, Lithuania, Romania, Slovakia and Slovenia. In 2008, at NATO's Bucharest Summit Declaration, the alliance clearly stated that it would accommodate bids from both Georgia and Ukraine: 'NATO welcomes Ukraine's and Georgia's Euro-Atlantic aspirations for membership in NATO. We agreed today that these countries will become members of NATO,' the official text from the event noted.[48] NATO membership offers are usually contingent on a country settling any outstanding territorial disputes.[49] A few months later, the Russo-Georgian War began.

The US military, by all accounts, is the most powerful in the world. It spends more than the next seven countries combined – in 2014 military spending was nearly three times that of China (second place) and more than seven times that of Russia (third place), according to SIPRI figures.[50] Russia's spending has increased enormously in recent years (up to 5.4 per cent GDP, according to World Bank data).[51] But it still lags. On top of that, US military bases have been positioned at a variety of points around the globe: in Japan, South Korea, Kyrgyzstan and Germany. Kyrgyzstan was home to the Manas Air Base until 2014 – which then-US President Barack Obama fought to keep open.[52]

National Security Archive documents declassified in December 2017 showed that politicians navigating the end of the Soviet Union and its relationship with the rest of the globe were repeatedly reassured that NATO would expand 'not one inch' eastwards. 'Gorbachev went to the end of the Soviet Union assured that the West was not threatening his security and was not expanding NATO,' said an analysis from academics at George Washington University.[53] However, there are circumstantial differences in how various countries have joined NATO. The Baltic states avidly sought membership, as opposed to being absorbed by a conquering military force. They were driven to join by their own desire for western military protection (a difference Russia does not seem to register). However, NATO has since taken some much less-eager member states under its vast wing too; public opinion in Montenegro is divided, and upon the country's accession to the military alliance, less than half the domestic population were in favour of joining. 'After the "Cold War" ended, three waves of the Alliance's expansion took place, and with each such wave its military infrastructure was getting closer and closer to the Russian borders,' said Lavrov shortly after the NSA documents' declassification.[54]

In early 2018, Gorbachev's chief interpreter Pavel Palazhchenko clarified his own take on the NATO issue, saying he could not agree with the opinion that Gorbachev was 'outplayed' by the west. 'How would Gorbachev look, if, as his accusers propose in retrospect, he had to ask for "contractual, legally binding guarantees of NATO non-expansion" from the west in 1991, when this issue was not even being discussed in NATO?' he asked. He added that there were, however, assurances and Russians had 'every right to take seriously these repeated and high-level assurances', but the chances of establishing written guarantees would have been basically nil. 'And when, shortly thereafter, with the arrival of President [Bill] Clinton, a campaign began to expand NATO, they [Russia] should have felt that they had been dishonored. It is not difficult to imagine how the west would react if it were in place of Russia,' he wrote.[55] Under Bill Clinton's administration there were efforts to integrate the countries of central and eastern Europe into the alliance – despite concerns that it would be poorly received in Moscow.

Any 'pro-western' popular uprisings close to Russia's borders came with a fresh set of implications for Russia – would NATO membership or loss of land follow shortly thereafter? Despite allied Second World War wins, the USSR lost its satellite states. And, in the case of Ukraine, what could a change of affiliation mean for Russia's Black Sea Fleet – the only southern sea route into the country? The 'Putin as defender' approach surmises that the Crimean operation in 2014 was just that – an attempt to prevent NATO's further expansion along Russia's western border and was largely born out of concerns that Ukraine's new government would evict the naval force based at the best strategic point on the sea route into the Mediterranean, through the Sea of Marmara and via the Bosphorus.[56] 'Putin's pushback should have come as no surprise. After all, the West had been moving into Russia's backyard and threatening its core strategic interests, a point Putin made emphatically and repeatedly,' wrote controversial American political scientist John J. Mearsheimer.[57] There are obvious flaws in this interpretation – it ignores Russia's domestic politics, transactional approach to its business partners, and styles an internal Ukrainian social movement as a conflict between 'east' and 'west' as opposed to a mass domestic expression of dissatisfaction with political elites. Seeing it solely through this prism plays straight into Putin's hands. But the fact remains, from where Russia is standing, NATO has been expanding its influence and edging closer to its borders. It sees – or at least pretends that it sees – the Baltics as being occupied by the alliance as opposed to being integrated into it. Russia has similarly beefed up its missile systems in Kaliningrad and modernized some forces in its Western Military District, as well as recently building a new helicopter base in the Baltic Sea, on the tiny island of Gogland (not to be confused with Sweden's Gotland) – a move that could be seen as aggressive, but in line with Russia's usual modus operandi, contains an element of posturing too.[58]

The Ukraine crisis began with the European Association Agreement. The Ukrainian government delayed signing the document that would create an economic and political alliance between the EU and Ukraine – a pivot away from Russia. It continued with Russia's counter-offer; Russia was eager to integrate a politically allied Ukraine into a regional customs union with Belarus and Kazakhstan. One of Putin's advisers, Sergei Glazyev, pointed out that 'Russia is the main creditor of Ukraine. Only with customs union with Russia can Ukraine balance its trade' – suggesting the importance of business interests and their integration with the political.[59] Gradually, tensions evolved into Euromaidan. The outcome had strategic implications for all parties involved, and there was opportunism on all sides. Russia placed a strong emphasis on an undated phonecall between Assistant Secretary of State Victoria Nuland and the US Ambassador to Ukraine, Geoffrey Pyatt, which clearly indicated that the US was seizing up opposition candidates in Ukraine. "I don't think Klitsch [boxer-turned-politician Vitaly Klitschko] should go into the government," Nuland can be heard saying in the recording. "I don't think it's necessary; I don't think it's a good idea." It indicated that Washington was monitoring events in Ukraine closely, and that Moscow was acutely aware of that fact. But to many participants it was never about 'east' versus 'west'. Amid Euromaidan's thick, pungent bonfire smoke smells of melting plastic, and piles of rubber tyres and ice, was the spirited atmosphere of a music festival with the youthful energy of volunteers distributing free tea and sandwiches and parents daring to take their children for walks in small snowsuits. One old lady, with white hair, plastic shopping bags and a beige quilted coat, wandered around laughing to herself, as if she'd been waiting decades for such mass activity. People were frustrated with high-level corruption; signs referred to now-ousted former President Viktor Yanukovych as a 'thief' and dark reminders of the activists who had disappeared and journalists who had been shot were dotted around the protest camps. Viktor Yanukovych's palace was deemed evidence of 'jaw dropping vanity and bad taste': a 'five-storey mansion, a luxury car collection, a greenhouse full of banana plants and a personal zoo including ostriches and peacocks . . . a hideous galleon-shaped banqueting hall moored on the river where visitors discovered personalised table-wear and a vast stock of expensive wines and spirits.'[60] There was a concerted suppression of the Russian language, as well as more radical elements – the Ukrainian Insurgent Army (founded by a man widely considered a Nazi collaborator – Stepan Bandera – in the 1940s) flags fluttered freely amid the yellows and blues of the European Union's flag and the slightly different shades of Ukraine's – although pro-Kremlin media vastly overstated their significance. There was a diversity of political alignment on the square, but they were united against a common enemy – a flamboyant Russia-aligned government, which, through the actions of the *Berkut* riot police, came to be seen as deadly in Ukraine. However, at home in Russia and in parts of Ukraine's east, they were fighting a 'fascist junta' in the capital.

Russia has a complicated relationship with the Baltics. As the first states to peel off from the Soviet Union, and the first former Soviet Republics to join NATO, they symbolize a historic betrayal of sorts. In Moscow in 1991, hundreds of thousands gathered on Manezh Square under the slogan 'today Lithuania – tomorrow Russia!' in support of the southernmost Baltic state. Their collective resistance became a symbol of resistance on a much more widespread level. In an echo of this, tens of thousands joined a March for Peace rally in Moscow in 2014 to protest involvement in Ukraine.[61] The Baltics were the 'western' Soviet Union – high-class holiday and spa destinations – but at the same time a showcase of the USSR's functionality for foreign visitors.

Generally, Russians perceive the Baltics as essentially 'western' or 'European' but are acutely aware of economic issues related to European integration and their reluctance to acknowledge both their Soviet heritage and the negative consequence of the split. They seem to view Latvia with the most negativity, and Estonia as the most progressive or successful (despite stereotyping Estonians as 'slow' too). Humorous Russian-language MediaWiki Lurkmore (similar to Encyclopedia Dramatica) colourfully states that: 'Taking a short break in the Baltics was [once] considered more prestigious than taking one on the Black Sea coast. Currently, it is also considered to be the most prosperous area in terms of former Soviet republics' living standards. However, this technically only applies to Estonia. Latvia, for example, has degenerated into such fucking shit that nearly a third of the population has fucked off out.'[62] Russia recognizes well that the loss of economic ties between the Baltics and Russia was in many ways detrimental to the region, and that Latvia especially has experienced longer-term issues as a result. There are related concerns that Latvia is the most likely candidate for simmering tensions to erupt, particularly on account of attempts to completely eradicate the Russian language in Latvian schools, to which Russia has responded very unfavourably.[63] In 2011, Russia-affiliated organizations and parties even gathered signatures for a referendum which aimed to make Russian an official language in Latvia (which did not occur). Political disillusionment means voter turnout in Latvia is often low, but on this occasion it was much higher. There is a proportionately large ethnic Russian population and there are Russia-leaning sympathies among several members of the political and business elite, who attempt to gain political influence. But similarly, there is a strong resistance among others to any small trace of pro-Kremlin sentiment, and any political in-fighting can melt into mass unification in the face of potential Kremlin influence. 'Perhaps like Kiev, Riga's elites are a worse adversary for the Kremlin than even the USA,' said Victor Mizin, a senior researcher, at the Center for Post-Soviet Studies at MGIMO – Russia's top university for foreign affairs. 'A terrible crisis is underway . . . it is getting even worse – with the Russian "vestige of alleged successes" and Western irritation with Moscow's intransigence . . . no one is ready to calm down so far.'[64]

Early in the twenty-first century there were shifting attitudes. In the year 2000, 5 per cent of Levada Poll Centre respondents viewed the Baltics as 'very good', 47 per cent 'basically good', 26 per cent 'basically bad', 13 per cent 'very bad' and 10 per cent 'difficult to answer'. However, in the year 2006 the more moderate options changed significantly, with only 35 per cent viewing them as 'basically good' and 37 per cent as 'basically bad'. A mere 2 per cent viewed them as 'very good'. Furthermore, when asked 'in which republics of the former USSR, according to your opinion, the rights of the Russian-speaking population are most seriously violated?' (also 2006), the majority (67 per cent) of respondents said they were in Latvia. In the case of Lithuania, some 60 per cent of respondents thought the rights of Russians were seriously violated, and in the case of Estonia, 54 per cent.[65]

The predisposal to view Latvia in a stereotypical negative fashion from inside Russia is the result of a variety of factors. Simply put, ethnic tensions run much higher in the country. Estonians and Russians integrate well even if more divided in spread by region, and Lithuania has a comparatively low Russian population. But in Latvia, the cleave is deeper, messier and wider. And socioeconomic differences between Latvians and Russians are more apparent to Russian visitors. 'When you enter Latvia from Russia, it seems briefly, as if you were in Europe,' wrote Gazeta.ru columnist Anastasia Mironova in late 2017. 'But when you travel there from Lithuania, [or] fly from Germany or the UK, you will immediately notice the devastation and desolation. Even if you enter the country from Estonia, poverty and poverty will strike you in the eyes. And Latvia, in comparison with poor Lithuania, is poor.'[66]

However, few Russians see any chances of a 'Crimea scenario' in the Baltics – 100 per cent of respondents (in a small survey of twenty involving residents of Kaliningrad to Yuzhno-Sakhalinsk and elsewhere) said they did not envisage this happening, even if they did consider parts of the Baltic states inherently 'Russian'.[67] 'Crimea was always a Russian region that was attached to Ukraine by Khrushchev,' one respondent wrote. Another independently cited 'Khrushchev's chicanery' as a major difference as 'Crimea used to be part of Russia and was given away to Ukraine'.[68] Academics have also conveyed that there is no particular strategic threat in a professional sphere. 'In the case of the Baltic states, Russia does not use history (or "compatriots") as a reason to justify this region as a sphere of Russia's strategic importance,' said one anonymous historian in an official capacity with regards to the Baltics (however, in an informal setting, the same historian told younger students that the Baltics were essentially part of Russia).

Rather, what matters for the Kremlin is 'geography and NATO's increased presence in the Baltic Sea region', the historian added.[69] Mizin agrees that 'no Pskov paratroopers division will move across the border in a sudden onslaught'. However, 'provocative overflights will continue ... psychological pressure, as well stirring up the ≈40 per cent-strong Russian speaking minority'.

Some Russians feel that the Baltics are attempting to carve out their own post-Soviet identity using Russia as a foil – an 'other' to which they are different or diametrically opposed. 'The Baltic states apparently consider being anti-Russian as their own defining characteristic. Which is not something that makes me like them,' wrote one survey respondent.[70] Defining statehood based on opposition to Russia is an especially bad idea when that 'other' is already a huge constituent part of the state. 'In the Baltic countries, censorship has been established ... anyone who speaks in favour of the Soviet past, or at least says that everything was not all bad, [that] there were not only Stalin and the Gulag there, but there were also good moments ... all of them have been immediately spat out, declared a Stalinist, a traitor, the executioner of his people,' said the director of VTsIOM Valery Fedorov, in 2014.[71] 'Therefore, it's hard [for people] to say something good about the Soviet times under these circumstances.' Russian academic work occasionally documents how the 'political elites' in the Baltic region implement 'anti-Russian discourse' in order to maintain their own political monopoly, which, in turn, hinders any cooperation efforts.[72] Some 82 per cent of survey respondents thought there was Russophobia in the Baltic states, and only 18 per cent said it didn't exist. 'Some people refuse to speak Russian, even though they know the language,' one commented.[73]

The Baltics are a minor issue for people who do not reside in the 'European' part of Russia, and in general, a much more trivial issue for Russia's vastness than Russia is for them as buffer states. Russians were taught very little about the Baltic states in school – most respondents to the survey said either 'no' or 'only in the context of the USSR' when questioned. Two recalled studying the Polish-Lithuanian commonwealth, and one covered the Grand Duchy of Lithuania.[74] However, overarching Russian perceptions of the Baltic states mention key similar, major problems: outward migration, unemployment, social issues such as ethnic divisions and lack of recognition provided to the Russian population (particularly cited in the case of Latvia), 'anti-Russian "hysteria"', and the consequences of EU integration 'which probably happened too early, and too quickly'.[75] Russians, like Europeans, clearly recognize the clash between the Russian Federation and 'Euro-Atlantic structures'. With regards to Ukraine, the EU and the US 'clearly underestimated Russia's willingness to actively oppose the process of forcibly drawing Ukraine into the economic and political influence of the EU by signing the Association Agreement' and Russia, 'did not presume such a degree of determination from the West … to give political support to the coup d'état in Ukraine in February 2014', according to one in-depth Russian analysis.

Projects such as the EU's 2002 *New Neighbours Initiative* – a 'proximity policy for wider Europe' that sought to create a 'ring of friends' around the EU, and which ostensibly included Russia – was seen in Russia as part of an effort to isolate and separate Russia in favour of cooperation and rapprochement with Ukraine, Moldova and Belarus. The paths of the Baltic states in the EU were fundamentally connected to the EU's plans for activities in the region: 'the EU, Poland and Lithuania, as well as Estonia, proclaimed it their mission to help post-Soviet countries rid themselves of the "socialist legacy", to carry out reforms, democratisation and distance from Russia. A new "anti-Soviet" and anti-Russian socio-ethnic identity began to be crafted purposefully. The closest targets for its impact were Ukraine, Belarus and Moldova,' declared the analysis published in *Perspektivy*, a development programme for journalists from Russia, eastern Europe and central Asia.[76] Some Russian media have even insinuated that the Baltic states are interfering in Russian affairs, rather than Russia in western countries. In February 2018, an article was published on a site (often derided by Baltic journalists as a propaganda outlet), RuBaltic, alleging that Lithuania was interfering in Russia's elections. 'The Lithuanian authorities for the past few years have been creating an infrastructure to support the Russian street opposition and are making their country a springboard for intervention in Russia's affairs,' it stated.[77] It went on to describe how two of Navalny's associates 'were detained on Tuesday at a Moscow airport after returning from Lithuania, where they had traveled to prevent their live feed from being interrupted by the Russian police', adding 'is it an accident that out of all the possible places abroad, Navalny's associates chose Lithuania for their work? Of course not.'[78] A newer angle in Russian media is that the Baltic states are preventing Russia from cooperating properly with the rest of Europe – perhaps in part related to controversy surrounding the Nord Stream 2 pipeline, which the Baltics and Nordics oppose, but from which Germany and Russia would both stand to benefit.

While there are some key Baltic issues presented in Russia's domestic media, the country's media are still dominated by topics such as Putin, Syria, the USA, Ukraine, and occasionally Belarus. Since the year 2000, the Kremlin started targeting media owners in attempts to wipe out all nongovernment national television. For the time, print media was left relatively intact.[79] However, Russia's domestic media have since been reined in tightly, and television carries particularly vitriolic messages through on-air debates, as well as more traditional broadcast television news stories. Vladislav Surkov, an influential Kremlin ideologist and assistant to Putin, is widely credited with constructing the domestic political theatrics which used a combination of nihilism and the avant-garde to create illusions of pluralism, participation and support for Putin. In Surkov's heyday, stunts were pulled such as pro-Kremlin youth group Nashi harassing the British ambassador, staged picket lines outside the Estonian Embassy and the public burning of books by Vladimir Sorokin, who wrote a biting satire of Putin's Russia called *Day of the Oprichnik*.[80] 'It is a strategy of power that keeps any opposition constantly confused,' said one journalist – the idea is shapeshifting, unpredictability to create a climate in which it is hard to establish what is real and what is staged.[81] This approach is a reflection of Surkov's deeper personality, it seems. 'He may shout and swear at one person, change his tone. With someone else he will speak softly, envelop them calmly and with a smile,' said a report in the *New Times*. 'My cellmates were offered $3,000 to tell how they supposedly raped me – he gave the "go-ahead" for that,' the late Boris Nemtsov told the magazine.[82] In *Nothing is True and Everything is Possible*, Peter Pomerantsev broadly documents his frenetic time working in Russian television too – a tumultuous combination of nationalism, disorientation, glitz and bizarre – yet effective – methodologies. The overall impact is chaotic and gripping, simultaneously. But there is a degree of public awareness of its ludicrousness. 'They cover the wrong topics and often the discourse on political talk shows is absolutely absurd,' said nineteen-year-old Kirill Li from Novosibirsk. 'All the major channels are monitored and regulated, and there is no freedom of speech. There is media censorship in our country, and I don't like it. Then, the authorities criticize the internet too because there is "too much freedom"'.[83]

While young Russians are generally plugged into the internet, often relying on it as their primary source of information, the rest of the country still watches a lot of television. The Russian state has been adept at bringing television under its control; Levada Centre polls indicate that for 85 per cent of respondents television remained the main source of information in 2015 (however, this was a significant decline from 90 per cent in 2014).[84] This means the messages relayed by television are still very powerful and carry a great deal of traction. 'I think a dangerous – really dangerous thing is that if you look at those terrible talk shows which are daily on several channels on the Russian TV, usually the Baltics are portrayed as the key element of very adversarial forces for Russia . . . something like a platform for the deploying of additional NATO forces which are encircling mother Russia,' says Mizin.[85]

The Baltic states generally have a poor representation on Russia's primary channels and propaganda messages are not confined to news programmes but rather penetrate all spheres of broadcast television; in late 2015, a Russian weather report infamously declared that it was good weather for bombing Syria.[86] These messages also spill over into drama shows. In the television series *Leningrad*, a 'journalist' is introduced who turns out to be an ideological accomplice of a German spy – that 'journalist' was calculatedly Estonian, and 'distributed anti-Soviet leaflets' expressing wishes for 'the Germans to be here'. Similarly, in *Motherland*, a terrorist accomplice is an Estonian.[87] 'Coverage of Ukraine and other international stories conforms to a meta-narrative that reconstructs Russia's past around the heroic achievements of the Russian (Soviet) state, reinforcing a collectivist culture and a sense of purpose in hardship,' stated a 2015 report from the European Endowment for Democracy. 'This is not simply the past. It is rather its extension, or a kind of present frozen in the past. It is a time during which the majority of the people who live in our country would like to live forever.'[88]

Kaliningrad-based 'analytical portal' RuBaltic started its work in January 2013. It presently has a low number of followers – just 16,000 likes on Facebook and nearly 52,000 on Odnoklassniki (OK), a Russian social network for former classmates to stay in touch, which is generally composed of conservative, pro-Kremlin older generations. RuBaltic was an initiative of Russian academics, students and journalists based in Kaliningrad and Moscow who specialize in studying 'post-Soviet space'. The Baltics (as well as more liberal Russians) often tout it as a propaganda platform. 'People are sitting in Kaliningrad. and there they make an incredibly malicious site about their own neighbours – Poland and the Baltic States. The degree of ideological intoxication is striking', wrote Russian journalist and blogger Aleksander Morozov on Facebook in February 2015, in response to discovering the site. Its chief, a young clean-cut academic named Sergey Rekeda, is only a little wary of conversing directly with journalists himself and is inflexible about the impossibility of speaking on the phone. 'I usually do not deny an interview about our portal. There were already many such interviews. But the experience of the previous interaction in such interviews indicates that it is better that the answers be recorded in writing', he said by way of introduction. His public position is that he simply wanted to create an internet platform 'where the opinions of experts from these countries on the situation in the Baltic region would be presented', he said.

RuBaltic has published stories stating that 'the Baltic states are pushing the US into a conflict with Russia', 'for the last 30 years there has been a policy of national revenge in the Baltics', and 'success story of the Baltic States: European leaders in homicide' – an article which 'refutes all mythology about the progressive and prosperous European countries on the shores of the Baltic Sea'.[89] This is not a false claim – Lithuania does indeed have the highest murder rate in the EU. The site quotes individuals who discuss the push for independence in more critical terms than that which is dispersed within the Baltics and in the global diaspora, and asks 'Russian historian' (and 'political expert' according to a 2007 *RT.com* interview) Vladimir Simindei what Sąjūdis (the party fronted by Vytautas Landsbergis who led the struggle for Lithuanian independence in the late 1980s and early 1990s) could offer people. He discusses Landsbergis' 'cult of personality' as well as the methods used. 'There were emotional slogans, a thesis of eternal victimhood and evil neighbors was exploited. These movements were in line with the ideology of eastern European nationalism, which carries a destructive potential, and involves conflicts with its neighbors,' Simindei told the publication.[90] Monikers such as 'historian' and 'political analyst' are common terms in Russian media to refer to unqualified commentators who can espouse opinions the state media generally sanctions.

Usage of the term 'emotional' is interesting. Vast swathes of Russian rhetoric apply feminizing language to the Baltics, or the western world as a whole. Politicians quoted in press reports often say that the US is acting 'too emotionally' or the Baltics are 'hysterical' in reaction to flyovers or other Russian activities – the implication being irrationality and weakness. Russian female opposition political figures are often derided as 'ugly, unattractive and hysterical' – for example dissenter Valeriya Novodvorskaya.[91] Foreign countries' apprehension is also widely denigrated as infantile. 'I read yesterday that the Swedish prime minister is becoming nervous that they also have elections very soon and that Russia would 100 per cent be involved in them. Childish, frankly speaking,' said Sergey Lavrov in an interview with the *National Interest* in March 2017.[92] The same interview also saw Lavrov say 'all these hysterical voices about violation of human rights, about discrimination vis-à-vis Crimean Tatars, is a lie,' and with regards to the relationship between Russia and the US: 'some absolutely artificial hysterical situation was created by those who severed all of the relationship'.[93] In labelling the western world in this way, Russian officials and commentators automatically self-proclaim a position of authority and maturity in relation to perceived feminine weakness – as Koni the dog to a nervous Merkel. The western world is a child, a girl, someone to be easily overpowered and intimidated by displays of machismo. Yet 'hysteria' also seems to be the intended outcome in some of Russia's actions, even if the state and its advocates use such chauvinistic language to mask intent. Internal Russian media reports often publish inflammatory stories, likely fully aware of the possible reaction. In June 2015 – amid heightened international tensions and following Crimea, when Baltic fears were higher than usual – Interfax ran an article with the headline, 'The Prosecutor General's Office of the Russian Federation will assess the legality of recognition of the Baltic republics' independence' (the Attorney General's office later rejected the request).[94]

Rekeda approaches the politicization of the Russia/west divide in the Baltic nations with a critical eye, and provides measured and calm responses. 'Russophobia is prevalent in the Baltics, primarily on a political level,' he says. 'First of all, it is a tool of political elites for achieving a number of goals – mobilizing their electorate (for this purpose it is easiest to create the image of an external enemy), attracting the attention of external partners (USA, Germany, EU ...)', he adds. The majority of Russian survey respondents agreed – 82 per cent said they thought there was Russophobia in the country, but some think it can be explained by Russia's historic actions: 'there are a number of reasons for it. 1. Annexation by the USSR 2. Fears of Russian expansion 3. Strive for self-determination, national building, creating own identity 4. Aggressive Russian policy in CIS countries,' wrote one.[95] Rekeda stipulates that the Russian population is essentially completely uninformed about the Baltics. 'To confuse the names of Lithuania and Latvia is the norm for the average Russian resident,' he says. According to Rekeda, the portal's funding comes in part from Immanuel Kant Baltic Federal University, vaguely referenced 'grants', and advertising. Several of its 'experts' (many of whom have questionable qualifications) are recycled on the more hardline Russian media circuit such as Russian Ministry of Defence television channel Zvezda (star) and Sputnik. 'Our authors are not our private property,' he states by way of explanation. 'This is the norm in the whole world ... if the authors are good, then they are in demand.' As can be the case with Russian media projects, the central chain of command remains opaque. Rekeda alleges that several experts and journalists in the Baltic region have been banned from cooperating with RuBaltic writers (I have found no evidence supporting this claim). Their positions 'differ strongly' he states. But this is 'necessary' as the Russian outlet ultimately creates 'a more objective information environment'.[96]

Lithuanian academic Viktor Denisenko maps Russian media patterns since the Soviet collapse, identifying five key trends and one overall pattern in approaches to the Baltics. The overall pattern, he says, is that Putin's ascension to the presidency marked a distinctive change in tone from inside Russia. 'In the 2000s, the Russian press started classified treatment of the Baltic States as "Other"', he notes.[97] Denisenko specifically identifies Russian media attempts to push narratives of Russophobia and nationalism in Estonia, Latvia and Lithuania, as well as narratives suggesting violations of human rights and failed economies. Two further key spheres are security (the Baltic States' membership of NATO is characterized as an action 'against Russia'), and history (narratives suggesting the free will behind Baltic membership in the USSR). He also notes that the nature of depictions of the Baltic states in Russian media fluctuates depending on contemporary political currents (security concerns become more visible in the periods of 1996 (two years after the Baltic States made a decision to integrate the NATO), 2003–4 (the Baltic States became NATO members) and 2008–9 (growing ideological confrontation between Russia and NATO)), he observes.[98] This does not relate specifically to NATO, but rather Russian print media as a whole. All his categories are still relevant today, barring the insistence that the Baltics joined the USSR of their own free will. The Russian state still does not use the term 'occupation' but it appears less inclined nowadays to insist Red Army soldiers were welcomed with open arms.

It is important not to overstate the overall impact of Russian media channels on politics both inside and outside Russia. Given the enormous population of Russia, the RuBaltic following is minimal – it equates to the size of an average British town like Tunbridge Wells. The majority of its traffic (18 per cent) comes from inside Russia. Second is Lithuania, and third is the US.[99] But, as Ivan Lavrentjev pointed out, local media often respond to or republish the stories too, even if they originate in negatively perceived outlets, which makes them appear more influential than they really are. This is an occurrence on a global scale; the highest proportion of web traffic to RT.com actually comes from inside Russia, according to Russian journalist Alexey Kovalev's research.[100] Rather, any strong international reaction to portals understood to be extreme or propagandistic outside of Russia can then be used inside the country as evidence of their effectiveness and global impact – when in reality their outreach is very low.

While 'European Russia' has this strong diversity of opinions in varying intensities and condensed into a small space, the Russian Far East is simply not as interested in the region as Moscow or St Petersburg. 'I live very far from Europe and I'm not quite aware of the problems of the European powers,' wrote one forty-to-fifty-year-old male based in Russia's volcanic Kamchatka region – a ten-hour flight from Moscow. 'Their problems seem to be microscopic in comparison with those of North Korea or Russia.'[101] Ira Smirnova, the student from Vladivostok also looks 'east' rather than 'west'. 'We're so close to Asian countries like South Korea and China, [that] people often move there because the pay here is too low to meet normal living standards. When I was a child, we'd often take the bus to China for weekend trips and stock up on cheap goods. The border town of Suifenhe is just a three-hour bus ride from Vladivostok,'[102] she said. Naturally, the gaze of the eastern side of the country points in a different direction to that of Moscow or St Petersburg and the Baltic states, towards Japan, China, the Koreas and Mongolia, rendering the Baltics far less important.

Yet, whether in the Baltics or across present-day Russia, the same blend of history, memory and fear conditions the way that Russia reacts – on an individual and geopolitical level. But the blend is subject to different present-day conditions in both countries, with Russia's military patriotism, and collective sense of military might presiding over the country with the sense that history was very much written in Russia, by Russians. In the Baltics, there is a much stronger sense that history was written from the outside.

4 BALTIC RUSSIANS

Liberal

On the second floor of one of Riga's many Art Nouveau buildings, the former editor-in-chief of one of Russia's most popular online news sites, Galina Timchenko, and one of her equally former departmental heads, Ivan Kolpakov, are Skyping with digital media and content company Buzzfeed to discuss a potential partnership. Timchenko was fired from the aforementioned news site, Lenta.ru, in 2014, in what its staff said was a politically motivated decision – an act of censorship – to dismiss an 'independent editor-in-chief' in favour of appointing someone likely managed 'directly from the Kremlin's offices'.[1]

'We, of course, assumed they would come for us,' the latter says ominously – a clear indication of the increasingly restrictive atmosphere under which they had been operating.[2] In the preceding years, editor-in-chief of Russian magazine *Kommersant Vlast*, Maxim Kovalsky was fired (2011), Russia's largest news agency RIA Novosti was liquidated in 2013, and independent television channel *Dozhd* (Rain) was evicted from its studio in January 2014. Pressure has been incremental, and extremely effective. Timchenko and some twenty other journalists left Lenta in March 2014 to set up the Latvia-based Meduza, which swiftly gained notoriety for its highly original reportage and objective yet critical eye. From the offset, it described itself as 'Russia's free press in-exile'. Since then, it has explored a wide range of topics, such as the dynamics of a support club for the parents of LGBT children in St Petersburg, published an editorial expressing solidarity with *Ekho Moskvy* journalist Tatyana Felgenhauer, who was stabbed in the neck in 2017, and conducted reportage which inspired a Pulitzer Prize-winning *New York Times* article about a computer programmer who refused to work for the Kremlin as a hacker, before fleeing to Finland fearing for his own safety.[3] In the past three years, the regional breakaway outlet has blossomed into a resource worthy of international acclaim and recognition, and finally published its first story as part of the long-discussed Buzzfeed collaboration in January 2018.

'We realized it would be stupid to make this media in Moscow,' says Kolpakov over glasses of tea set in very Russian *podstakanniki* (tea glass holders). 'In 2014 everything looked stupid. Even the idea of creating new media in itself was extremely stupid . . . We realized there is no place for us in Russia.' Despite their reporters being Russian, they still may have to start registering with the Russian Ministry of Foreign Affairs for accreditation, 'just as [with the] BBC and the *New York Times* – it's crazy.' A lot of people won't talk to the outlet, e.g. those serving in the presidential administration, because they are technically now classed as 'foreign media'. And, Kolpakov believes, because Russian propaganda has created an image of Meduza itself being an 'anti-Russian propaganda' outlet. Russian state media, or Kremlin-linked media such as LifeNews and *Izvestia* have published a variety of pieces attacking them, but Kolpakov does not specify the exact stories that various outlets ran. 'Do you know the phrase "я не разбираюсь в сортах говна" (I am not an expert in different kinds of shit)?' he jokes sardonically, in response to further questioning. The negative press inside Russia has adversely affected some of the journalists' personal relationships back home, with relatives expressing political disagreement.

Meduza chose Riga for a variety of reasons, after having drawn up a long list of pros and cons. Its close proximity to Russia and great air transport links meant Riga, as the largest Baltic capital, became the number one choice. 'There is a local Russian community here . . . it was really cheap, in that period before the economic crisis in Russia – Riga was twice cheaper than Moscow,' says Kolpakov. Furthermore, it was much easier to move to Riga than to countries further west. 'We couldn't move to Germany for example because it's a hell of a mess of bureaucracy,' he adds.

This thought process is not unique to Meduza's journalists, but can be applied to a new (mostly) young generation of more liberal-minded Russians making conscious decisions to relocate to the region, prompted by the politics of recent years. They stand apart from the descendants of ethnic Russians who were born in the Baltic countries, who have tended to stay in their own calcified communities, despite nowadays living in a different nation from that in which they were born. 'I like a sentence that one of the local political scientists said one day – Latvia is a country of two minorities – Latvians act like a minority even though they are the biggest part,' says Kolpakov. 'I feel sometimes that people here identify me as part of the Russian minority . . . I don't have any personal connections with the local Russian minority and community.'[4]

These recent Russian immigrants to the region cite the prevalence of the Russian language, shared histories, transport links, ease of migration, freedom of movement in the EU as (positive) contributing factors for their departure, and the domestic situation in Russia as a 'push' factor. The more liberal dissidents all had a different point at which they decided moving was their best option. For Meduza, it was the situation at Lenta amid tightening media restrictions in Russia nationwide. Vilnius-based activist Vsevolod Chernozub cites the prospect of being sent to prison as his main reason to relocate. He was a key member of the Bolotnaya protests in 2011–13, which were Moscow's iteration of the largest mass protests in Russia since the fall of the Soviet Union. They took place as a response to alleged electoral fraud and Putin's announced intention to run for the presidency in March 2012. 'I was a member of the Russian opposition movement which was established by Gary Kasporov, Boris Nemtsov, Ilya Yashin and other human rights activists and politicians,' recalls Chernozub. 'We had a big criminal case against the opposition after Putin's election . . . I went to Vilnius and I got political asylum.' He says that his high public profile with regards to the protests in Russia eased the process of his application.[5]

Film director and head of Russian documentary film festival ArtDocFest, Vitaly Mansky, says that the invasion of Crimea prompted his decision to buy property in Riga. 'I remember the exact moment when I took the decision to emigrate from Russia,' says Mansky – a good-humoured, insightful, grey-bearded fifty-something-year-old – with the air of someone who has told this story many times before. 'It was actually in one minute that I decided.' He orders ice for his apple juice in Russian and the waitress looks blankly at him. He repeats his request in English, just a hint of exasperation, and she dutifully complies. This scenario later repeats itself in an Estonian café, much to the frustration of its Russian clientele.

'I was in Spain, we were in a hotel and I was watching a Federation Council meeting [Russia's upper house] – it was a livestream. The question was raised on the nation[al affiliation] of Crimea. And a vote was taken on whether it would be reasonable to use armed forces in this conflict, and the candidates had to vote. There were sixty seconds for voting . . . on the sixty-first second I saw that it was a unanimous decision to use armed forces. On the sixty-first second I called my wife and I told her that we're going to emigrate.'[6] While Mansky cites widespread Russian-language usage, proximity to Russia, and the ease of obtaining residency shortly after purchasing land, he notes there was another draw which put it firmly ahead of countries further west. 'What is very important to me is that Latvia is now at its building state, in its development state, and it is much more liberating for a person to come into this developing country than come into a concrete jungle where everything is already structured,' he says. He is much more vocal on local politics than Kolpakov, who doesn't deem it his place to comment. Mansky compares Latvia's pro-Russia (former) mayor Nils Usakovs' populism with that of Donald Trump. 'He knows well his electorate, the people who elect him and why they're electing him,' he says, the implication being that playing the ethnic Russian card is his primary – and perhaps only – selling point.

The ownership of property in Riga has now become almost synonymous in Russian media with corruption and national betrayal. Fifty-seven-year-old Pavel Grudinin is the director of the Lenin Sovkhoz (state farm) on the outskirts of Moscow. He was also the Communist Party candidate in the 2018 elections. Despite an entrepreneurial background he swore to tackle corruption across Russia, and his popularity rose dramatically in the run-up to 18 March; Grudinin was polling second with just over 7 per cent of the vote, putting him in second place. He may have become a little too popular; in the preceding month or so, Russian media started placing a strong emphasis on his or Grudinin's relatives' Latvian assets. Frequent and widespread stories are published about how 'the eldest son of Pavel Grudinin, Artem, owns a house in the Latvian city of Marupe, which is literally ten kilometers from the center of Riga.'[7] In some sense, the Baltics are still, inside Russia, somewhat synonymous with betrayal.

Among those who selected the Baltics to live in, there is a strong sense that none of the Russians who uprooted themselves would have done so if not directly nudged – they still consider Russia their homeland, and somewhere to which they are inherently faithful – perhaps more so than their compatriots who managed to adapt to the changing, constricting atmosphere. Dmitry Kuzmin, a Russian critic, publisher and poet, who moved to a forested village outside Riga sometime between 2013 and 2014, said in 2015 that his move there would have been 'a brilliant change . . . if it were not forced'. But, rather than feeling like he has turned his back on Russian society, or a Russian 'world' supposedly bound by shared national values, he believes his departure is ensuring aspects of Russian society that are being erased at home are through him, preserved. 'I'm helping aspects of Russian culture to survive,' he said. Estonia too is now home to environmental activist Yevgeniya Chirikova, who campaigned against the construction of a £5.34 billion road linking Moscow to St Petersburg in 2010. She received political asylum in 2013, saying in 2015 that 'it is difficult to work in Russia because they can come for you at any moment – like, they blackmailed me once with my children'.[8] Among the Russians who have also moved to the northernmost Baltic state are music critic and journalist Artemy Troitsky, another journalist, Vadim Shtepa, as well as an artist, Vladimir Dubossarsky.[9] There is a certain amount of poetic historical continuity in this; in the Soviet era, Nobel prizewinning writer Joseph Brodsky developed a long romance with Lithuania after eighteen months of exile – culminating in a series of poems, one of which paid atmospheric tribute to the religious hordes exiting churches in the Lithuanian dusk.

Vsevolod Chernozub lost faith in the Russian opposition movement's potential, in the past few years resigning himself to *zhertva* (martyrdom, or becoming a casualty of the increasingly repressive situation) if he had stayed in Moscow. It reached the point in Russia, he said, when the situation was getting so bad that 'your risk doesn't have any sense'. Nowadays, he does not particularly regret his choice to leave, but he still considers it 'emotional. You were part of this movement and you live this movement, you have this призванные (calling) ... [and then] you lose your friends, you lose your situation, you lose your favourite city.'

Lithuania, as well as being home to Chernozub, is also home to Russian journalist and blogger Alexander Morozov, the same Alexander Morozov who took exception to RuBaltic. Morozov recognizes a division between society's Russians in his Baltic home too. 'The old community is the Russians who lived here many, many years, and they were born here. And the new community is the political community – the ones who came to Vilnius ... after the beginning of Putin's third term,' says Morozov. 'Now – they say – in Vilnius [there are] more than twenty families ... it's often popular with people and I know here there are [both] liberals and nationalistic Russians.'[10] Morozov believes Lithuania is much safer for Russians than Latvia, on account of its much smaller Russian population, and less heated ethnic divide. He recognizes, despite his awareness of

Russian propaganda, that some Latvians can harbour harsh attitudes towards the Russians in society, purely on the basis that they are Russian. A handful of these Russian liberal dissidents often come from places of relatively high standing. The 'educated' or 'liberal' 'urban intelligentsia' can afford to make such a move even if under conditions of persecution back home. They are still focused heavily on events in Russia, rather than the Baltics, and many own centrally located apartments in areas housing their 'creative' Baltic counterparts (Morozov very briefly lived in the trendy self-proclaimed republic of Užupis, high on most foreign tourists' visit lists). They are not directly confronted by pressing social issues such as unemployment and poverty in the region – the issues that hit hard the marginalized, calcified local communities of Baltic Russians and leave them enduring a different degree of socioeconomic hardship and segregation from their Baltic peers. 'Apparently, I should be referred to as "privileged,"' Morozov later added. 'In my opinion, all Russians who have a working contract . . . are in a better position than many others trying to leave.' He has now moved to Prague, where he is employed by Charles University. 'I am a famous journalist and I can count on the support of various public and state institutions in Europe,' he said.[11] Chernozub, as a political refugee, cannot.

Ethnic Russians and inequality

The streets in Narva, according to residents who frequently cross the green banks of the river into the fortressed Russian city of Ivangorod, are much, much better maintained than those over the 4-kilometre border where Russia lies. Local rumour has it that the Estonian government keeps Narva's streets so immaculate in order to flaunt how much better the quality of life is in Estonia to the local Russian community. Before the Second World War, Narva had the same beautiful red roofs as Tallinn. But the city was completely razed and now only two pre-war buildings remain. Sparse, homogenous concrete structures house the residents of the region. Inside they look just as distinctly Soviet, with the diagonal flooring patterns, wooden furniture, floral wallpaper, and boxy kitchens that characterize so many homes of the same era. People were noting the contrast in development between Russia and Estonia more than ten years ago. 'The difference is much bigger when you come back from Russia [as opposed to Finland],' said one thirty-five-year-old icon painter named

Ivan. 'Order, buses that go on time . . .We are becoming bourgeois.'[12] Over the border in Ivangorod, the city is plagued by 'devastation and decline', writes Russian opposition blogger Ilya Varlamov after a trip. He paints it as a 'transit city' with cars and trash clogging the barely-there, crumbling roads, 'The city is weedy and falling apart, it is gloomy and miserable,' he adds.[13]

Narva is located in Estonia's northeastern Ida-Viru county, and as of January 2017, 73.1 per cent of the population of the entire county was Russian.[14] Foreign journalists have frequently been drawn to Narva since Russia's annexation of Crimea, angling for stories; in 2015, a Foreign Ministry employee rolled his eyes when I mentioned I was planning a trip there. It is a local running joke that soon there will be no 'Narvites' who have not communicated with some foreign journalist and, to some, visitors mentioning the idea of Narva seceding, or becoming 'the next Crimea' is dangerous. 'Theorizing about its autonomy, is a dangerous step back into the past, which neither Narva nor the rest of Estonia needs,' said communications adviser Lavrentjev.[15]

My host is a Russian man, Roman, who – despite severely decreased mobility in one leg – picks me up from the bus station himself. With typical Russian chivalry, he will not let me carry my own case, and he struggles with it up five flights of stairs while I repeatedly protest and unsuccessfully try to intervene. He prepares tea from flowers and linden leaves that he personally harvested from the city's 'clean' areas, and we discuss mentalities in the city. Later, as we walk around Narva, he tells me that he believes people in the city can idealize Russia, and while it is so close, many of those who do idealize it have not visited the country themselves, but rather developed a pro-Russia point of view through the propaganda propagated via television. He finds it odd, yet entertaining, that despite the high proportion of Russians in the region, all street signs and billboards are required by national law to be in Estonian, and not Russian – much to the inconvenience of the Russian majority, who cannot necessarily understand them. Nobody agrees on where Narva's city centre really is, he says.

We temporarily part ways, and I linger around Narva Castle, from which there are incredible views of Ivangorod Fortress, a vast medieval Russian structure erected in 1492 (in part to ensure sea access). Narva's own castle had been constructed in the late thirteenth century, under the rule of Denmark, until it became a stronghold of the Livonian Order, which Russia defeated in the 1550s. The country held onto Narva for less than twenty-five years; the Swedes took the city, and Russia did not conquer it again until 1704. In a 1917 referendum, Narva voted to become part of independent Estonia until the Soviet occupation, Now, just one single statue of Lenin hides in the corner of Narva Castle's courtyard, his outstretched right hand pointing in the direction of Russia. People cheerfully fish on both sides of the sparkling waterway marking the border, and guards boat up and down it at night, flashing their torches for signs of a breach. My aim is to visit Kreenholm Manufacturing Company – a redbrick industrial complex inhabiting an island between two waterfalls, and south of the thick clump of train-tracks extending enticingly from Tallinn to Russia and beyond. The company was first founded as a mill in the 1850s and became a cornerstone of the Russian Empire's cotton industry. It closed before the Soviet occupation, but under the Soviets, the facility became an enormous industrial enterprise again. After independence, the factory once became unprofitable, resulting in hundreds of layoffs in 2004.[16] Now, it's slowly being developed into something of a creative hub – in part to consolidate 'European' Estonia's presence in the Russian-speaking region. In September 2018, a 'boutique music festival' called Station Narva was held for the first time at the complex, spearheaded by Tallinn Music Week founder Helen Sildna and featuring Liverpool post-punk legends Echo and the Bunnymen, as well as local acts from both sides of the border. Narva even launched a bid to become European Capital of Culture in 2024.[17]

But en-route, I meet a group of men wearing white vests as they squat in the hot sun drinking beers and chain-smoking. It's midday. Thirty-year-old Evgeniy, or Zhenya, twenty-seven-year-old Gennady and another Zhenya (who quickly goes inside a nearby housing block preferring not to speak to journalists) are affable, humorous, and mostly eager to converse. They offer me a can. It quickly materializes they are Russian nationalists to the core, and three of Estonia's 80,000–90,000 'grey passport holders'. The grey passports or 'alien passports' are so-called because they are the preserve of people – usually ethnic Russians – who never assumed Estonian citizenship after the collapse of the Soviet Union. The Estonian government forbids dual citizenship, forcing Russians to make a hard choice – either apply in full to be a citizen of Estonia, or procure a Russian passport. Only in 2016 were laws amended to ensure that newborns with Russian parents were automatically considered 'Estonian'.[18] Unemployment among non-Estonians is still higher than among Estonians, and the average salary for Estonians is approximately 17 per cent higher than for Russians who have the same qualification.[19]

These grey passport holders are not subject to conscription laws, but neither can they vote. 'We are without citizenship,' they state matter-of-factly. They do not know any Estonians as there aren't many in Narva, and only speak Russian, despite the best efforts of local signage and having been required to learn Estonian in school. Practising it away from school was never really necessary for them; they stayed in a calcified Russian-speaking community and say citizenship exams are very difficult to pass. 'Narva's a Russian city!' Zhenya declares with great conviction, in a manner reminiscent of Tomas, the not-cigarette-smuggler in Lithuania's Dieveniškės appendix. However, a few moments later he contentedly adds that 'here, it is the European Union'. Despite his technical lack of citizenship, he is perfectly comfortable living just as he is – in a Russian city in the European Union. He does, however, recognize the problems his situation entails, and has been impacted by divisions between Russians and Estonians as a national minority. He is convinced there is sweeping Russophobia in Estonia. 'Nobody loves the Russians,' he states matter-of-factly, adding Estonians think 'Russians are bad people'. He likes Putin – who is a 'very good man' purely because he is Russian – but does not like Trump, whom he deems 'cunning'. He then tells me that if Russia ever invades, he'd immediately side against Estonia.

The ethnic Russian and 'native' communities in both Estonia and Latvia are somewhat location-dependent. At the fall of the Soviet Union, one famous 1980s Estonian power ballad called *Mingem Üles Mägedele* ('Go to the Mountaintops') repeats the line 'Peatage Lasnamäe!' ('Stop Lasnamäe!') in its chorus and bemoans how Tallinn is 'swollen' and 'evil has taken hold'. Lasnamäe is a Russian-majority administrative district on the outskirts of Tallinn. There, I meet with another pair of ethnic Russian grey passport holders who have also struggled with learning the Estonian language and perceived socioeconomic subjugation. 'We haven't a normal connection,' one says, of the relationship between Estonians and Russians in the area. He has no Estonian friends. 'I am speaking Estonian not so perfect,' he adds slightly regretfully in broken English, even though he can sort-of understand the language. He wants to go and live in Russia – St Petersburg, rather than Moscow – but has never been there himself. 'I think there's [Russophobia] in Estonia,' he says. 'Ninety per cent.' It's mostly language-based in his opinion and present in everyday interactions. Their complaints echo Russian film director Mansky's frustration. If they go to the shops they can only correspond with salespeople in Estonian – which is a frustrating problem for them.

But these opinions are not shared by all Estonian-Russians. In the same district, a twenty-two-year-old Russian mechanic reminisces about an Estonian ex-girlfriend, and how they used to communicate freely together in English. He's calm about relations between the communities, and thinks people simply have a tendency to speak their own mother tongue. Otherwise there is very little animosity, he believes. And in Latvia, one eighty-year-old Russian lady says the most striking animosity towards Russians in the Baltics came from Russians at 'home' who feel negatively about the region. Minaida Veyde arrived in the Soviet era with her parents when she was just a child, and now rents out a student apartment complex in the centre of Riga, along with her husband. She was likely herself once regarded by native Latvians as an 'occupant', and could have returned to Russia at any point, but says she loves Latvia and has no intention of leaving. She has visited family back in the Russia over the years. But her face changes as she recalls one particularly vicious interaction with her brother. 'He called me a traitor,' she says. Neither do native Estonians in Lasnamäe register any particular difference between the communities. They seem more inclined to believe that the situation is calm and uncomplicated – perhaps the privilege of a majority group as opposed to a minority group.

Some socioeconomically subjugated native Estonians are avid Putin supporters though, too. One ethnic Estonian man, visiting his family in Lasnamäe (he works in Finland), tells me drunkly, and bitterly, 'I love Russians. Fuck, I love Putin! I hope if we go to war, that Putin will fucking bomb this place.' A sense of disillusionment and disaffection with their current lives can leave some people seeking an external solution. In Latvia too, research conducted by the National Defence Academy's Center for Security and Strategic Research has found that people with 'low incomes and a low or medium level of education, unemployed, physical workers, Russian speakers, people living in Latgale and Riga, 18–25 years old, as well as people over 46 years are generally the most exposed to Russian influence.'[20] It identifies a sense of alienation between society and the state (the vertical gap) as a factor in why an individual may feel the political elite does not care about the population, therefore, leaving them potentially open to exploitation.

In the more impoverished areas there is a certain sense of unity between those native to the Baltics and those who class themselves more broadly as Russians; Belarusian-Ukrainians receive the same meagre state pensions as their Latvian counterparts, for example, and many still have to work well past retirement in order to supplement them. There's a sense that everyone is in the same creaky and unstable boat. 'It's not only Russians who suffer from state policies; Latvians do, too,' said fifty-nine-year-old Irina Gorkina (Latvian-born father, Russian mother), from the Latvian town of Daugavpils – a two-hour drive from the Russian border.[21] A general sense of attachment to the region and one another could be, in part, attributable to the diverse nature of the Soviet Union. And after its immediate collapse, it is likely that Baltic residents felt more 'Soviet' than Russian, so did not forge as strong a link with the new Russian identity as they had with the Soviet. The sense of attachment to either a Soviet, Russian or Baltic identity and its intensity can be influenced by other factors such as length of residence in the Baltic region, language practice, occupation, and nationality.[22] The linguistic issue is clearly at the forefront of the divide between ethnic Estonians and 'native Russians'.[23] Integration between the calcified communities is increasingly necessary – but for it to be effective, it requires heightened efforts to communicate on both sides.

In the 2017 film *Stebuklas* (*Miracle*), directed by Lithuania's Egle Vertelyte, a Soviet woman named Irina, played by theatre actress Egle Mikulionyte, is singlehandedly shouldering the impact of perestroika. An American Trump-like figure named Bernardas struts into her parochial backwater town where she runs a pig farm with her alcoholic husband, gradually falling into debt, and her farm descends into neglect. Bernardas, who believes the land is his (from his Lithuanian parents who fled the occupation), pledges to buy it off her, and in the process solve all her problems, he says. His charisma, loutishness and shiny red Cadillac bewitch the townspeople, yet he has no practical plan for the property. In the aftermath of his visit there is an anticlimactic atmosphere with the protagonist left feeling naive, exploited and misunderstood. Some former Soviet citizens also initially felt this kind of intrusion from former Soviet Baltic landowners who fled their territory, perhaps believing they were granted land in exchange for their hard work before the 'wise old elves' returned with a sense of propriety that they believe subsumed that of the new landowners. 'We are non-citizens. They called us occupiers, but now they turn out occupiers themselves. This is Russia's land,' said one eighty-year-old in 2014.[24]

The number of stateless persons in the Baltics is slowly declining, but weak integration and the inhabitation of different 'information spaces' is still ensuring the communities stay ostensibly separate from one another; almost 75 per cent of Estonia's Russian speakers get their information from Russian news sources. While handfuls contemplate returning to their over-idealized vision of what Russia might be able offer, the trend is beginning to change, say some. 'When we were filming in Narva ten years ago, the youth were looking more towards St Petersburg, but now they are looking towards Tallinn,' Estonian film director Aljona Surzhikova told local media.[25] Further to that, fewer are migrating back to Russia nowadays in search of permanent residence and more are travelling to EU countries since the Baltics attained EU member status (although this is much more difficult for grey passport holders). However, grey passport holders also have some troubles getting to Russia too; non-citizen of Latvia Oksana Karaja was deported from Russia because of having no visa in 2016; while non-citizens of Latvia and Estonia (former Soviet citizens) as well as their minority-age children had the right to enter Russia without a visa, their majority-age children do not. The issue instigated debate in the Baltics and Russia. 'We should even consider a law giving such people priority for Russian citizenship,' said Russian nationalist writer (and 'Russkiy Mir' advocate) Pavel Svyatenkov. 'Unless the Russian authorities lift this ban, all of their promises to protect their compatriots will be just dust,' he added.[26] Between 1989 and 2003 Russia saw a positive net migration of just over 243,000 people, with the largest migration arriving from Latvia (118,500), followed by Estonia (70,000) and Lithuania (54,000).[27] Between 1998 and 2013, migration to the EU increased in all three Baltic countries, rising the most in Lithuania – Latvia and Lithuania saw the largest outflows (relative to their populations), spiking at 40,000 Latvians and 83,000 Lithuanians in 2010 in this period.[28] For the grey passport holders both directions are equally 'open'.

In Lithuania, the atmosphere appears considerably less terse for ethnic Russians in the country than in Estonia and especially Latvia, likely in part due to the immediate assimilation of non-titular populations, whereas there are still tens of thousands of these grey passport holders in the other two Baltic nations. They are also less concentrated in specific Russian-majority regions. 'Russians living in Lithuania have virtually no risk of rebellion and only a small likelihood of protest. One factor contributing to this situation is the fact that Russians in Lithuania are geographically dispersed,' said a Minorities at Risk assessment in 2006. 'The current treatment of the group by the government is largely positive . . . [it] has adopted a number of positive measures vis-à-vis their Russian minority and the levels of protest by the group have sharply declined as a result.'[29] It is generally regarded as having the best policies for national minorities in the Baltic region – however, the local Poles (and Roma) would not necessarily agree. The leaders of Electoral Action of Poles (EAP) have been agitating for better rights for the domestic Polish population for years. In Klaipeda, on Lithuania's coast, the proportion of ethnic Russians is much higher than the national average – some 20 per cent of the population. They have been more active in lobbying for local changes, such as Lithuanian-Russian street names (as opposed to just Lithuanian).[30]

Historically, the Baltic coast was filled with spa and resort towns popular with Soviet citizens, even then as a 'window to Europe' of sorts. The most famous was Latvia's Jurmala – known as 'a playground for Russia's well-connected wealthy'. Renowned for its concerts, it is today almost equally renowned for some of its shadier residents. 'Jurmala isn't really a music festival. You don't need to go to Latvia to listen to Russian pop stars. You can do that in Russia,' investigative journalist Leonid Jakobson told the Guardian in 2008. 'In reality Jurmala is an important moment. The Russian mafia and Russian government are together in one place.'[31]

Russia's entertainment industry has been slowly trickling out. Popular Russian festivals KVN and New Wave left the region in late 2014–early 2015, and the ruble crash severely impacted the prospects of potential Russian buyers of real estate. But there was still a demand. Russians could gain residency rights in Latvia for an investment of €150,000 until mid-2014, and more than 10,000 Russians obtained residency under the programme.[32] By 2015, estate agents said numbers began to decline. 'There are far fewer Russian clients,' a Moscow-based realtor said in 2015.[33] The high-end tourism market is still benefitting from the presence of Russians. The Grand Palace Hotel is an elaborate boutique building in the heart of Riga's old town, attaining a five-star superior rating in 2015. Regional director Bernhard Loew says that Russians still spend the most there cumulatively, even if there have been numerically more American visitors than Russian in recent years.[34]

Wealthy

The Latvian coastal city of Jurmala is not the most obvious place for anyone to store their wealth. A tiny white-sand Baltic pine forest beach, it's pretty, but surely has low business appeal. Yet the chairman of

Gazprom InvestHolding, Alisher Usmanov, has property in Latvia to the amount of €3.9 million – he bought his resort in Jurmala from the CEO of a cosmetics company, Ilya Gerchikov, in 2014. Usmanov now lives in London and is a major shareholder in Arsenal Football Club. Arkady Rotenberg also obtained a residence permit from 2010 to 2013, after which he did not request its renewal (possibly on account of Finnish citizenship acquired via marriage, according to the Organized Crime and Corruption Reporting Project (OCCRP)). His brother, Boris, acquired property in Garkalne (east of Riga, rather than west, in Jurmala). Up until the introduction of sanctions, the Rotenbergs owned SMP Bank in the country, which they founded in 2001. Political analysts, former Duma members, and an Aeroflot manager are also among the Russians who presently own real estate in Latvia. 'There is a good corporate tax system for business in Latvia, and I'll consider whether I should transfer part of my business operations there,' said former Vice-Governor of Irkutsk and professional investor Alexander Rudik in 2015. 'I'm not thinking about living in Latvia permanently, it's more a summer home thing. I will seek a residence permit though, as it's useful for travelling freely around Europe.'[35] Russia's super-rich own properties all over the world, and tend to reside in the UK or Switzerland over countries in the Baltic states or central and eastern Europe, but there's no denying they have a strong presence in the region, especially in Jurmala.

In 2008, one of these rich Russians disappeared. Multi-millionaire Leonid Rozhetskin was one such tycoon who also enjoyed Jurmala's thick pine forests, beautiful sunsets and white sand dunes. A Soviet Jew who migrated to the US in the 1980s, he amassed his fortune during Russia's wild 1990s. A founding shareholder of London's *City AM* newspaper, he previously served as executive vice chairman of Norilsk Nickel – Russia's largest mining company in which Vladimir Potanin, Oleg Deripaska and Roman Abramovich have all had stakes. On that March weekend in 2008, Rozhetskin's secluded Jurmala mansion on Kapu Iela (Latvia's most prestigious neighbourhood) was in complete disarray: furniture was overturned and there were conspicuous traces of blood on the floor. Further blood was discovered in a car abandoned in Riga's city centre. Russian media quoted police sources suggesting that his US citizenship, combined with the fact that his private jet had departed the country after his disappearance, pointed to the fact that he may have faked his own death.[36] His wife, former model Natalia Belova, and their son moved to their £3 million Mayfair apartment, with five bodyguards.[37] His body was missing.

Just ten days after his disappearance, Latvian police confirmed the blood found at the villa was that of Rozhetskin. 'Murder is one of the possibilities that we are considering,' Dailis Luks, head of Latvia's central criminal police department, told the *Moscow Times*. However, 'only a moderate amount of blood was found – it is difficult to define whether there were spots or drops', Evita Spalvena, head of Jurmala's criminal police unit, told the same reporter.[38] Rumours and speculation filled the region – that he was a closeted homosexual, the victim of a contract killing, or that he was still alive, free under the auspices of a new identity. For five years, nobody knew of Rozhetskin's whereabouts. He had been involved in a diverse range of activities, acting as a co-producer on US comedy film *Hamlet 2*, starring Steve Coogan. In 2007, he co-founded a movie production company with Eric Eisner, son of Disney executive Michael Eisner, L+E Productions. Their next project was set to be *Three Wolves* – a film about the Russian mafia.[39]

In 2013, police discovered skeletal human remains in a forest 40 kilometres from the villa. Inside the jacket pockets was Rozhetskin's credit card. His mother, Elvira Rozhetskin, expressed certainty it had been 'a professional hit by hired Russian agents'. The extensive security apparatus at her son's luxuriant home had somehow been bypassed, yet very few items were missing.[40] He was confirmed dead in November 2013.

There is, of course, no concrete evidence in the public domain to confirm Rozhetskin's death was related to any specific one of his complicated business interests.[41] But the entire affair pulls back the curtain – if only a little – on the dark underbelly of Russian business deals and their spillover into Latvia. In Russia, the state and criminal networks often bleed into one another, and their activity permeates societies beyond Russia's borders. Russia-based organized crime groups in Europe have been used for a variety of purposes, 'including as sources of "black cash", to launch cyberattacks, to wield political influence, to traffic people and goods, and even to carry out targeted assassinations on behalf of the Kremlin,' says an ECFR policy brief. The brief specifically fingered Latvia as a favoured money laundering hub for Russia-based organized crime. It cautioned that EU defences against money laundering in some constituent countries were 'becoming less robust' because of the absence of a common European approach and that some EU countries lack the 'awareness and skills (and sometimes, by implication, inclination) on the part of the financial sector to play its role', suggesting Latvia could be undertaking greater efforts to combat corruption and money laundering.[42]

Highly dubious money has been gushing through Latvia since the Soviet collapse. An extensive OCCRP report in 2014, documented its money laundering capabilities in detail. The 'Russian Laundromat' report as it came to be known explored the activities of shady Russian companies seeking to divert their funds into more secure European banking systems, using a network of various businesses and banks. The laundromat was an enormous operation, in which Latvia was merely a cog, but the overall system worked well enough to 'clean' roughly $20.8 billion from 19 Russian banks – some $13 billion of which had been transferred via a bank called Trasta Komercbanka in Latvia.[43] Trasta Komercbanka's 'location in the European Union made the transactions less likely to be questioned by other banks'.[44] The money ended up passing through 5,140 companies with accounts at 732 banks in 96 different countries.[45] The illicit operations of Latvian banks are a reflection of corruption in Latvia, not Russia. But their use by Russia, and their willingness to cooperate is a mutually beneficial arrangement that can help Russia circumvent sanctions and furthers links between criminal networks and official institutions. This is taking place in a geopolitical climate which is seeing growing links between said criminal networks, the Russian state security services, and Russian business interests.

'My daughter started having her geography classes in Estonian last year,' Maria, an ethnic Russian based in the northeast of Estonia, told Amnesty International. 'The school said that this was part of their phasing out of Russian as a language of teaching in secondary schools.' She was in a conflicted position, wanting her Russian-speaking daughter to not only learn geography to a high standard, but also improve in the Estonian language – higher education is not available in Russian to people who only speak Russian. 'I want my daughter to go to university, and realize that she needs to speak better Estonian,' she said, adding that while her teacher was supportive at the expense of his own time, 'it usually ends up with me having to explain her geography homework to her in Russian to ensure she understands everything.' She expressed hope that language reform would help her daughter learn Estonian. But, 'without the right resources, she won't be able to study in Estonian. I'll have to explain all of her subjects to her in Russian', she said.[46]

Language and educational policies across the Baltics do not cater to their native Russian populations well, despite some attempts at inclusivity. After the collapse of the Soviet Union, restructuring education became one of the key cornerstones of new national reforms in an externally inflicted atmosphere of diverse languages. However, all three states differed in their approaches, juggling varying degrees of internationalism and protectionism, especially in higher education. Each Baltic state set about reintroducing their own languages as the only state language in a variety of ways. European officials have since expressed concerns that language policies are contributing factors in marginalizing Russian individuals in society. 'Difficulties in learning in their second language might increase the rate of school dropouts and failure in the final exams, which in turn amplifies the difficulties in accessing higher education. It may also carry an increased risk of social exclusion', noted Alvaro Gil Robles, the then-Council of Europe Commissioner for Human Rights in 2004.[47]

During the occupation period, the proportion of native Estonians in the population dwindled from 97.3 per cent in 1945 to 61.5 per cent in 1989, and in that time Russian was elevated to a 'second native language' as opposed to a foreign language. Instead of assimilating to the occupied territory, the occupied territory had to assimilate. Non-Estonians did not consider it necessary to learn Estonian in that period, but Estonians were required to learn Russian to keep their jobs (of which there were far fewer for Estonians, as they were not trusted to serve in several senior positions).[48] This Baltic-wide phenomenon became known as 'asymmetrical bilingualism' as the Russian-speaking population remained largely monolingual inside the Baltic borders. Language became a political issue. Estonia's constitution established Estonian as the country's sole language in 1992, while the 1995 Language Act (renewed 2011) regulates state apparatus, language rights and proficiency requirement.[49] The 1995 Universities Act stated that the language of instruction at universities is Estonian, but their councils could establish other languages. Latvia's Education Law (1998) and the Law on Institutions of Higher Education (1999) dictated that Latvian would be the primary language of instruction in higher education, but any programme may teach 20 per cent of its courses in any other official EU language. In 1991, Lithuanian was deemed the official language of higher education instruction after the Law on Research and Higher Education was passed.[50] While Amnesty suggests the Russian population should be catered to, in order to reduce the possibility of social exclusion (feelings of social exclusion could particularly be the case among Baltic Russians born prior to the end of the occupation), there's a sense of injustice among the descendants of Baltic refugees; over the course of writing this, one told me that if people come to England they are expected to assimilate, rather than receive an education in their own language. Why on earth should Russians be taught in a language that is simply not the state language?

In Latvia and Lithuania, the numbers of schools are decreasing and in Latvia, even more restrictive language policies are still in the process of being discussed. Both nations implemented acts of their own after the fall of the Soviet Union: in Latvia, the Official Language Policy Guidelines 2015–20 laid out plans to ensure the 'development and stability of the Latvian language' while citing a commitment to a multilingual society, while the Law on the State Language (1995) in Lithuania decreed that all public oral and written communications should be in Lithuanian. State language exams have been implemented in each country.[51] There is no such law in place in Latvia, but in 2016, Latvia's State Language Center fined Mayor of Riga Nils Ušakovs €140 for using Russian on Riga council's official Facebook page. 'The law on the state language doesn't say a word about regulations on the language of the government's communications with its citizens over foreign social networks,' Ušakovs pointed out.[52] The State Language Center enforces the laws governing Latvian language use; in the first half of 2016 it fined 180 individuals for language offences, 139 of whom had failed to speak Latvian while performing official duties, according to the centre.[53]

Resident Russians' attitudes to learning languages in the Baltics has fluctuated over the years; generally, Russians can be sympathetic to the reasoning and have been receptive to Baltic language policies in the aftermath of occupation. In a large-scale survey conducted in the year 2000, over half of Russian respondents agreed that people wishing to become citizens should pass an examination in the titular language and disagreed with the position that they 'should not be made to learn'.[54] Native Russians are well aware of the fraught history and actually possess a degree of sympathy with native Balts.

While Russian speakers in Lithuania appear generally happy with their country, Russian teachers have expressed concerns about the future of the nation's schools, which themselves can strongly impact both students and staff. In Lithuania the number of Russian schools has been declining. There were around eighty-five Russian schools and 103 mixed schools in 1990–1, which declined to fifty-five Russian and forty mixed schools by 2013. English is replacing Russian as a second language.[55] In 2015, the former chief of Lithuania's State Security Department (VSD) Gediminas Grina, compared the minority schools to 'education ghettos' and demanded their dissolution. Russian teachers universally condemned the statements. 'It has sowed fear and apprehension over the future of the schools. Quite undeservedly. It hurts all of us here,' teacher and chairwoman of the Lada Russian community in Klaipeda, Svetlana Vasichkina, told Lithuanian media. However, Grina insisted that a hostile country in the east could be responsible for filling ethnic Russian schools' curriculums with propaganda. 'Sowing seeds of distrust and fear might encourage some to take an action against the schools, many of which are proud of so many achievements,' Vasichkina countered, saying they foster a strong sense of citizenship, despite the linguistic differences. 'After graduating from a Russian school and excelling in her major in Lithuanian at Klaipėda University, my own daughter now successfully works in the city's business sector.'[56]

Naturally, the tone and form of educational practice can be contingent upon individual teachers who use their own beliefs about nationhood and education in order to teach their subjects; on occasion it can be the native schools that have an insular approach. Merilin Piipuu from Estonia's Museum of Occupation recalled speaking at an Estonian school on 9 May and the teacher closed the blinds to prevent students from seeing the Russian Victory Day parade outside. Piipuu said she would have made a sociological adventure out of it for the kids and would have rather encouraged them to speak to the Russians, to understand why they were celebrating the occasion. But the teacher thought it best to ignore the entire holiday. Furthermore, English has surpassed Russian in the other two Baltic states as well as Lithuania. It is now the chosen second language in the region, but more specifically in higher education, where practices are inclined towards English as the dominant foreign language rather than in the younger years. Knowledge of the English language has grown across the region, although levels of fluency in Estonia are higher than in Latvia or Lithuania.[57] The University of Tartu, Vilnius University, and the University of Latvia all deliver programmes in foreign languages, and specifically English, and while multiculturalism is recognized, Russian on a more specific level is sidelined and even ignored in policy documents.[58]

The use of Latvian and Russian languages in Latvia has been an extremely topical issue in the past year. In January 2018, the Latvian government endorsed sweeping reforms of Russian language schools in the country, prompting a serious backlash inside Russia. The Ministry of Education and Science proposal's draft amendments aimed to ensure that Latvian would be the language of all educational instruction across the country. 'Language is an element that unites the nation, and only a cohesive nation can develop successfully,' argued Minister of Education and Science Karlis Sadurskis. The country phased in new language reforms in 2018 which stated that by September 2021 all sixteen- to eighteen-year-olds will be taught only in Latvian, and the push to achieve this will begin in 2019. Russia threatened sanctions, with the MFA terming it 'part of the discriminatory policy of the forceful assimilation of Russian-speaking people that has been conducted for the past 25 years'. Russia regarded the move as part of an ongoing wave of attempts to minimize Russian language usage across the country – even though Latvian is the only official state language already,[59] prompting thousands to protest in February (according to Russian media, which does not always cite the most reliable protest figures). It passed its second reading on 9 March. 'The absurdity surrounding private schools is just beyond any common sense. Have you ever seen a country that prohibits national minorities, whose children make up a quarter of all students, from studying in their own language even for their own money? There is no such country,' Andris Morozovs, a lawmaker from opposition Social Democratic Party 'Harmony' told TASS.[60] If signed into law, the legislation will be enacted in September 2019. The divide between Latvian and Russian media spaces is therefore a reflection of the 'discursively created divide in identity politics' between 'Latvians' and 'Russians'.[61] This is not the first time Latvian language policies have roused the ire of local Russians: in 2004 education reform in Latvia saw attempts to ensure that up to 60 per cent of school subjects were taught in Latvian and up to 40 per cent in Russian, much to the outcry of demonstrators. However, protesters failed to prevent the reforms.[62] The support for Saskana (Harmony) within Latvia is also emblematic of the divide in society. There is a clear ethnic divide as Russian voters generally vote for either 'Harmony' or 'Latvian Union of Russians', while Latvian voters generally avoid these parties. Harmony officials have previously expressed cynicism about mainstream 'western media' as well as impending language reforms favouring Latvian over Russian – a hot topic which has seen heated responses from Russia. If Saskana sees success, there could be doubt cast on the future of these language reforms, Latvia's place in Europe, and even the country's support for sanctions against Russia. But as Mizin mentioned in the previous chapter, Latvia's political elite pose a formidable challenge, and often unite against perceived Russian influence.

The Russian-speaking population in the Baltic states, while calcified in its own communities is far from homogenous. Some of its members integrate well with natives, some are socioeconomically sidelined, and some reject attempts to learn the local languages despite the fact that this can improve their domestic socioeconomic prospects. This reduces integration prospects but is not the sole factor in bringing down the capacity for a cohesive identity. Rather, 'political factors have a moderate tendency to reduce this capacity, whereas cultural factors generally increase the potential for a consolidated group identity'.[63] In a way, this works well in favour of the Baltic states. A coherent, consolidated group identity would potentially make any Russian state operations in the region more efficient, with a greater capacity for them to be mobilized. But, it seems Russians in the Baltics see several positives to being in Europe and have a sense of nuance with regards to their own presence in the Baltics.

5 THE BALTIC FUTURE

Tommy Cash is reclining shirtless on a black-and-white leopard print throw, hands tucked behind his long bleached hair. At precisely 4:20am in Tallinn, inconsistent cell phone buzz tears through his speakers. It's a call from St Petersburg. 'Hello, Tommy Cash,' states the voice on the line. It is not a question. 'We wanna invite you. To Russia.' Cash arrives in the woods at daybreak, met by a little woman in a red dress and matching *kokoshnik* (traditional headdress), flanked by two men in red tracksuits, one of whom is carrying a bottle of vodka. The other gives Cash three cheek kisses. Cash whips out a PPK. 'I heard it's dangerous in Russia so I took a gun, man,' he says wide-eyed, with a slightly maniacal grin. 'This is gun?' his host says disdainfully in thickly accented English. 'I had this gun when I was a baby.' He shows Cash a badly edited photograph of a child cradling the same pistol. 'Look at my gun.' He pats the tank stationed behind him.

Estonia's Tommy Cash, or TOMM¥ €A$H, as he styles his name, is collaborating with Russian mainstream rave staples Little Big. Both Cash and Little Big have earned frequent (and thoroughly warranted) comparisons to South African hip hop group Die Antwoord – but with an added aura of Serbian film director Emir Kusturica. In the 2015 video for *Give Me Your Money* the foursome drive the tank through city streets drinking vodka, interspersed with comically exaggerated references to several distinctive Russian tropes, churning out lines like 'in the supermarket / try'na find wall carpet', while visiting the *banya* (Russian steam room). The video features the infamous Stas Baretsky (an enormous gravedigger-turned-songwriter 1990s Russian gangster cliché) biting a beer can in half with the aid of his metal tooth. The end of the video shows the three Russians, in black tie and wearing earpieces, looking out over St Petersburg's Church of the Saviour on Spilled Blood. 'Yes, the guest was met and shown everything necessary,' says the tank owner over the phone in considerably subdued tones. He chuckles sensibly. 'Yes, Estonia will be afraid of us,' he says.[1]

Cash was born Tomas Tammemets in 1991, a 'compote of Ukrainian, Kazakh, Russian, and Estonian,' rising to domestic notoriety in 2013.[2] Even that early, Estonian media was awash with a degree of certainty he would break the international market. Cash remained typically stoic, saying 'if a boy is ready, then he's ready,' at the time.[3] He was 'ready' in 2017, with his specific satirical style of 'post-Soviet rap' fitting into the western zeitgeist well enough to land him *Guardian* coverage describing his music videos as both 'surreal' and 'idiosyncratic'.[4] YouTube clips of his solo work have now reaped tens of millions of million hits, he has 540,000 Instagram followers, and even *Vogue* jumped on the bandwagon in early 2018, compelled by the contortions, amputee ballerinas and blades of newly released 'sinister-meets-sexy' video PUSSY MONEY WEED. The magazine's headline? 'Meet "Kanye East"'.[5]

Of course, Cash's collaboration with Little Big was just that – a carefully thought-out creative collaboration – a meeting of like-minded rappers with a similar attitude and edge. Around 2013–14, the rave scene was kicking off in Moscow. In a design factory in the north of the city just outside the second ring road, Flacon, Russia's black-clad 'Generation Z' congregated to dance wildly and freely to the thick, hypnotic beats of Радость Моя ('My Joy'), IC3PEAK (with whom Cash later also collaborated) and CROSSPARTY, among others, at various instalments of a brilliant party series called VV17CHØU7. In 2016–17 'western' publications started to pick up on the witch house and rave movement, along with its proponents' aesthetic tastes. Chaotic Russian 'street style' – largely born out of the necessity to buy second-hand or at flea markets due to low wages or debt – became the height of western fashion from 2016 onwards, manifested in the meteoric rise to popularity of Russian designer Gosha Rubchinskiy. He first hit the Paris catwalks in 2014, and eventually ended up collaborating with fashion powerhouse Burberry in early 2018. The *gopnik* hooligan subculture that emerged after the collapse of the Soviet Union ('gopnik' is similar to the British slur 'chav') inspired the badly fitting denim, puffer jackets and sportswear styles stamped with Cyrillic letters that soared to such great heights, accompanied by the lurid, ironic and sometimes deeply unsettling details prevalent in both Cash's videos and those of both underground and mainstream Russian rave scenes. However, its ascension has since produced a somewhat predictable backlash – frequent criticisms from people with Eastern Bloc roots – disparaging the 'moneyed Westerners fetishizing commodified poverty that they have the privilege of discarding once it's not so cool anymore', according to one apt observation.[6] Additionally, the concept of 'post-Soviet' as a fashion statement rather than an epoch of academic exploration has proven problematic among some youth from Baltic countries who resent the idea of being pooled together with Russia once again as a post-Soviet state by definition.

The 'former Soviet republics' vehemently dislike being described as such. Free of the shackles of the USSR for more than a quarter of a century, the reputation persists to date, but their wariness about the possibility of a repeat scenario and continued association with the USSR heightens concerns that they will be ignored in the case of foreign aggression. In September 2017, ambassadors from all three countries jointly sent a letter to French newspaper *Le Monde* calling on the publication not to refer to any one of them as 'former Soviet republics'.[7] They sent a previous petition to Germany similarly asking media to stop referring to them as 'former Soviet countries', and in January 2017, to their relief, the United Nations officially classified all three countries as Northern European countries, instead of Eastern European.[8] 'New East' fashion serves to both dilute the stigma attached to Russia in the current geopolitical climate and continues to present all former Warsaw Pact countries and former Soviet republics as part of the same cultural aesthetic.

Tommy Cash grew up on the poor, 'Detroit' side of Tallinn, as he terms it.[9] Kopli is a run-down area in the northeast of the Estonian capital located a little further along the coast from the colourful wooden houses, independent coffee shops, and designers of Telliskivi 'Creative City' and the 'hipster district' of Kalamaja, Kopli is a mass of graffitied and boarded-up stone and wood buildings and is yet to gentrify – but local authorities and businesses have been trying. Just two years ago the area was incredibly dangerous – narcotics problems, homelessness and squatting, as well as dangerous and deadly fires and the occasional murder. 'All the fucking bums and junkies look like they're wearing the latest Balenciaga,' Cash tells me.[10] Two security guards were shot in the area as recently as 2017.[11] It was originally built for workers at the nearby Russo-Baltic shipyard in 1913–17, which is one of the most prominent features of Tsarist Russia's legacy in Estonia. Vast docks and shipbuilding basins, limestone production facilities, factories and a service network made it one of the biggest industrial complexes in the Baltic Sea region at the time.[12]

'I've been here since I was six, now I'm seventeen,' says Susanna, a cheerful, laid-back resident with cropped blonde hair and black-rimmed glasses. She lives on the other side of the tram tracks from the "Kopli lines" – the part of the area that is still inhabited, known as the 'Professors' Village'. 'The lines area, I remember when people lived there . . . of course you were a bit afraid, because you knew there were homeless people but they were, like, peaceful. They had to live somewhere, right?' She adds the houses are under protection 'but they're in such a bad state that they're not safe. I like the rust and wooden houses, and it's like beautiful, I think. You can take really nice photos there.'[13] The coastal breeze and overgrown vegetation still hold a little human activity. A woman is attempting to walk a stubborn, chubby calico cat on a red leash. Eventually she gives up and starts brushing it in the wrong direction. There is also a workshop on the grounds of an old hospital that restores European classic cars. They moved to the area because of the amount of space. 'Rooms are available, and with quite a reasonable rental price . . . it has already increased a bit,' says a man named Taavi, in the midst of renovating a dark green 1952 MG TD in a sort of bunker. 'This is the place where the dead bodies got held . . . I figured it out earlier this year,' he says. 'History comes again. [Now] the dead cars come here. We wake them up.' He says he has seen the area change rapidly, and he believes it's quite safe now. 'People lived in these houses, and I don't know where they moved or where they are . . . now, it's a security company, and the tramlines have been closed for a year,' he says.[14]

A developer, Fund Ehitus, plans to invest some €55–65 million in the district over the next twelve years to turn it into an up-and-coming residential area with easy links to the centre of Tallinn.[15] After the fall of the Soviet Union, suburbanization started taking place at different paces across the Baltic capitals; private interest encouraged new developments in areas previously reserved for other functions, and in Estonia areas along the shore were often militarized; secret 1946 and 1955 regulations restricted border coastal belt access.[16] The Department of Urban Planning confirmed that it would preserve 'the most valuable' houses, according to Anna Semjonova from the Tallinn Chief Architect's Office. 'Some of them had these brick staircases. We will preserve the staircases and build similar houses [around them],' says her colleague, Mihkel Kõrvits. 'This Kopli peninsula – in ten years there will be living more people – maybe even these hipsters will go there,' he adds. The youngsters are starting to get irritated by the number of cars crowding their traditional stomping grounds in Kalamaja. 'I see that they are step-by-step going somewhere here and here,' he points out movements eastward on a map. I ask what happened to the homeless people. 'It's a sad story,' Kõrvits says, pausing. 'Nobody knows.'[17]

The creative, somewhat 'hipster' side of the Baltics is beginning to shine through in various ways, with youngsters bonding together in their own communities to create 'spaces' for them to thrive, from the bottom up, taking advantage of the somewhat sparse populations, exacerbated by high levels of outward migration. The aforementioned Kalamaja district in Tallinn is home to Telliskivi Creative City, a complex of repurposed industrial buildings containing bright murals, cafés, performance spaces and shops selling a variety of clothing and furnishings. The Balti Jaam market is the site of one of Tallinn's best street food stalls, Baojaam, and the Põhjala craft brewery sits further west along the coast. Vilnius has its own 'creative' space in the self-proclaimed 'Republic of Užupis' with its own similarly colourful graffiti, statue of Frank Zappa and an absurdist constitution ('Everyone has the right to live by the River Vilnelė, and the River Vilnelė has the right to flow by everyone'; 'Everyone has the right to die, but this is not an obligation'). Established as an April Fool's Day joke in 1997, the micro-nation has since been one of the country's primary tourist spots. It started out as an organic haven for artists and other visionary types seeking cheap accommodation in a run-down region, but more than two decades later the area is now one of the most expensive places to live in the city.

In the front yard of one of Riga's many unused Soviet buildings, a man in his early twenties is hammering a sign reading 'swamp' into the muddy ground. The wetter patches have been fenced off by low-lying black and yellow tape, and a makeshift swing of plank and climbing rope is dangling haphazardly from a nearby tree. Another boy in a bright shirt sets up a sound system and a young woman in an apron organizes a screen-printing table. The venue, an interwar building known as D27, has been repurposed by a movement called Free Riga, seeking to breathe life back into the city's empty buildings by providing space for creative initiatives unable to pay high rents. Free Riga maps these otherwise uninhabited properties and functions as a point of contact between landowners, politicians, creatives and the public. D27 houses a 'free market' as well as artists' studios, accommodation and Riga-based comic publishing house Kuš! (pronounced 'Koosh') which tonight is celebrating its tenth birthday.

Kuš! singlehandedly created the comic arts scene in Latvia and has since fostered the talents of new generations of young illustrators and artists making surreal, sweet, deeply foreboding, or sometimes just plain confusing collections of images using a wide range of mediums. Swiss-born David Schilter edits the publications alongside the woman in the apron – Latvia's Sanita Muižniece, who became involved nine years ago. Over the time it has been active, it has established itself as enough of a national leader to be granted government support. 'We cannot now call ourselves fully independent,' says the soft-spoken Schilter. 'I moved here in 2006 – there were no comics.' Schilter made the decision after completing his Erasmus studies in Lithuania in 2005, during which he fell in love with the Baltics. When he first arrived there were 'a couple of translations from *Tintin* and *Asterix* but there were no comic shops here, no publishers. The only comics you could find here besides Kuš! was this Mickey Mouse magazine,' he says.

The scene has grown along with Kuš! which has extended its network to work as a platform for book illustrators, staff and students from the Art Academy, as well as more random recruits. In their first year they distributed for free, backed by Schilter's savings, so aspiring artists quickly learned of its existence. Oddly, neither of its leaders make comics themselves. 'David [Schilter] and me are the only ones who don't draw,' says Muizneice.

The initial absence of 'comic culture' meant that at the beginning Kuš! had problems sourcing Latvian artists to fill the book's pages. 'The first issue, only the cover was a Latvian artist,' he says. Nowadays, it showcases vastly more. The majority of artists in the 'Celebration' anthology, released in honour of its tenth birthday, are Latvian. It also includes illustrators from Canada and Switzerland, but nowadays they are outnumbered. Kuš! has also started travelling abroad to comics conventions in several other countries, such as Russia and London. The artists come from a variety of backgrounds and disciplines: students, academics or professionals (Roman Muradov, for example, has had illustrations in the *New Yorker*, the *New York Times*, and the *Washington Post*), while others work in completely unrelated fields.

Reinis Pētersons illustrates children's books for one of Latvia's only independent publishing houses, *Liels un Mazs* ('Big and Small'). He says that the publishing house is unusual, as most places tend to rely on new editions of old children's classics. 'Not many houses do original children's books,' he says. His comic in the Kuš! anniversary 'Celebration' collection is a striking and richly coloured affair, showing tribesmen capturing a giant hog. It is one of only a few text-free comics, relying solely on its imagery to tell the story, suggesting that its unclothed hunters would also be able to understand the simple narrative. 'It's very primal,' he laughs.

Pētersons draws his inspiration from a variety of sources – both 'western' and Soviet. But this can change with the arrival of new generations onto the scene. 'The generation quite active in comic book art now, they don't have direct memories from Soviet times,' he says. Pētersons was born in 1981, so retains memories from the era – and they influenced his work deeply. 'It was a big shock when we got this whole western culture coming in this big way with the Disney animation, with western comics . . . you see there is this different kind of approach.' He notices that things seemed somehow more advanced, but he still honours the positive aspects of his past. 'Lots of animation films in the Soviet era were not only for children. They were . . . very philosophical sometimes,' he elaborates. 'The best I thought for me was the Sci-Fi animations, films in the eighties – there had already started to appear some Sci-Fi – they were very intriguing, about visiting different planets.'

Space exploration displaced religion in the Soviet Union and images of rockets, colonizing the moon, and space adventures penetrated popular culture deeply in the form of children's books, cartoons, songs, and even playground equipment.[18] Several illustrators comment on the Soviet legacy as a source of their inspiration, especially the ideas aimed at children. But some of them are too young to remember the actuality of Soviet times and some were not even alive under the occupation. Nonetheless the visual culture remained. 'I remember we had old Russian books from Soviet times,' said one young artist, Liana, born in 1994. 'They would have these crazy illustrations and I remember, it wasn't so much the story [that appealed] as the pictures.'[19]

While Free Riga had origins as a grassroots community organization formed in September 2013, it has slowly acquired legitimacy because of the benefits it can offer to both landowners and wider society. 'I got involved in Free Riga when it was formed as an NGO,' said Project Manager Jāzeps Bikše. 'First it was more or less in the huge worldwide breeze of Occupy and the city did this huge action around empty buildings.' Activists attached yellow stickers to the facades of buildings. 'Occupy Me stickers, you can still see them around – it was very much a movement, some sudden collective social urge to get space and come together.' However, Free Riga is not the only initiative of its kind. Both *Pagalmu Renesanse* (Courtyard Renascence) and *Labas Vietas Talka* (Nice Place Clean-up) were launched in 2014 with a similar goal of using resident engagement to revitalize urban space, and to complement the city's European Capital of Culture status – but these initiatives both began with a much clearer organizational structure, an action plan, and a source of funding.[20]

D27, in Bikše's opinion, is a great showcase of Free Riga's work; there are some problems with water and electricity, but generally the rooms are in very good condition. This was the fourth building they took under their guardianship after a long series of conversations with its owner, who stands to benefit greatly too. 'First of all we cover his maintenance costs – it would be guarding the property, taking care of it, warming it in winter. But, actually, the big real benefit for him is that we give him 90 per cent tax reduction for the property, land.' Ninety per cent is high, even for Riga – pensioners, the disabled, and 'performers of economic activities' all receive varying levels of tax relief from 25 per cent, up to 90.[21] 'If the user of [the] property is [a] socially beneficial organization that does revisions yearly, activities – which we have, are doing – then the land or building has this tax reduction,' says Bikše.[22] The D27 project has since drawn to a close, but Free Riga has two newer projects where it has repurposed old buildings in a similar way, at another interwar structure on 57 Kalēju Street and a creative complex at 34 Miera Street.

Some 750 metres away from D27 is the beautiful Kronvalda Park, split in two by a canal linking Rīga Stradiņš University buildings to the University of Latvia's Zoological Museum. It is named after nineteenth-century Latvian author Atis Kronvalds, a linguistic nationalist writing around the time of the 'National Awakening', who urged his readers to view the usage of the Latvian language as a 'sign of participation in a deeper – a national – consciousness that linked them all' regardless of their location.[23] The largely German Northern Crusades in the Baltic states aimed to Christianize these lands from around the twelfth century, and later Enlightenment Romanticist and nationalist trends depicted the Teutonic Knights and Livonian Order as part of a civilizing mission, spreading the German *Kulturraum*.[24] By the end of the fourteenth century German was overwhelmingly used in Riga and Tallinn, especially by the predominantly German-speaking aristocracy – largely the result of *Ostsiedlung* – that is, medieval German eastward expansion (not dissimilar to the more modern idea of *Lebensraum*), as well as the Teutonic Order's campaigns.

In a high-ceilinged building close to the park, I am waiting for Latvian soprano Kristine Opolais. She made her Royal Opera House debut in 2011 as the tragic Cio-Cio-San from Puccini's *Madama Butterfly* and planned to return to sing the lead as Elsa in Wagner's *Lohengrin* in summer 2018, before withdrawing due to routine surgery.

Latvia is fast becoming a musical superpower. Sopranos and mezzo-sopranos such as Kristine Opolais and Elīna Garanča have attained stunning acclaim in leading roles at the globe's opera houses, taking centre stage at New York's Metropolitan Opera among several others. Latvian director Alvis Hermanis and conductors Mariss Jansons and Andris Nelsons (Musical Director of the Boston Symphony Orchestra, to whom Opolais was married until early 2018) have also received widespread recognition. Lithuania's Mirga Gražinytė-Tyla has received acclaim as a conductor and music director of the City of Birmingham Symphony Orchestra, while Estonia's most renowned classical musician is of course Arvo Pärt, whose calm and coruscating compositions, 'shifting patterns and permutations cloaked in immense stillness' give a sense that the passage of time and incremental change are softly making peace with one another – music often associated with death and its acceptance. String orchestra the Scottish Ensemble and the independent theatre company Vanishing Point made an entire performance out of a selection of Arvo Pärt's compositions towards the end of 2017 based in part on this perceived link.[25] His most famous piece of work, *Spiegel im Spiegel* is immediately recognizable from myriad documentary soundtracks. While Pärt's music has an ethereal, religious tone – in part inspired by Gregorian chants, and which occasionally set him at odds with the secular Soviet regime – some critics also identify the Soviet legacy as a key factor in the musical aptitude of the region. 'There was only one good thing the Soviets gave Latvia, and it was specialist music schools,' Ivars Cinkuss, director of the Rigas Tehniskas Universitates Viru Koris Gaudeamus choir, said in 2015. 'In a way, our large number of top musicians is a direct result of the Soviet system.'[26]

However, Opolais seems to regard herself as someone who has succeeded in spite of the old system, rather than because of it. 'All my life people are saying to me I "can't do that",' she recalls. 'Not only in the Academy of Music [but] also in the [Latvian National] opera house when I started to move from the choir to a soloist,' she says with palpable (and slightly acidic) regret at the perceived injustice. When she was younger, the academy did not let her prolong her studies, which she now views as one of the most valuable occurrences of her career; it gave her the determination to prove her worth. 'I hate systems. Because when you're in the system you cannot do anything special. Because the system is killing the talent,' she states. 'Only when I started to sing at Covent Garden. When I made my career debut at the Metropolitan Opera. In Munich, *Russalka*. Only when all other opera doors were open for me, only then did I become really, for real, welcome in my country.'[27]

Opolais has just arrived from Jurmala, the allegedly mafia-soused coastal resort city 25 kilometres west of Riga and home of the Dzintari Concert Hall. In 2019, it is set to host the international Rīga Jūrmala classical music festival for the first time, But when Opolais comes home to Latvia, she doesn't like to perform, and would rather recuperate and spend time with her family. Apologetic about traffic, and brisk and smiling, she begins by reeling off all the required formalities – tour dates, where she's been, critical reception and where she will be heading next. She comes across as inherently impulsively open, but an initial degree of caution suggests that people around her have not always responded favourably to her combination of self-assurance, perceptiveness, and glib openness. As our interview progresses, it becomes clear Opolais is refreshingly comfortable in her own skin – in fact, she considers it imperative to her voice – and a reflection of her career. 'If you are strong, if you are a personality. If you have special charisma, there will be always people whom you are disturbing ... this is fantastic. You can be sad about that, but you need to be proud of that.' Opolais finds several of her roles very physically and emotionally demanding – while she clearly adores her profession and the music, she is slightly bemused and perplexed by people who tell her to 'enjoy' singing *Butterfly* before she goes on stage. Many of her heroines are sick, die or kill themselves. She has a self-professed love for drama, and a clear understanding of the value of her own mixed experiences in Soviet and 'post-Soviet' Latvia, their value to both her deeply expressive and tormented performances, and her public identity.

'Puccini – you really love it and understand this music only if you know what means suffering and passion in your life,' she says, but remains vague about the precise nature of this suffering when pressed. 'I will not explain in which way and why, but I know what [it] means.' Nowadays, she's receptive to it, believing sombre experiences hold a key place as important, necessary events that contribute a certain depth and richness to existence. With a comfortable background – perhaps wealth, and intelligence, or some combination thereof – she theorizes that any aspiring actor or singer is missing something fundamental that they cannot learn. 'You just need to go through a lot of difficulties in your life, emotional difficulties, to understand what this life means, generally in all [its] colours,' she says, later touching on the grim poverty of the Soviet Union that she was exposed to in her youth.

Opolais holds her talented compatriots in high regard despite ambivalence towards her home country's domestic system. 'A lot! Isn't it?!'

she enthuses when I broach the subject of Latvian classical music stars. 'We have a lot of great singers singing outside of Latvia ... and I think Elīna Garanča is the best mezzo soprano in the world.' She says that she is not a 'real Latvian' (her mother came from Belarus), but she still considers it her country. 'The culture in Latvia is at a very high level. I think we have something in the blood,' she says.

Latvia, Lithuania and Estonia all have a strong tradition of song and dance festivals – Baltic song festivals even have a space on the UNESCO Intangible Cultural Heritage List. Held every five years in Estonia and Latvia, and every four years in Lithuania, they are widely regarded as a celebration of Baltic cultural identity that managed to subversively prevail even under the USSR – Estonia 'sang its way out of the Soviet Union'.[28] 'We have also an amazing tradition of our choir,' says Opolais, a little dutifully. 'I think the Latvians are very deeply musically sensitive people, and our amazing choir song festival is something, really.' However, she does not seem to believe it heavily impacted her. Rather she was a big rock and pop fan as a child, and an aspiring actress. 'Only the words of my mother, that she wanted me to be an opera singer [encouraged me]. And the second thing for me was the CD of Maria Callas,' she recalls, dismissing the song festivals as a key cultural influence. When she receives thunderous audience applause in America, she feels more like Tina Turner, or Lady Gaga, than a product of either the Soviet system or a more traditional cultural heritage.[29]

In Estonia, the fall of the Soviet Union became known as 'The Singing Revolution'. A choir of some 25,000, and up to 100,000 spectators, still join together at the *Lauluväljak* (the song festival grounds) in traditional national costume to sing and dance together. Thousands of dancers swarm the stadium together forming fluidly kaleidoscopic patterns for onlookers, and there are open-air concerts on every one of the three days it spans. Each festival ends with an enormous, celestial rendition of *Mu Isamaa on Minu Arm* ('My Fatherland is my Love'), which was first set to music for the first Estonian Song Festival in 1869. A new melody was written for it in 1944, which sounds strikingly similar (at least at the start) to the Estonian national anthem.

After the first period of Soviet occupation authorities prohibited all independent societies, among them choral societies and *Eesti Lauljate Liit* (ELL, the Estonian Singers' Union). In the 1920s and 1930s, the goal of the ELL was to develop Estonian national choral culture through local and general song festivals, and to introduce new Estonian choral music, which had its roots in nineteenth-century parish churches (despite its later secular nature), somewhat influenced by the German choral movement.[30] However, the Soviets had to offer their own take on the song festival – while thousands of people coming together to sing was strong embodiment of the Soviet ideal, cultural nationalism received mixed responses – it had to be administered top-down in the occupied republics from a central government more interested in developing the idea of a collectively Soviet people. The General Committee for Song Festivals was established, and several traditional festival songs were censored. The 1947 festival included two Soviet songs and one Ukrainian – in previous years the only non-Estonian songs had been Finnish and Latvian.[31]

Traditional song and dance is by no means the preserve of older conservative generations, and is universally revered in a different way from the triumphantly patriotic anthems you might find in countries with an imperial past. My former (twenty-something) Estonian teacher in London, and a relative in her mid-teens in Tallinn, are both very passionate about the dancing celebrations. And the song festival is a deeply, viscerally felt affair, with countless pairs of wet eyes visible during the rich solemnity of *Mu Isamaa on Minu Arm*. Few overtly 'happy' old songs seem to exist, and there is a very specifically emotional element to the type of unbreakable bottom-up nationalism the songs channel; 'a song festival is a matter of the heart. Like the Estonian language and mentality, like love,' said late former President Lennart Meri in 1999. 'Songs have been our weapons, song festivals our victories.'[32]

Latvia and Lithuania both place a similarly central emphasis on songs as a cornerstone of their traditional culture, alongside folk customs, costume and local myth. Most families are in possession of at least one set of traditional costumes and through their colours and finer weave, you can pinpoint where someone is from too – this traditional dress almost acts as a wearable postcode. While historically, intertribal variation in clothing style is minimal, concentrated in jewellery and ornamentation, not garment construction and shapes, it is likely this changed during the nineteenth century.[33] Latvia and Lithuania's *daina* folk songs (*dainos* in the Lithuanian plural) are fundamental to both cultures, and just as is the case in Estonia, their present-day prominence has an intensely political history.[34] The songs feature fairy tales and folktales superstitions, proverbs, and descriptions of daily life that have taken on a revered, almost religious nature.[35] The late-nineteenth and early-twentieth-century 'National Awakening' in the Baltic region with its heightened focus on national cultural independence saw folksongs, art and local stories used as collective expressions underpinning national identity and historical memory in the face of cultural domination by Polish, German or Russian neighbours.[36] Folklore especially was intrinsically connected to the National Awakening. Friedrich Reinhold Kreutzwald first published the Estonian national epic *Kalevipoeg* (*Kalev's Son*) in 1857, while the Latvian national epic *Lplsis* (*Bearslayer*) was created by Andrejs Pumpurs in 1888. National epics were a conglomeration of folksongs and legends 'attributed to a pre-national community, something that had preceded the nation' – they became a great source of pride and a 'foundation for the emerging nation'.[37]

There are some beautiful modern twists to these local manifestations of folk culture and traditional music for social or political purposes, as well as religious. Composer and sound artist Arturas Bumšteinas spent 2008–10 travelling to twenty-two parishes in Lithuania with organist Gaile Griciutev on an 'Organ Safari' recording the sounds of various organs in churches around the country. 'There's no personal religious agenda. It's more an interest in the phenomenology of space or sound … the collaboration between the church space and the organ is what is the most interesting,' he says. All the organs are somehow different. Not only are they made by different masters, but they have been treated in a plethora of different ways under the different epochs. 'Some of them have been played and taken care of and some of them have been neglected for many years – during the Soviet times in churches there were a lot of nailed-down, boarded-up instruments because there was no priority to preserve cultural heritage … it's just easier to pretend it just doesn't exist,' he says, recollecting his friend's discovery of a bell inscribed with Lithuanian wording hidden in a rural church tower.[38]

Lithuania is home to televised choral competitions – like a religious or community version of *X-Factor*. The 'Battle of the Choirs' sees (for example) police, city or student choirs, or the Choir of the Blind (which won in 2015) vie for the position of the nation's best singing group.[39] Bumšteinas is disparaging about the choral heritage and the 'propaganda event' that is the song festival – bringing smaller choirs together to make a 'super choir'. However, he has himself written one piece for choir – which bizarrely, was last performed in Berlin's legendary club, Berghain. 'It's crazy. It's a dance club, and there's a choir,' he says. He describes the piece as a 'twenty-minute-long whispered version of art history written by a crazy French man in the sixties' – a reference to Robert Filliou's proclamation that art was born one 17 January, when someone dropped a dry sponge into a bucket of water. He adapted the work and asked choristors to sing it. 'I invited every choir singer [from an international group] to the sound studio individually – they came one by one and I gave them this text, and they just improvised,' he says. He then took the different parts and mixed them together.

The Christian choral tradition has managed to persist in this wide variety of forms, as well as the older folk *dainos*. Baltic paganism has also been well preserved and has even seen something of a revival in each country since the Soviet collapse, as residents sought to develop connections with their own organic 'historic roots'. Fostering a connection to the land, old languages and old gods and tradition is intrinsically linked to identity and community, and Baltic pagan religions have enjoyed a recent resurgence. Estonia's Maausk neopagans, along with Estonia's other prominent neopagan group, the Taaraists, tripled in size from 2001 to 2011 (the most recent figures available from the national census), while Lithuania's Romuva community has seen an increase in membership from 1,200 in 2001 to 5,100 in 2011.[40]

Across each country, there is an overwhelming presence of magical and mythical natural sites embedded in the geography of everyday life. Sacred groves and hills scatter Estonia, Latvia and Lithuania while certain objects contain spirits or gods. Trees, stones and rocks can all take on a sacred or magical quality, strangely sentient in Baltic folklore. In Latgale (the easternmost region of Latvia), there is a certain fabled tradition of rocks acting as tailors – that is, they (or a spirit residing in them) are able to make clothes if cloth is left on them overnight. In one other tale local to the region, a furious landlord pushes a stone into the river, but it climbs out on the opposite bank.[41] Devils often described mending their clothes sitting on stones, and there are similar parallels in regional Lithuanian and Belarusian folk literature. Across Latvia, the Devil lends his name to dark or mysterious locations. Among the sites are 'Hell's Hills' and a 'Devil's cave' – and sandstone caves are often thought to have been used as pagan cult sites by local peasants.[42] The country's Pokaiņi Forest, some 90 kilometres southwest of Riga, allegedly exudes a 'cosmic' or 'healing' energy, and is home to the 'mysterious' Pokaini Stones, thought to possess magical properties. During the autumn solstice hundreds of Latvians head to the forest and shamans from the Far East Russian region of Yakutia have also reportedly attended.[43] Bullaun stones – that is, rocks with man-made hollows in – are peppered around the Baltic region too. Groves, rocks, springs and trees were the sites of grain and milk offerings and occasional animal sacrifices to the spirits and gods and goddesses.[44] In Estonia, two of Tartu's most beloved attractions are its Sacrificial Stone and Kissing Hill – students from the university ritually burn their notes at this particular Sacrificial Stone after exams. There are some 400 sacrificial stones scattered around the country.

Jaanipäev is one of the most important dates on the Estonian (Jāņu diena in Latvian and Joninės in the Lithuanian) calendars. The word means St John's Day, or Midsummer, and marks the solstice, the longest day of the year. Despite the name, it is not particularly related to any Christian sentiment. 'In the Latvian case, the church ... imposed the name of the saints,' says Aldis Pūtelis, a former researcher at the University of Latvia's Institute of Literature, Folklore and Art. 'St John is the patron of midsummer's night and all the pagan activities there, and St George is the name of the day that different pagan cults related to horses are observed, but again neither of these saints are responsible for what these pagans are doing. It's just a name.'[45] Those who celebrate Midsummer light large bonfires, and use tree branches and boughs as décor. Different trees have different meanings, for example the thunder god Perkunas is linked to oak trees. A choral song, Saule, Pērkons, Daugava (Sun, Thunder, Daugava) is one of Latvia's most beloved festival songs, the Thunder in its lyrics symbolising a father. In Estonia, the ash, lime and oak are considered particularly sacred, and women make wreaths for their heads, and people search for the elusive fern blossom which according to local lore only blooms that one day. While a variety of mystical superstitions surround the date (as well as it marking the more practical change in farming seasons), the best-known tradition is jumping through or over the bonfire after lighting it. It appears to be an extremely dangerous activity when it takes place on a larger scale, but nowadays people are more likely to build miniature bonfires they can jump over instead of diving through giant, all-consuming flames. The ritual is thought to guarantee prosperity and stave off bad luck (and to some women, even increase fertility). The bigger the fire, the further away mischievous spirits are supposed to stay.[46]

The heightened interest in the Romuva in Lithuania, the Dievturi in Latvia, and the Maausk and Taaralased movements in Estonia are all essentially polytheistic but have some minor distinctions too. In November 2009, a small Maausk group from these pagan denominations congregated on the sacred hill of Kunda in Mahu, northern Estonia. Attendees cooked and sang folk songs while praying to their ancestors, Maaema (the god of land), Uku (the god of rain) and other ancient deities.[47] But its proponents see it less as deity-focused and more connected to community and life itself. 'Something much more than a religion. Maausk is our vernacular, our songs, our customs, our beliefs, our archetypes and culture. Maausk is thousands of years old, a tradition that binds us to our land.'[48] Lithuania's modern strands of paganism have stronger links to Hinduism and Sanskrit – whether real or imagined, there are indeed linguistic links between Lithuanian and Sanskrit, and Latvian and Sanskrit, but the evidence of a quasi-religious connection is more tenuous. For some Romuva a connection 'proves that Lithuanian or Baltic culture is as old as India's old spiritual traditions', according to Egle Aleknaite, a researcher at Vytautas Magnus University in Kaunus, Lithuania, who was a Romuva community member as a teenager. Romuva became a manifestation of traditional Lithuanian culture and identity, including paganism in the post-independence era, and is now pursuing 'official religion' status.[49] The Dievturiba movement in Latvia is was created by using the Latvian *dainas*, the aforementioned ancient songs and poems and established around the first independence period, and was again a way of consolidating an ancient association with the land in the face of external forces. Banned under the Soviets, it even has a branch in the US (Wisconsin. The Romuva community is likewise active in Indiana). 'In reality, one could say that the *dainas* are our holy texts as they hold explanations of our god, life and living. *Dainas* have very many hidden meanings and symbols, but not everything that is written there has to be taken literally,' Riga-based folklorist Gunta Saule told *The Baltic Times*. 'It is important to mention that modern Dievturi are not members of some kind of new religion – it is only new in the way that it has formed recently, but the foundations are as old as the proto-indo-European language, and since the first Balts arrived in the region,' she said.[50] Latvia's new religious movement is somewhat unique out of the three; instead of being pantheistic, polytheistic, shamanistic or inherently linked to the 'spirituality of nature', its proponents search for an 'individual path to God', even if ensconced in folklore and national ideology.[51]

Contemporary Estonian writer Andrus Kivirähk in his bestselling work of fiction *The Man Who Spoke Snakish* well encapsulates the medieval Christianization of pagan Estonia, symbolized in the conflicts between new village residents and nature-tethered forest-dwellers during the Teutonic crusaders' invasion. Early in the novel a tall, grand and 'enviably well-dressed' man tells the forest-dwellers that 'all the sensible people' are moving from the forest to the village. 'What will become of you if you don't learn to talk German and serve Jesus?' he asks.[52] In the protagonist Leemut's rapidly changing world (he himself is traversing the line between childhood and adulthood) this conflict is heavily symbolized by the types of food consumed: in the villages the people till fields to make bread as a mark of sophistication – to 'appear terribly fine'; the 'normal people' live under the open sky and 'not in a murky forest' where the backwards bumpkins feast voraciously on elk and hare and drink wolves' milk. Leemut's family are some of the few final forest-dwellers who speak the dying language of Snakish, which allows them to control local wildlife. He has a conversation with a colossal ageing fish, while bears seduce women, and deer offer themselves as food in this shambolic self-parody. The novel becomes a marvellously absurd satirization of modern, nationalistic over-romanticization of Estonia's ancient roots – just as the German 'civilizing missions' were romanticized in the National Awakening period, today it is more fashionable to romanticize the pre-Christian. Resistant to both the new religion and the mythology of the forest spirits, Leemut finally exclaims in frustration, 'I agree to do all the work, till the fields, and prepare the same bread, which doesn't actually taste good but fills your stomach – everything that is tangible and edible, and thus real and actual. But I don't need new sprites!'[53]

In the more tangible world, a Baltic food scene with elements that resonate deeply in Kivirähk's fiction is booming. The 'slow food' scene in the region places a profound emphasis on the seasonal and the local, often procured in person from the wild directly by restaurant staff. Elk, moss, guinea fowl, caviar and even iced beeswax all hold places on Baltic menus. In November 2017, White Guide Nordic confidently stated that 'there is no better time than NOW to visit Baltic restaurants'[54] and in the space of just one year, the number of recommended restaurants in the region rose from just sixty to 160, with Estonia (despite being the smallest country) having the largest representation in the rankings, topping the list with NOA Chef's Hall, which now has its sights set on a Michelin Star.[55] Twenty-six-year-old head chef Orm Oja and his 'forager', Maret Allikas often harvest mushrooms, berries, wild edible herbs from the Estonian countryside for the restaurant – the practice is less common in the UK, but in the Baltics foraging is much more of a regular habit, with young and old heading out to the woods and coasts to collect nettles and flowers to make tea. 'Estonian cooking is quite, like, peasant based,' Oja told Scandinavian food blogger Anders Husa. 'We don't have any luxury produce. Wild plants in the peak season – we use them fresh. Some of them Maret [Allikas] dries so it's easier to use them in the winter time.'

There is a similar attitude in Latvia. 'I explore this country in terms of wild food – what is there, what is edible and what's not edible ... to go out and pick something myself,' said Dzintars Kristovskis, the head chef at Annas Hotel some 80 kilometres east of Riga.[56] Oja definitely considers Baltic cuisine a sibling of Scandinavian. 'Estonian cooking links to Nordic cooking – the biggest similarities are foraging and using the really wild products, because Estonia actually has the most edible plants per square kilometre in northern Europe – so it's the one thing that gives us food on our plates,' he said. 'I still have a dream, that I will get a star someday.'[57]

Vincents, in Riga has counted Britain's Queen Elizabeth II, the Emperor of Japan, Elton John and BB King among its guests. Former head chef Martins Ritins once described traditional Latvian cuisine as essentially 'pork, pork, pork, pork'. His food has a French twist, but in early days was sent back by the locals for, he thinks, not being heavy enough. 'Vincents has always been the business card of Latvian fine dining cuisine,' said its head sommelier Raimonds Tomsons, who won the accolade Best Sommelier of Europe in 2017.[58] Ritins, despite his recent departure from Vincents, is widely considered the leader of the 'slow food' movement in the country and has been vocal about his opposition to mass-produced food's role in diluting national identity. 'The seller must be able to tell from which fields and from which farmer he has taken a product,' he said. 'The opportunities for our farmers are quite extensive, for example, they are growing asparagus again now, which was mentioned in old cookbooks. But in Soviet times, asparagus flowers were taken to graves. We have parsnips, Jerusalem artichoke, black salsify, and then many varieties of cabbage with immeasurable nuances in their flavor.[59]

It's August in Estonia, and I'm driving back from watching the sunset from a point on the northwestern Tallinn coast with two relatives. As we drive through the winding, forested streets of the suburbs, we pass a cute, chubby white box with antennae, wheeling itself along. These beetle-like delivery robots trundle through Estonia's streets on a regular basis dispatching food to customers using a combination of internal cameras and GPS. Tallinn-based company Starship was set up by founding members of Skype, and Estonia was the first country in Europe to introduce them to the streets – hardly surprising for a country where you can become a digital citizen (there are 33,000 to date), vote online, board a driverless bus, or that established the world's first 'data embassy' in Luxembourg. The country is regarded as a bastion of technological progression in Europe, and far beyond its own borders, earning it the monikers 'e-Estonia' or 'E-stonia', and securing it top spot out of sixty-eight countries in terms of digital life in a 2018 Digital Life Abroad report.[60]

While little vehicles can even stop at traffic lights by themselves, not everyone is welcoming of the prospect of introducing these delivery robots to city streets; in May 2017, San Francisco's city supervisor Norman Yee proposed legislation to keep delivery robots machines off pedestrian pathways – allegedly because of the potential threat to public safety, but it is highly likely the city's complicated relationship with technology, regulation and space plays a role. While Starship did manage to acquire a permit for testing, it hasn't yet been taken further. 'It's all about trying to get ahead of the curve before it gets out of hand,' Yee said. 'Basically when you give them space, you never get it back.'[61] However, the Council of the District of Columbia has voted to approve a bill that would legalize the robots within the city's boundaries – as long as they travel at a maximum speed of 10mph.[62] They are also set to be welcomed in San Jose. 'It's tempting to regulate when there's a new technology that's deployed in such a visible way but it's important to understand whether the disruption is such that really requires regulation,' Mayor Sam Liccado said.[63]

Tallinn was the first home of internet-phone service provider Skype, which was bought by Microsoft Corp. for $8.5 billion in 2011 but continues to have a development office in Tallinn. The founders of TransferWise, a global money transfer startup that has been valued at more than a $1 billion, are Estonian. Tallinn is also home to Toggl – a time tracking app for freelancers and companies to record time spent on various tasks. PC Mag gave it an 'excellent' (4.0) in February 2018, calling it their favourite time-tracking tool for freelancers.[64] Its innovative hiring process attracts the type of workers that it perhaps appeals to as a tool – it only uses remote workers. The company has nearly seventy employees across the US, Europe, Asia and Australia – and only twenty of those are based in Estonia. However, it still ensures they all maintain face-to-face relationships, and new hires are flown into Tallinn for a couple of weeks. 'We always get people here, they hang around the office, go to lunch, to the bars. Then they go back home and it's a lot easier to communicate with them because they now know the people they are chatting with,' cofounder and product lead Krister Haav told Forbes.[65] This idea of remote, international business minds 'meeting' in Estonia underpins the famous 'e-Residency' project too, wherein digital entrepreneurs can be issued a government identity to run a business from the EU country, even if not physically located there.

In total, tech companies leased 21 per cent of all office space taken up in the city between 2012 and 2017, according to JLL. However, Estonia's presence at the forefront of the tech scene in eastern Europe can be overstated (after all, it is not uncommon to complete administrative tasks online in several countries), and there are still small holes that need patching. At the end of 2017, a group of Czech security researchers managed to exploit a ROCA vulnerability to still information from electronic ID cards. Estonia had to recall 760,000 digital IDs in the aftermath. Former President Ilves maintained that other countries were impacted by the same issue, but the only difference is that Estonia happens to be transparent, while 'others [countries and organizations] remain silent about the very same flaw'.[66] Proximity to Russia can still be viewed as an issue by the international community and the NATO Cooperative Cyber Defence Centre of Excellence in Tallinn, Estonia holds annual live-fire cyber defence exercise Locked Shields 2017 in an attempt to maintain the technical defence of virtualized infrastructure against potential threats.

While Estonia is a startup haven (the country is third in Europe in terms of the highest number of startups per capita), Lithuania is geared more towards accommodating foreign companies. Lithuania had the fastest public WiFi in the world in 2015, 2016 and 2017 based on average download speeds in megabites per second (mbps). According to Silicon Valley communications company Ooma, average download speeds stand at 15.4 mbps and average upload speeds at 14.17 mbps. Estonia is third in the world (Croatia takes second place). There has been a flurry of construction of modern offices in Vilnius lately and the Lithuanian capital is now attracting technology development operations by big firms such as Uber as well as smaller firms like American software maker Unify Square Inc. and Belgian data science company Sentiance NV. Vilnius Tech Park – with some 9,000 square metres of office space – is the biggest ICT startup hub in the Baltics, and home to several different companies – including Bored Panda, the viral content site started by a Lithuanian business administration student in 2009. Alongside that, the Barclays-backed Rise Vilnius, a 'startup incubator' FinTech community, aims to act as a draw for the larger companies, providing coworking spaces, meeting rooms and podcast recording facilities. Its head, Darius Kavaliauskas, believes Lithuania's size facilitates a tight support network and a good climate for experimenting with new ideas.[67]

So far, efforts to attract more FinTech companies have been working. Lithuania recorded a 43 per cent increase in new registered startups in

2017 compared to 2016 – thirty-five FinTech companies were registered in 2017, according to the Lithuania Fintech Report 2017.[68] One of the report's compilers believes this is because of 'a growing talent pool, hassle-free regulation, flexible banking infrastructure, and the ability to access half a billion customers in Europe' – that is, acting as the key to the EU market.[69] Toon Vanparys, chief executive of Sentiance, said they chose Vilnius because the city has a large pool of engineers and data scientists locally, plus they can attract senior engineers living elsewhere who want to move away from the chaotic lives of large tech cities. 'We will probably build smaller tech hubs in the future, based on the quality of living and the availability of talent,' said Mr Vanparys. The INFOBALT association of IT companies conducted a recent study along with Invest Lithuania and the Research and Higher Education Monitoring and Analysis Centre (MOSTA) which showed that 13,300 specialists will be needed in the information and technology market over the next three years, adding that investors about to settle in Lithuania include Booking. com, Centric, NKT, and Telia.[70] It is clear the Baltic nations are keen competition for the accolade 'Silicon Valley of Europe'.

Baltic conservatism

For all of this technological progress, the Baltic states are still socially conservative in several ways. Women's rights have a long way to go, wages are low and outward migration is extremely high, various professions are underpaid, overcrowded and mired in nepotism. Alcoholism is rampant, suicide and homicide rates high, domestic violence apparently regarded as unremarkable, and the LGBTQ+ community still struggles with acceptance – even in recent years activists have faced significant opposition from locals. A late-2018 Pew Research Center poll indicated that 61 per cent of Estonians aged eighteen to thirty-four opposed gay marriage, as did a much higher 70 per cent of Latvians and 74 per cent of Lithuanians. The same poll indicated a mere 25 per cent of Estonians, 19 per cent of Latvians and 16 per cent of Lithuanians would be willing to accept Muslims as family members.[71]

Lithuanian poet Aušra Kaziliūnaitė's name means 'dawn' in Lithuanian. She was around three years old when the Soviet Union collapsed and a new era rose. At that point, her parents decided to move from Vilnius to a more rural area in the country's north, establish a farm, and raise (and later kill) rabbits. Her father used to read Goethe to her at night as she fell asleep. When I first saw her speak at the Piccadilly Waterstone's in early 2017 during a renewed cultural emphasis on modern Baltic literature, she read her poems in her native Lithuanian through a long and heavy curtain of bright pink hair. Here, in Mint Vinetu, a cosy second-hand book shop and café-workspace (named in part, after German author Karl May's Winnetou), Aušra is visibly more relaxed, speaking fluent English with her trademark pink hair tucked neatly behind her ears. With us are Lithuanian-American writer, translator and editor Rimas Uzgiris and poet and editor of Literary magazine *Vilnius Review*, Marius Burokas.

'Aušra was in a way brave enough to actually write about the anger, the sense of violence and rupture,' says Uzgiris, reflecting on the social problems in Lithuania that occurred after the Soviet collapse. 'A lot of people ... sort of got stuck in the past writing about the same old neoromantic stuff,' he adds. 'We don't have a lot of strong women poets from the old generation because in Lithuania and the Soviet Union period there was a lot of sexism and we [are] dealing [with] this problem these days as well – a lot of homophobia, sexism, a lot of unkind stuff.' He added that there's a palpable sense that people are 'angry'. 'I still feel it. Not so much here, in the old town [Vilnius] – there are a lot of young people here – but like in my old neighbourhood ... I felt every day a low level of aggression, that in America I don't ever feel. Just angry, grumpy people ... you put these things together and you see there's some underlying problem. People are somehow unhappy and they don't know how to deal with it.' In the whole of the EU, the Baltics hold the proud positions of highest proportion of household expenditure on alcohol. 'Households in the three Baltic States devoted the largest share of their total expenditure to alcoholic beverages: Estonia (5.6%), Latvia (4.8%) and Lithuania (4.2%),' according 2016 Eurostat figures.[72] Estonia was struggling with a serious fentanyl epidemic until 2017. The suicide rate in Lithuania is the highest in Europe and the homicide rate is higher than anywhere else in the EU. Women are often blamed if they are victims of domestic violence, with a general lack of support available in the event that they do seek it.[73]

Aušra recalls her first brush with the less progressive side of society. 'I started to write poetry very young. My first publication came when I was fifteen years old ... I had a lot of comments about my publication and all the things in these comments was nothing about the quality of the verse or poems but more about my gender. So, for example, I remember one comment very good because it was very painful for me – it was written. "Oh,

this little girl, maybe you gave a blowjob to the editor for this publication"...
I recognized which person wrote it and it was like an older writer – it wasn't
just [some troll] ... I think it's a lot of hidden, and not actually hidden
sexism in our culture.' She refused to name the writer. 'Now for me it's not so
painful but I'm just trying to think about it and I think it's a very good topic
from which you can try to recognize this situation and what's happening
now – I think after the Soviet Union we had a lot of people who were angry.
A lot of forms change but this anger exists in some people.'

The Baltic states are still socially conservative countries in many
respects, for examples displays of LGBTQ+ pride are still difficult for the
wider public to register as acceptable. As *Passport* magazine put it, 'LGBT
visibility gets stronger the higher you go' – that is, Estonia is the most
progressive in this sense.[74] However, even Estonia has not yet properly
implemented its civil partnership law (the Registered Partnership Act)
which is gender-neutral and was passed in Estonia in 2014 in a 'landmark'
move, according to Aili Kala of the Estonian LGBT+ Association – it was
the first former Soviet republic to do so. 'It [says] to Europe that we are with
you,' Kala told Buzzfeed. 'Russia can see that we want to [stay] in the EU
and get more support from EU countries.'[75] The country has also recognized
same-sex marriages conducted abroad since 2016, and the same year put
on an exhibition at the Museum of Occupations called 'NSFW: A
Chairman's Tale', which documented the life of an Estonian Soviet farm
chairman, found murdered in 1991 (possibly by a male prostitute).[76] The
Conservative People's Party of Estonia (EKRE) has predictably vocally
opposed the law and attempted to get it repealed (in protest, a local
beverages company depicted two EKRE MPs Martin Helme and Jaak
Madison as *Brokeback Mountain* characters on its rainbow label).

'When people think of the Baltic States, they think of three similar
countries, but Estonia is miles ahead of us in Lithuania and Latvia,'
Kristine Garina, chair of Mozaika, Latvia's LGBTQ+ rights and advocacy
organization, told NBC. 'In Estonia, politicians never used homophobia
as their only political platform, at least not as strongly as here. In Latvia,
from 2005 to 2007 there were whole political movements that built their
success only on open homophobia, and they are largely responsible for
the extremely slow progress – and even regress – of LGBTQ rights here.'[77]
It was therefore quite surprising when Latvia's Foreign Minister Edgars
Rinkēvičs came out in 2014 – which he announced two days after the
(heterosexual) live-in partner of a rescue worker killed in a shopping
mall collapse was denied inheritance and state benefits. To Rinkēvičs, it

highlighted the issues surrounding non-traditional partnerships: 'Our country has to create a legal framework for all types of partnerships, and I will fight for it,' he wrote in his tweet.[78]

Aušra wrote a poem called *Holiday Make Up*, within which are the lines: 'I saw eight-year-olds sent by their parents / running up to human rights activists / shouting – give us back the rainbow.'[79] She recalls the activist event that inspired it. 'this one wasn't a very huge event – maybe thirty-five or forty, but you know, people in Lithuania aren't very active. One child just ran into the small crown and shouted – "give us back the rainbow!" It was very interesting to think about because this child cannot decide for themselves.' The family structure in Lithuanian law is generally quite restrictive about what constitutes a family – single mothers, LGBTQ+ relationships, a grandparent and a grandchild all don't 'count'. Aušra cites the Catholic church's role in some of Lithuania's more socially conservative policies. 'Our government is like a secular country . . . but a lot of priests have a lot of influence on government. We protested near Parliament because our government wants to forbid abortions, like in Poland, so we did a huge event and fought a lot,' she recalls, adding that women eventually retained the right to abortion.

In some ways LGBTQ+ rights and an acceptance of homosexuality has become an inherently political issue in eastern Europe; many Russia-leaning individuals see it as symbolic of a depraved Europe and support for LGBTQ+ rights is now almost synonymous with 'western values'.[80] 'Homosexuality has become a political tool that Western countries use to break up our society. It's unacceptable in our culture and it should stay as a taboo. If you start discussing it, it will divide us and eventually break up the society,' said Vadim Topalov, a twenty-year-old political science student at the Donetsk National University in eastern Ukraine in 2016. Russian television has been increasingly terming the continent 'Gayropa'. Tolerance for the rainbow flag in the region has somehow become a divisive political issue as opposed to a civil rights topic.

But social activism in Lithuania also comes with an odd downside – anti-government action can be construed as pro-Russia even if the activism is completely unrelated; lobbying for rights that the Russian government would never condone, you can still be accused of doing Putin's bidding. 'If I am a patriotic person I can criticize the decisions which in my opinion are not good for our country!' Aušra says. 'But after I hear "oh, you are working with Putin"! if you are critical . . . if you act not in the same way as the government we can say "Oh, is Putin paying you?"'

6 THE BALTICS IN EUROPE

Entering the age of 'Great Power'

Politicians and analysts are becoming increasingly attuned to the idea that the world is making a return to 'Great Power' politics. The US is starting to regard China as a key player on the world stage, both militarily and commercially. Russia's lack of internal stability somewhat hinders its 'Great Power' status but it is still a formidable presence in its near-abroad, and increasingly in the Middle East. North Korea and Iran's nuclear programmes are often deemed a threat to the US, with Pyongyang having developed a nuclear arsenal that could potentially reach US soil.[1] Europe has fallen behind in the world order since both World Wars, with its constituent states largely functioning under a power structure that is presided over by the US and NATO, although its larger nations, for example France and Germany, are renewing old alliances in the face of a perceived weakening of relations between the US and Europe. Since the UK's Brexit, EU states are becoming increasingly attuned to the importance of European solidarity, as well as the need to somewhat counterbalance larger continental powers involved in running the bloc. Right-wing populism has gained a footing both in Europe and on a global level. Inside Russia, the world's twentieth-century institutions and the political or strategic ideals underpinning them are generally deemed obsolete, and the identity of Putin's successor remains uncertain – should he even plan to leave his role. So how do all these intersecting currents impact the future of the Baltic states on the global stage, their place in Europe, and their potential exploitation. Is the new 'Yaltaphobia' justified?

In *Sunday Times* political editor Tim Shipman's book, *Fall Out: A Year of Political Mayhem*, he recalls then-UK Foreign Secretary Boris Johnson and his team meeting with Steve Bannon and Jared Kushner. One Brit asked, 'What do you give Russia to get them to the table?' 'Steve Bannon, being mischievous, said if they want to move into some Baltic state, 'We're relaxed,' a source present said.[2] The Russians want 'the old sit-down like they had with FDR at Potsdam and Yalta, working out what's their piece of real estate and what's ours', Fiona Hill of US research group Brookings Institution told *The Atlantic*. 'They want to have the U.S. acknowledge that they're a great power and have the right to have a veto over things that they don't like.'[3]

The US Department of State's top official in Europe, Wess Mitchell, resigned in January 2019, supposedly on account of 'personal reasons'. However, his departure sparked murmurs on both sides of the Atlantic: an anonymous Democratic staffer in the Senate said Mitchell's departure was 'unfortunate for those of us who want a responsible Russia policy', adding 'I'm surprised he lasted as long as he did ... he was much more forward leaning than the White House on Russia.' Upon his departure, Mitchell told the *Washington Post* that, 'We're entering an era of big-power competition.'[4] The following day, on 23 January, the US House of Representatives approved legislation aimed at preventing US withdrawal from the NATO alliance. Twenty-two Republicans voted 'no' – in essence, voting in favour of letting Trump leave the alliance. The *New York Times* published an article the previous week alleging that 'several times' over the course of 2018, Trump privately told his advisers he wanted to withdraw from NATO.

In a time in which US support for NATO seems to have been wavering, the strength of Europe as a cohesive entity has never been more important, or complicated. Different blocs within Europe are beginning to form in an apparent response to the perceived fragility of international institutions. Within Europe, one such emerging bloc is the New Hanseatic League, or the Hansa. Established in February 2018, it encompasses the Republic of Ireland, the Netherlands, Denmark, Sweden, Finland, Estonia, Latvia and Lithuania, the coalition of fiscally conservative northern European governments developed in the wake of the UK's Brexit crisis. The new monetary union was based in part on the original Hanseatic League, an old, medieval commercial and defensive alliance between guilds in the northern, largely coastal European regions until the sixteenth century.

The northern European states are regarded as something of a counterweight to the dominance of France and Germany on the European continent by countries such as the Netherlands. The UK acted as a 'counterbalance [to] the French statist approach and the legalistic methodology of the Germans', according to national daily *NRC Handelsblat*. But as Brexit became a reality, new relationships had to be forged.

Dutch Minister of Finance, Wopke Hoekstra, took the initiative to seek and unite new European allies. He concentrated on 'the northern eight', which existed close to the country from Ireland, Denmark, Finland, Sweden, Estonia, Latvia and Lithuania. Together they form a strong counterweight against the Franco-German axis with 50 million inhabitants. The Dutch press at the time noted that the Hanseatic League was banished from London by Queen Elizabeth I in 1597.[5] Despite the temporal distance, the sixteenth-century move has an air of present-day familiarity. Then, England had come to resent the trading bloc and rival trading groups began to emerge internally amid fears that the League was beginning to threaten the country's maritime prowess.

While history is not repeating itself, as the old adage stipulates, it does rhyme. 'In order to keep influence in Brussels, we have to leave our comfort zone. We go to countries where we used to come rarely. Like Spain. Or the Baltic states. Pretty exciting, actually,' one Dutch official told *NRC Handelsblat*.[6] The Netherlands has again been looking towards smaller EU states to form a coalition that counters the dominance of France and Germany, and which functions independently of today's shambolic United Kingdom. However, these 'Hansa' states are still small countries in the north, and analysts suggest that partnerships with larger countries such as Spain and Italy remain necessary.[7]

Germany and France consolidated their strength in the EU in January 2019, signing a sixteen-page treaty in the German border town of Aachen to bring ties to a 'new level'. It was ostensibly regarded by officials in both countries as a positive symbolic step in the wake of growing right-wing populism on the continent, but also heralded in the creation of a Franco-German economic area and commitments to defence cooperation via 'joint councils of military chiefs and economic experts' and forging of a 'common military culture'.[8] The roots, perhaps, of a new joint European army. Energy and financial policies on the continent, as well as small-scale migration issues are among the currents that continue to cause contention in Europe, especially with regards to a potential new natural gas pipeline from Russia, Nord Stream 2, which 'Scandinavian' Europe, including the Baltic countries, is firmly against, but Germany has appeared in favour of, despite concerns that it will increase European dependence on Russian gas, and Denmark has not yet agreed to let the pipeline pass through its exclusive economic zone.

Baltic 'power', past and present

The Baltic states in recent years have been set on diversifying their energy dependence away from Russia. Up until recently, the Baltic states relied heavily on Russia. Estonia, Latvia and Lithuania essentially maintained their entire energy infrastructure after the Soviet Union collapsed, integrated into the 'BRELL' (Belarus, Russia, Estonia, Latvia, Lithuania). They remained dependent on Russia for their energy resources, retaining the same links to the old electricity grids and gas supplies in Belarus and Russia – meaning that Russia has basically had the capacity to cut their supplies at any point over the past three decades and beyond. Vitally, Russia has only done this once, in 1993 (Estonia – in apparent retribution for a residency law),[9] and has not threatened to do so since. This may be in part because the Russian exclave of Kaliningrad's power network is synchronized with Russia via the Baltic states, but generally, it is not in the country's economic, political or energy interests to create such a major dispute with its neighbours, and negatively impact its energy markets.[10] There are also points of cooperation. A Latvian underground gas storage facility, Incukalns, is a compound located some 40 kilometres northeast of Riga and is owned approximately 34 per cent by none other than Gazprom via a stake in operator Conexus Baltic Grid. The Underground Gas Storage (UGS) facility is part of Gazprom's network of facilities in Europe which it uses to store surplus gas and provide it on demand. In the summer months, when less gas is required it accumulates in the storage, and in the winter months, the unit supplies parts of Latvia, Estonia and northwestern Russia. Gazprom also has access to sites in Germany, Austria, the Netherlands, Serbia and Czechia, while owning facilities in Belarus and Armenia too.[11] The plant is similarly owned just over 34 per cent by Latvian electrical operator Augstsprieguma Tikls after the Latvian government opted to increase its share in Conexus, via a treasury loan to Augstsprieguma Tikls. The most important stated goals at the time were to develop the regional natural gas market, continue to integrate the Latvian energy market in the EU, and bolster both energy supply security and national competitiveness. However, the Baltic states have made a concerted political decision to disconnect from the 'BRELL power grid' by 2025, and the Baltic and European power grid synchronization project has already seen some €323 million of European Union financing.[12]

Russia certainly uses energy politics as a foreign policy tool in the region. Gazprom (natural gas), Rosneft (oil) and Rosatom (nuclear) are all sort of ambassador companies of the Russian government – especially Gazprom which has overtly styled itself as a guardian of Russian interests, and is Kremlin controlled.[13] Gazprom owned 37 per cent of Estonia's Eesti Gaas, 34 per cent of Latvia's Latvias Gāze, and 37 per cent of Lithuania's Lietuvos Dujo in 2014 (however, it sold its stake in Estonia in 2016).[14] Gazprom's ownership has seen some fluctuations, but generally its presence has lowered in the past few years as opposed to increasing, although Russia apparently hopes to continue using its energy companies to exert influence in post-Soviet space – as they are small countries, they are not necessarily the biggest consumers of gas, so there is a lingering sense that this could come into play in a conflict situation.[15] As a result, there remains a strong interest in reducing Baltic energy dependence on Russia as a form of potential damage minimization, and the countries have been incrementally successful.

After a liquefied natural gas (LNG) terminal opened in Klaipeda, Lithuania, in 2015, and the Klaipeda-Kiemenai pipelines' capacity increased (these pipelines ensure the flow of gas between Latvia and Lithuania), the Russian gas monopoly in the region was severely dampened, and Gazprom was finally edged out of the market. The LNG situation in the region led to Latvia, in 2016, finally managing to adopt a law implementing all the requirements of a third round of EU energy market legislation.[16] In August 2016, Lithuania took a leap away from Russia when its first shipment of LNG arrived from the US. 'We want to cement our relationship with the United States in many aspects in addition to defense and security – energy trade is one of the strategic areas for cooperation,' Minister of Foreign Affairs Linas Linkevicius noted at the time.[17]

Just as the Baltics are keen to minimize energy dependence on Moscow, Brussels is too, and the Baltic Sea region has become a 'showcase of the EU-Russia diversification race', as Russian academic Tatiana Romanova put it. Russia and the EU both have multiple LNG terminals in the Baltic Sea region, with Russia using them to supply EU member states. EU member states are all eager to develop their own terminals; Lithuania opened its floating terminal in Klaipeda in 2014. Poland had a project in Swinoujście. Finland and Estonia have been developing a shared LNG project, while Latvia has also been contemplating the possibility of one of its own.[18] Estonia is in a slightly better position than both Latvia and Lithuania as it aims to have the joint gas line project with Finland in operation in 2019 (and on top of that, Estonia's consumption of 100 per cent imported Russian natural gas is comparatively very low).[19] The flexibility and firm connection with global prices that LNG projects afford EU member states provide them with a greater opportunity to challenge Russian prices.

The Baltic states (in addition to Poland and Ukraine) have expressed opposition to the proposed German-Russian pipeline Nord Stream 2. Germany and Austria believe they would stand to benefit from the possibility of constructing a new energy pipeline from Russia that would increase the supply of gas to Europe, via the Baltic Sea. Germany's energy groups Uniper and Wintershall, as well as Austria's OMV, Anglo-Dutch group Shell and French company Engie have all invested in the 1,225 kilometre pipeline.[20] Russia's geopolitical actions in recent years mean that the Nordics and Baltics consider the move concerning, and Estonia has warned against letting it become 'a tool for political pressure'. 'Before the project goes any further, we have to analyze the consequences very closely,' said Estonian Foreign Minister Sven Mikser in July 2017. 'If this analysis shows that Nord Stream 2 puts Russian suppliers in a position where they can exert pressure on any country in Europe, for example, Ukraine, then we have to take this very seriously,' Mikser added.[21] Estonia (along with Latvia and Lithuania) is eager to see the West limit business cooperation, and most importantly stick to its guns in terms of sanctions on Russia, out of fear that any lapse in severity could be conveyed as a message of tacit approval that it is okay for Russia to commit acts of aggression against neighbouring states. The US is also opposed for similar reasons – that sanctions against energy companies were part of sanctions imposed after Russia's annexation of Crimea – even if they do not at this point apply directly to Nord Stream 2. 'The United States opposes the Nord Stream 2 pipeline. We see it as undermining Europe's overall energy security and stability . . . Our opposition is driven by our mutual strategic interests,' said US Secretary of State Rex Tillerson at a joint news conference with the Polish foreign minister in Warsaw.[22]

Russia argues that the project should be free from any geopolitical insinuations. 'We support the implementation of this project, which is undoubtedly absolutely free from politics. This is a purely economic and moreover purely commercial project,' Putin said in 2018.[23] The Baltic states do not agree that it is an apolitical issue. Nord Stream 2 will help Gazprom minimize transit risks, and is certainly an economic project, but Gazprom is effectively Kremlin controlled, and to ignore the geopolitical environment would risk overlooking EU authorities' decisions which can themselves be informed by myriad geopolitical currents.[24] EU regulation is based on cooperation between EU member states and is inherently political.

Ukraine's Deputy Minister of Foreign Affairs, Olena Zerkal took to the stage at a conference in Kyiv in late 2018, speaking impassionedly against Nord Stream 2, emphasizing its inherently political essence. On 5 April that year, Ukraine's Parliament, the unicameral Verkhovna Rada, called on the world not to support the construction of the pipeline. Russia could increase its military presence in the region during construction, 'as with the Kerch bridge', said Zerkal. 'And this could happen in the Baltic Sea with the Baltic states.'[25]

The Kerch bridge, or the Crimean Bridge, was the Kerch strait-spanning construction that opened in May 2018 between Russia and the Crimean peninsula. The contract for the bridge's construction, worth billions of dollars, was granted to Arkady Rotenberg's Stroygazmontazh (SGM Group) – the same Rotenberg brother known to be Putin's former judo 'sparring partner'.[26] Its construction was hailed as a project that would 'symbolically cement Russia's control over the territory and demonstrate the country's re-emergence as a geopolitical power willing to challenge the post-Cold War order'.

Over the course of its patchy construction (a section collapsed in October 2018 and there are doubts that it will last a long time on account of the region's poor geological conditions), amphibious troops were dispatched to guard the project termed 'illegal' by Ukraine. Russia's National Guard, trained to look for 'terrorists' and explosive devices, would also deter 'amateur divers' and 'enemy saboteurs'.[27] Another key task, falling into the 'explosive devices' category, would be to find and dispose of unexploded ordnance and ammunition from the Second World War – this would also be a potential issue in the Baltic Sea. Divers from explosive ordnance disposal teams are continually having to clear munition from shipping channels in the North and Baltic Seas, and the construction of Nord Stream 2 brings with it the risk of setting off Second World War unexploded ordnance, causing potential damage and chemical contamination to the regional ecosystem.[28] Concerns about this have been aired inside Germany too, where environmental group Nabu filed a lawsuit in 2018, stating the pipeline would harm underwater sea life.[29]

However, to many the situation is simply 'business as usual', operating entirely outside the realm of geopolitics, and despite threats of US sanctions construction looks increasingly likely to go ahead. Despite Washington having threatened to impose sanctions (in July, and then in September 2018, US Energy Secretary Rick Perry responded in the affirmative when asked if the US could implement punitive measures against Nord Stream 2 and other projects), its operator says the project has been developing as expected.[30] The Swiss-based Nord Stream 2 AG told Reuters 'The project is progressing according to schedule,' and gas is to start flowing at the end of 2019, bypassing routes through Ukraine. Shell, as well as four other European energy companies (ENGIE, OMV, Uniper and Wintershall) have all signed up for the project. Business 'circles' paint a vastly different picture to political 'circles', and the role of commercial self-interest with regards to the project should not be underestimated. 'We have regular connection with Gazprom with that. The investment in Nord Stream 2 is not obviously strategic for Shell. If we can participate in this project to improve energy security supply and reduce the cost of bringing gas to Europe, then we will consider,' Shell's Chief Financial Officer Simon Henry said in 2017.[31] Collectively, the five energy companies have financed nearly half of the project, risking opposition from Washington.[32] And they seem more than willing to take this risk.

The town of Visaginas, Lithuania, lies less than 30 kilometres from the Belarusian border. It is Lithuania's youngest municipality, developed by the Soviet government in 1975, originally named 'Sniečkus' after Antanas Sniečkus, a former first secretary of the Lithuanian Communist Party. It is known as the 'butterfly city' as the shape into which it has developed somewhat resembles that of a butterfly's wings. The vast majority of residents speak Russian as opposed to Lithuanian. 'As a child I grew up in some place, without really thinking what country that place was in,' says director Olga Černovaitė in the trailer for short film *Butterfly City*. 'I figured it was Russian because everyone was speaking Russian.'[33] The skinheads back in Vilnius would later tell me Visaginas is 'full of *vatniki*' (pejorative Russian slang for blindly, fervently patriotic Russians). The city was constructed solely for the enormous nuclear power plant at its epicentre – a near-identical twin of the ill-fated nuclear power plant at

Chernobyl, Ukraine, which suffered a catastrophic meltdown in 1986, releasing at least 100 times more radiation than the atom bombs dropped on Hiroshima and Nagasaki.[34]

Ignalina's two units contained the same class of mechanism – the Soviet-designed RBMK 1500 reactors. The presence of the plant at Ignalina was understandably, therefore, of great concern to Europe. Lithuania agreed to close the plant as part of the country's EU accession agreement. Unit 1 was shut down in December 2004 and unit 2 in December 2009. Inside the plant, one worker sums up its situation drily and succinctly: 'We build it, we turn it on, and close it,' he says simply. Since 2004, the number of employees has plummeted, from 5,000 people providing the country with 70 per cent of its power, to a mere 200 involved in the decommissioning process. The removal of the last used fuel assembly from the reactor of unit 2 took place in February 2018,[35] and residents are increasingly perplexed by the situation. 'Here there's a problem – there's no work, everything's at a standstill … you can't live here,' one local tells me in Russian.[36]

The town is indeed a shell of its former self. Apartments have emptied and unemployment is rife, schools are closing, and people are leaving in droves. A local journalist in Vilnius later says that a lot of foreign publications dispatched correspondents to the town after Crimea's annexation, looking for the 'next place to fall' – a Lithuanian Narva, or Daugavpils perhaps. But there was no story as the Russian-speaking population 'know what it's like on the other side'. The skinheads were wrong about 'vatniki' in the area. My host, Olga, is very typically Russian in some ways. She insists on me wearing tapochki (slippers), feeding me chicken lapsha (noodle soup), arranges all my transport plans for me against my will, and generally treats me like a confused child who somehow ended up in Visaginas by sheer error, and who, if left unattended, might continue to make further ridiculous mistakes. But even though she harbours a lot of love for several Russian cities, she sincerely dislikes her Russian compatriots over the border because of their temperaments, which she deems rude. She has no desire to 'break away'. The overarching antipathy towards Russia may be related to a more generalised local opposition to the plant, which became a rallying point for environmentalists and anti-Soviet sentiment, bolstered by concerns about its impact on locals. Activists 'discredited' the project, especially after Chernobyl, and by extension the Communist regime. The plant's employees penned a protest letter to Gorbachev in the late 1980s describing the negative impact of mass opposition on their work. They mentioned a thousands-strong protest action called the "Circle of Life" which took place on September 16–18, 1988, saying that meeting attendees had made 'derogative and threatening statements' and that they were 'constantly concerned' about the security of their homes and families.'[37]

The plant is 10 kilometres from the town centre. Its communications specialist, Beata Voitechovskaja, takes me around. As we walk through the vast halls we meet barely anyone else. The plant is eerily deserted and our white overalls slowly turn black from the accumulated dust in the air. She is herself part-Belarusian. 'I cannot separate the history of the town and the plant,' she says. 'It was just a forest, lakes around' prior to that. 'The first people who arrived were very young specialists . . . we called them the brains of the Soviet Union,' she says, adding that her dad was among them.

But, she says, after Chernobyl in 1986, international anxiety intensified enormously. 'Specialists from Switzerland came here – it was a psychological moment; they were very afraid. When they realized what power we had and that the third reactor was nearly built – 60 per cent of it . . . they didn't allow us to use that.'

The plant's decommissioning is being financed by an international donor fund managed by the European Bank for Reconstruction and Development. The Ignalina Decommissioning Support Fund, which was established in 2001 and has received more than €750 million to date, is backed by the European Commission as well as Austria, Belgium, Denmark, Finland, France, Germany, Ireland, Luxembourg, the Netherlands, Poland, Spain, Sweden, the United Kingdom, Norway and Switzerland.[38] Bulgaria and Slovakia also agreed to shut down plants as part of their EU accession plans. However, the Czech Republic did not, and its Temelin plant has been a frequent bone of contention with the EU. In the decommissioning process each country was left to work out their own safety procedures on an individual basis – and Ignalina had no suitable leading examples to work from. 'We are the first,' says Voitechovskaja, somewhat proudly. Its uniqueness today, and similarity with its historic Ukraine sibling, would later make it the perfect location for HBO to film parts of the award-winning Chernobyl television series.

As we are decontaminating and disrobing, a cloakroom attendant starts talking about her life to us in Lithuanian. Voitechovskaja translates. 'One daughter lives in London and another one, in Switzerland. They say that they want to come back, but they don't know where to come back

[to],' she says. 'If you don't have work there's nowhere . . . that's why she's lonely. Her husband – he left this work because there was such little pay that he needed to go back to Finland to at least get some money for them to live on. And now she's alone,' Voitechovskaja says. The woman starts to tear up.

As the plant is being decommissioned, just 20 kilometres over the border in Belarus, another nuclear plant is being built. Two reactors, each with a capacity of 1,200 megawatts, will be operational in Astravets from 2019/2020. Moscow is almost entirely financing the project via the Russian state energy corporation Rosatom, much to the distaste of the Lithuanian government. Vilnius has repeatedly said the project breaches 'international nuclear and environmental safety requirements.'[39] Russia is often criticized for using energy issues in an attempt to influence its neighbours. Prior to Chernobyl, Belarus had plans for a plant near Minsk, but temporarily shelved them – the new project in the country's northwest is closer to Vilnius than any major Belarusian settlements.[40] Lithuania is making it very clear that it has no desire to use any of its output. 'In accordance with the law, no electricity from the Astravets nuclear power plant will be able to enter the Lithuanian power market, nor the European electricity market,' spokeswoman of Lithuania's energy ministry Aurelija Vernickaite told AFP in 2017.[41] Vytautas Bakas, chairman of the Lithuanian parliament's Committee on National Security and Defense says that the plant is extremely dangerous. 'Fake news that was released several weeks ago was that the IAEA [International Atomic Energy Agency] had recognized Astravets nuclear plant to be a secure facility,' he said in 2017. 'This came just a very brief period of time before the Seimas [Lithuania's parliament] looked into a draft law recognizing the Astravets nuclear power plant as a threat, as an unsafe facility, before deciding not to buy any electricity produced there . . . the very construction is unsafe and doesn't comply with at least three international conventions,' Bakas says.

Money, environment, employment in the EU borderlands

Out of the three Baltic states, Estonia is faring the best economically, which can occasionally lead people in the other two Baltic states to express a hint of bitterness or envy regarding the 'slow' Baltic nation's comparative progress; in 2014 Estonia's GDP per capita was the highest at €21,400 – 76 per cent of the EU28 average in purchasing power parity, while Latvia's was €18,500 – 64 per cent of the EU28 average. Lithuania's was close to Estonia's with €21,200, 75 per cent of the EU28 average. The Lithuanian economy adjusts the most rapidly, and Latvia's the most slowly, while Estonia is most exposed to international fluctuations and Latvia most affected by internal national shocks.[42]

One such shock was the global financial crisis in 2007/8 which triggered the collapse of property markets. Up until that point, the three countries had been known as the Baltic Tigers on account of the preceding period of economic boom they had witnessed. Latvia's second-biggest lender (and the Baltic states' largest independent bank) Parex Banka folded and was forced to seek state protection. Large swathes of the population used EU freedom of movement policies to earn better money abroad, often to pay off loans. While nowadays the economy can weather such crises better, the Latvian banking sector is still mired in scandal and subject to claims of money laundering and corruption; in 2014, leaks exposing the 'Russian Laundromat', as it came to be known, suggested that dirty money flowed directly from Russia through Latvian institutions. However, the banking sectors in all three countries are generally dominated by Scandinavian subsidiaries: the three largest banks (SEB, Swedbank and DNB) hold 68.6 per cent of the Lithuanian banking sector, 71.4 per cent of the Estonian sector and 35.9 per cent of the Latvian.[43]

Estonia has also suffered financial scandals in recent years, being home to the branch of Danske Bank that played a vital role in a €200 billion money-laundering scandal which saw that amount in 'suspicious payments' through the Estonian branch between 2007 and 2015. The payments were predominantly from Russia and the sheer amounts of money involved make it the largest money-laundering scandal in history. In 2019, Estonia ordered Danske Bank to close its Tallinn branch following the scandal, after some tensions over culpability within the new 'Hansa'.

The Baltic nations' integration into Europe after the Soviet period has had massive economic consequences, as well as environmental – good and bad. The Baltics are home to odd former mono-industrial towns besides Visaginas. Estonia is famous for Sillamäe, an old closed Soviet city and key Baltic sea location. Shrouded in mystery, it slipped off and on Soviet maps, sometimes represented by a name and sometimes a code. Sillamäe was the site of the USSR's first fully operational uranium processing facility (largely for the nation's first nuclear bombs), and Soviet authorities tightly controlled access. Sillamäe has distinctly Soviet town planning and is home to a cultural centre built according to the neoclassicist elements of the Soviet architectural style. Like Ignalina, the decision to 'construct' it was a direct result of a USSR central government decision. And like Ignalina, Estonia had to close it down. Europe charged Estonia with removing 'one of the greatest threats of pollution to the Baltic Sea' between 1998 and 2008, because of its Soviet-era activities. 'Sorting out the environmental problems related to the site aren't only important to Estonia but to all of the countries on the Baltic Sea,' said Tõnis Kaasik, the director of state environmental company AS ÖkoSil in 2008.[44] At that point, ten years of remediation work on the radioactive tailings pond had just been completed as a direct result of cooperation between Estonia, the Nordic countries and the European Union. 'The Sillamäe uranium site has been one of the EU's regional pilot projects,' said Kaasik, adding that there had been similar remediation projects undertaken in Hungary, Slovenia, the Czech Republic and elsewhere in central and eastern Europe.[45] The Baltics have a big responsibility to the rest of Europe when it comes to ensuring the safety of former Soviet sites which could potentially be dangerous pollutants to the rest of the continent. The Baltic Sea is also one of the major common features between the three Baltic states, and a cooperative network has been developed there, in the form of the Council of the Baltic Sea States (CBSS). This is important not only for other European nations but also for Russia and maintaining links. CBSS became the foundation for cooperation among the Baltic Sea states, which together account for approximately 40 per cent of total Danish exports, according to the Danish government. 'The active participation of Russia in this cooperation is of great political importance for Denmark,' it adds.[46] The EU Strategy for the Baltic Sea Region (EUSBSR) was established in 2009. It describes itself as striving for a 'more intensive cooperation between the countries in the Baltic Sea Region' and it 'shapes the region into a cooperation model for the whole EU'. EUSBSR aspires to cleaner water and efficient shipping methods in the region, as well as good connections, reliable energy markets, and increased prosperity.[47]

However, the Baltic states' own de-Sovietization as well as European Union membership requirements, have had some major socioeconomic repercussions. Plant closures and decommissioning various facilities ultimately means the destruction of those jobs – Sillamäe and Ignalina are not unique cases. Estonia, Latvia and Lithuania were all admitted in the 2004 enlargement under certain conditions which had some painful economic repercussions. 'Sweet sugar, bitter price: what did we pay for the EU sugar reform?' one article asked painfully in late 2017. In 2000, a quota system was introduced with the aim of balancing sugar production in Latvia. The country had three refineries – in the central city of Jelgavas, the southeastern city of Jēkabpils and the western coastal city of Liepāja. The EU compensated sugar factory owners a total of some €48.5 million to halt production and close, effectively putting an end to the sugar industry in Latvia, despite widespread local support.[48] In 1999, Riga's Sarkandaugava glass factory closed too, and the Kreenholm manufacturing company sitting on the Narva River was once home to the world's largest cotton spinning mill. In 2010, Swedish textile group Borås Wäfveri, responsible for privatizing Kreenholm, filed for bankruptcy. While Kaunas, in Lithuania, is set to be European Capital of Culture 2022, Narva has been angling for the moniker in 2024, attempting to rebrand Kreenholm as a potential artistic or creative space in the face of the region's high unemployment levels (more than twice as high as in the rest of the country). Narva has established a new arts residency program, and the under-construction Vaba Laba theatre is set to accommodate theatre groups from Petersburg and Moscow as well as host after-school theatre workshops.[49]

Migration and the rise of the right

Socioeconomic problems in the Baltics resulting from EU-backed industrial reform and factory closures may in part be responsible for any currents of unrest in the region. However, right-wing sentiment has been rising across Europe on a more general level, and the Baltics are no exception to this trend. On the continent, entities such as National Rally (RN, formerly National Front) in France, Alternative Fur Deutschland (AfD) in Germany and the Dutch far-right Freedom Party, have all gained a stronger footing. The increasing visibility of far-right sentiment has been bolstered by political currents such as Brexit and the election of US President Donald Trump, stirring concerns about the future of Europe and the 'nationalists international' that appear to be rising within it. Since 2017, the anti-immigration and Islamophobic Alternative for Germany (AfD) has become the third-largest party in Germany's Bundestag, and in

May the same year, Marine Le Pen garnered some 34 per cent in the presidential election run-off that saw Emmanuel Macron elected. Commentators worldwide have been mourning the rise of global populist nationalism, linking it to both the challenges posed by migration and increasing numbers of refugees in Europe, as well as the lingering after-effects of the European economic crisis.[50]

Parallel to heightened visibility and subsequent concerns are concerns about Kremlin influence on the continent. German state broadcaster Deutsche Welle has termed the Freedom Party of Austria (FPÖ) 'Putin's Friends' on account of its good relations with Russia (after Russia's annexation of Crimea, FPÖ politicians recognized it as part of Russia); in January 2017, *The Atlantic* published an article titled 'Putin and the Populists' (after publishing 'Trump, Putin, and the Alt-Right International' just a few months earlier), while NBC have been staid and direct, stating simply that 'Europe's Far-Right Enjoys Backing from Russia's Putin'.[51] While right-wing parties carry slightly more sway in Latvia and Lithuania than in Estonia, local media says that it suspects the Kremlin plays a hand. An organization known as Skydas ('Shield') in Lithuania started emerging in 2017 – hiding their faces behind masks, they openly displayed Nazi symbolism and homophobic and anti-Semitic placards.

Right-wing populism and anti-EU sentiment in the Baltics takes a slightly different form from populism on the rest of the European continent on account of history and proximity to Russia. That said, the shared sentiments connecting right-wing parties in the Baltics and their European counterparts inadvertently link them to Russia nonetheless. And there are some variations between them on account of domestic population composition. Lithuania's Order and Justice Party cannot necessarily be characterized as an exclusionist or nativist party.[52] However, the Electoral Action of Poles in Lithuania – Christian Families Alliance (EAPL–CFA) that sits with the Order and Justice Party in the Seimas exists to enhance the rights of the Polish minority and could be construed as populist. However, its influence is limited as the segment of the population at which this populism is targeted is too narrow. In August 2013, Latvia's National Alliance, Lithuania's Nationalist Union and the Conservative People's Party of Estonia (EKRE) signed a joint declaration promoting more traditional values in the face of 'post-modern multiculturalism', indicating a strong strain of localism and nativism prevalent in the countries, rejecting both the EU and Russian dominance. In Estonia EKRE has been rising the most notably in recent years.

Founded in 2012, it saw a spike in popularity in 2015, as a 'newcomer' party. It managed to garner 8.1 per cent of the vote, landing it seven seats in elections for the Riigikogu (Estonian Parliament).[53] It polled as the third most popular party throughout 2017 and 2018, and remains a stalwart of 'conservative values' with a strong anti-migration and anti-'homosexual agenda' stance.[54]

EKRE holds something of an anti-Russia stance and is much more interested in forging links with right wing populist parties in both Latvia and Lithuania than with the eastern neighbour. However, it is very Euro-sceptic and critical of the continent's 'liberal elite', opting instead to sympathize with more overtly pro-Putin politicians such as France's Marine Le Pen.[55] In 2019, the party managed to gain nineteen seats in parliament, propelling it into power for the first time and granting it five key ministries.

While Estonia appears to be becoming more socially liberal on a surface level, EKRE's popularity was bolstered after the formal recognition of same-sex unions in 2014.[56] Analyst Kristi Raik also points out that Estonia is far from heading in the same direction as Hungary, for example. 'Mainstream parties' broad commitment to the rule of law, the separation of powers, and an independent media – make it unlikely that Estonia will travel the same path,' she writes. 'Nonetheless, given the ongoing volatility of European politics, one cannot take the survival of existing political systems for granted.

There is also a low-level degree of xenophobia which is comparative to that on the rest of the European continent. During the height of the refugee crisis in Europe, the Baltic states seemed somewhat reluctant to integrate refugees into their populaces, prompting an outpouring of indignation from the international community which pointed out swathes of Baltic nationals were once themselves refugees, and a degree of distaste among refugees themselves, many of whom expressed preferences to be accommodated in 'western' European countries such as Germany. Mekharena, an Eritrean, ended up in Latvia after a long journey through Uganda, Ethiopia, Israel and Italy. 'We all know that in Germany they give you an apartment and €400 (£350; $450) pocket money. But in Latvia they don't give us anything – just €139 a month,' he told the BBC's Russian service.[57] A former shopkeeper in Syria, fifty-two-year-old Mohamed Kamel Haj Ali, also said that 'when we left from Turkey to Greece, our final goal was Germany or Holland,' as opposed to Rukla in Lithuania, not far from Kaunas.[58] 'But the land route from Greece was already closed, so we had no choice but to enter the relocation programme.' Out of the 349 asylum seekers taken in by Lithuania by 2017, 248 left after receiving official refugee status, and in Estonia, seventy-nine of the 136 refugees who arrived under the EU programme also left.[59] As of February 2018, Estonia had taken in 141 from Greece and six from Italy. Latvia had taken in 294 from Greece and thirty-four from Italy. And Lithuania had taken in 355 from Greece and twenty-nine from Italy.[60] In March 2018, seventeen refugees were sent back to Lithuania from other European Union countries after violating the requirement that they settle. 'They have no right to legally stay in Germany and they have been granted asylum by Lithuania. As they have the right to live in Lithuania, they were sent back,' Evelina Gudzinskaite, director of the Lithuanian Migration Department, told BNS.[61]

In 2015, Eero Janson of the Estonian Refugee Council said that even that meagre number had put the current system under pressure and there had been some domestic negative responses to their resettlement. He said, in emailed comments, that what has been lacking since the start of the crisis was 'effective communication to the public, causing misunderstandings and driving overall hate speech around that question', adding that negative attitudes could also be furthered by 'general xenophobia (and Islamophobia in particular), the wide circulation of a lot of myths, half-truths and incorrect information around that question, the feeling of being overrun by the EU bodies.'[62] That said, Muslims have managed to survive in the Baltic states – not just as migrants but historically as Tatars. In Lithuania, the town of Keturiasdesimt Totoriu ('Forty Tatars') just southwest of Vilnius is home to a mosque which was built in 1558.[63]

EU membership has facilitated migration in both directions, though, and low wages and few job opportunities at home can often push educated Estonians, Latvians and Lithuanians abroad in search of both. In a gaming café just out of the centre of Riga, teenagers congregate to play tabletop RPGs and trade card games like Magic the Gathering. Anime posters and posters from comic book movie adaptations and cult franchises such as Zelda line the walls, and a console and projector are set up for playing Street Fighter, and other videogames. Teenagers are swapping hentai (pornographic cartoons) and denouncing imageboard and former notorious hacker hangout 4chan as 'boring'. One boy holds a tall glass soft drink bottle, pretending it is vodka. He staggers around melodramatically.

'I'm Russian!' he proclaims. A meek, yet clearly bored woman in her mid-twenties serves behind the bar, as a seventeen-year-old girl chats exuberantly at her and orders milkshakes. The café is responsible for holding the Latvian version of Comic Con.

The bar-woman is a medical resident, and maintains the café job to support herself. Unenthused about the prospect of a formal interview, she somewhat defeatedly mentions in passing that when she starts looking for full-time jobs, they will likely be given to people who have family high up in the medical profession, and several of her colleagues are contemplating leaving the country to practise abroad after they qualify. She echoes all Lithuanian medical resident Elena Landsbergytes statements about the practice in Lithuania completely unprompted. In June 2017, Elena (who is also working in a café to support herself) uploaded a pay slip to Facebook showing that she earned the same salary as a cleaning lady. 'And people are surprised, why all the doctors are emigrating,' she wrote facetiously.

Lithuania is having a serious outward migration problem – both skilled and unskilled workers are suffering the impact of low wages and nepotism, Latvia is witnessing a similar pattern. Since Latvia's EU accession, nearly a fifth of the nation has uprooted itself to move abroad; in the year 2000, Latvia's population was around 2.38 million, whereas in 2010 it was around 2.1 million and in 2017 it stood at 1.95 million.[64] In December 2007, all three Baltic states joined the Schengen area. The following year, negative net migration more than tripled, from -7,946 in 2007, to -22,367 in 2008, and an even greater -34,477 in 2009.[65] Ambassador for the Diaspora, Atis Sjanits has commented that the country is losing people 'fast', while journalist Otto Ozols has expressed more extreme concerns, speculating that 'at this rate, in 50 years or so, Latvia may cease to be a nation.'[66] The highest group migrating abroad over the past fifteen-odd years has consistently been twenty-five to twenty-nine-year-olds, giving rise to concerns about a youth 'brain drain'.[67]

The highest support for free movement of EU citizens is in the Baltic countries, with 94 per cent of Latvian, Estonian and Lithuanian poll respondents all being fully supportive of the practice. Despite expectations that Estonia, Latvia and Lithuania should be seeing a population rise with 'fertility rate that is well above replacement level', leading post-Soviet nations in terms of life expectancy, combined they have lost a staggering 20 per cent of their population since gaining independence in 1991.[68] This is largely down to outward migration from the region, particularly since they joined the EU. Russia is, perhaps surprisingly, a key destination still for migrants from the Baltic nations. Out of a total of 446,620 people migrating to Russia from Northern Europe in 2015, some 143,677 left Estonia, 137,224 left Latvia, and 59,466 moved from Lithuania.[69]

It took Rasma, a Latvian doctor, nine years to qualify. She lives in a Soviet apartment near the coast, just outside of Riga, which she shares with a man called Walter and a noisy, and slightly unhinged, cat. She watches American medical drama shows. 'The closest reality was *Scrubs*,' she laughs, remembering her residency. 'When we start the residency, we are helpless.' I ask her whether she is planning to leave the country too. 'It's a complex question,' she says. 'I like this country and I would like to stay here. I have ideas but there are limitations in my career and also my salary – I can't survive here. I would like to stay here, but I just *can't*,' she says emphatically. She is, however, less cynical about nepotism in the profession than her Lithuanian counterpart. 'They are legally getting these places because of points,' she says of the most coveted positions. But there are some specializations in which it is still common. 'Like gynaecology for example, you have to have connections,' she says. 'Maybe that's not wrong? Maybe that's how it should be. That's legal,' she adds. She also recalls the long hours that some people in medicine suffer, with (what I hope are) some possible exaggerations. 'There are doctors who work, like, three twenty-four hour shifts in a row, and then they have one day free when they go home and wash themselves, and then they come back.' She doesn't do it herself (understandably), believing the quality of her work to decline under such circumstances. She is one of many struggling doctors, eventually destined to leave the Baltics.

People seeking employment and business opportunities at home still have to contend with the domestic situation. The Baltic nations still struggle with corruption – especially Latvia. 'Smaller municipalities have problems recruiting hardworking and honest candidates for local councils and the executive, and there have been patterns of nepotism. Controlling corruption and ensuring transparency are often difficult,' a Freedom House report stated in 2006.[70] While there is now increased optimism about the falling tolerance for corruption in the country, the 2017 Freedom House report still underscored the presence of 'recurring problems with corruption, tax evasion, and tax fraud'.[71] Estonia is 15 places higher than Latvia and 14 places higher than Lithuania in the Corruption Perceptions Index 2018, indicating Estonia's comparative progress in this sphere, and Latvia and Lithuania's need to 'catch up'.

In relation to other former Soviet Republics or Warsaw Pact nations, the Baltic states' initial transitions were characterized by much deeper output decline, and across the region, growing inequality still 'threatens to cause long-term difficulties for social cohesion', according to assesments.[72] 'While later the average growth has been rather strong, also the volatility across the business cycles has been strong, as shown by the highest growth rates in European Union during 2004, 2007 and the deepest GDP decline in 2009,' stated a Growing Inequalities' Impacts (GINI) report.

'The attitudes that people in the Baltic countries hold towards inequality, political institutions, participation, and each other, should be viewed both in the light of country's Communist past, as well as the huge political and economic transformations the three countries experienced as part of becoming democracies,' it summarized, but noted the hardship of the massive transition period the countries have been undergoing. 'The experience of state socialism left a significant demand for high levels of state provision and a tendency to blame the state for individual hardship. However, with time people in the Baltic countries have become more aware of their own responsibility for their fate. Nowadays, except for Latvia, citizens of the Baltic countries do not expect from the state more than citizens of other European countries.'[73]

CONCLUSION

As of 2019, Felicia remains in surprisingly good health. Her son has returned to Lithuania, despite any geopolitical reservations, and the graffiti on the café walls still greets incoming travellers. The time elapsed since the annexation of Crimea has fostered an attitude of comparative calm, even as war persists in eastern Ukraine and soldiers continue to die. But even with the growing sense of reassurance, the Baltics can never quite forget the one simple fact: that Russia can militarily overpower the region. And Putin's government would be very happy to do so – if there was any certainty that it could without facing a wider international backlash. There is dismissiveness -and even negativity towards the Baltic region inside Russia, but in the face of these protestations that the Baltic countries are 'useless' to Russia, they are strategically important as a sea route from Europe to the 'Northern Capital' (St Petersburg) and Kaliningrad, and carry historical significance, especially to a leader who stokes the embers of regret for the collapse of the Soviet Union. Russia has wielded military power in both Ukraine and Syria in recent years, investing in new weapons systems as part of a military modernisation programme, and engaging in 'snap' military exercises.[1] The country is undoubtedly a formidable presence on the eastern borders of Europe.

However, an invasion or outright conflict in the Baltic region remains an incredibly unlikely scenario at present. Internationally, Russia has more immediately pressing concerns. The Baltic states remain eager members of both NATO and the EU, the former of which far outstrips Russia in terms of collective total defence spending. Meanwhile, NATO's Enhanced Forward Presence serves as the tripwire that it was intended to be, and the presence of very few soldiers on this 'frontline' is not a sign of weakness, but of strength – it is a consistent, pressing reminder that 'an attack against one Ally is considered as an attack against all Allies'. Testing that alliance is still too risky for Russia, even with Trump in the White

House. Still, 'Russian armed forces are consistently practicing for an extensive military conflict with NATO', stated a recent Välisluureamet (Estonian foreign intelligence service) report.[2]

The twenty-first century has brought with it new means of warfare. While Russia may not be contemplating an armed attack on the Baltics, it is more than willing to employ 'hybrid warfare' methods and stoke internal instabilities. In March 2018, NATO started examining whether a cyberattack would constitute an invocation of Article 5. The alliance has been 'dealing with the issue around this and in cyber and working to define an understanding of what would be a trigger', according to General Curtis Scaparrotti, the commander of NATO forces in Europe.[3] If the scope of Article 5 increases it could somewhat paradoxically become more fragile. At present Article 5 draws a clear boundary, but as the concept of what constitutes an attack broadens, so does its potential to be fudged or made less clear.

In terms of 'hybrid warfare' methods, Russia has focused on fomenting internal instability through the perpetuation of misinformation, such as suggesting that NATO forces present in each Baltic country pose a threat to the resident populations (both Baltic and Russian), focusing especially on deeply emotional or difficult topics such as the supposed threat they pose to children. Astroturfing is also an issue; in the Russian-language Facebook equivalent Vkontakte, estimates indicate that only 14 per cent of the 'public messaging on the platform about NATO' in the Baltics and Poland comes from 'recognizably human' units.[4] Russia also constantly perpetuates the idea that Estonia, Latvia and Lithuania are 'backward' countries, focusing selectively on present-day social and economic issues as well as promoting highly questionable, selective interpretations of history. A narrative incorporating the ideas of 'Soviet investment' and 'ungrateful Baltic people' is being pushed, as well as a heavy focus on the Second World War, especially ideas that native Balts were sympathetic to invading Nazi forces. This is accompanied by more modern notions of hysterical 'Russophobia' around the globe, as pushed by *Russia Today* in the West.[5] It's worth noting that a lot of these ideas are being pushed in Russian, which serves to keep separate the already-calcified communities within each country: the Russian-speaking populations and the 'native' populations.

What many in the west do not realize is that the Baltics are adept at recognizing the methods employed by the modern-day Russian Federation and their capabilities and pragmatic responses have made these countries some of the best in the world at counteracting Russian disinformation and espionage tactics, methods other global players could do well to learn from.[6] While there is a significant degree of support for Putin's Russia and sense of victimhood among parts of the Russian populations in the Baltics, many also appreciate the value of the EU membership, the importance of learning the native language and many also harbour sympathy towards the former occupied populations. Their supposed loyalty to Russia is far from black-and-white. The fact that Soviet and native populations spent so long living side by side means that older generations can feel more Soviet – rather than feeling any degree of loyalty to the present-day Russian Federation (although many do still look towards Moscow).

Neither David nor Goliath

Apart from being a formidable military power, Putin's Russia is a uniquely unpredictable and dangerous country in current global politics. It has displayed a glib disregard for civilian lives in Syria, has seemingly poisoned 'traitors' abroad (Sergei and Yulia Skripal in March 2018), and conducted reckless aviation manoeuvres. It has annexed part of a sovereign foreign state and is, of course, still one of the world's foremost nuclear powers. Domestically, several journalists and opposition figures have been murdered or hospitalized, diplomats subjected to acts of intimidation, and police routinely crack down on people sharing or posting opposition to Russia's activities abroad. To take just one recent example, journalists Kirill Radchenko, Alexander Rastorguyev and Orkhan Dzhemal were killed in the Central African Republic in July 2018, allegedly investigating the activities of a private military company with links to the Kremlin. Yet, Russian influence is often overestimated. The country is clearly capable of significant levels of destruction both at home and abroad, but it is limited in scope and often chaotically executed. Think of the clumsy nature of the Skripal poisonings, and its impact amplified by the reactions of western media organizations. 'Instead of a single master plan, we face a plethora of gambits, ruses, plots and adventures, most of which are pointless, or fail,' as Mark Galeotti succinctly writes.[7] Its authoritarianism is often mistaken for efficiency, and organizations second-guess Putin's wishes to gain recognition, often to little or no effect. The climate for innovation is poor, with a tendency to punish or undermine dynamic and innovative firms, encumbering the nation's vast potential.[8] Instead, tried-and-tested methods continue to be deployed both at home and abroad, intimidating opponents into submission, creating an atmosphere of nihilism and uncertainty by flooding the information sphere, 'on-the-ground' espionage increasingly employing civilian actors or 'economy-class' agents (the Russian state has allegedly even started enlisting civilian ships to undertake 'provocative behaviour' at sea on behalf of the government).[9] And, of course, the aforementioned cyberattacks. But the Kremlin is also credited or held responsible for events outside the realm of its complete control, although it may enjoy believing that it has an enormous degree of influence given recent international media coverage.

Divisions in Europe, such as Brexit and the rise of far-right nationalism, may be exactly what Putin's government seeks, with the presence of a strong EU-wide alliance on Russia's western border posing a potential problem to the country (alongside the continued existence of NATO). Coverage in Kremlin-backed media on the topic has been clearly skewed in favour of right-wing populism on the continent and troll farms encouraged higher visibility of the pro-Brexit vote, spreading pro-Leave sentiment. Several questions remain unanswered, such as the sources of Arron Banks' funding (the UK's largest Brexit donor was allegedly 'wooed' by the Russian ambassador Alexander Yakovenko).[10] The UK's Electoral Commission stated in November 2018 that it had 'reasonable grounds' to suspect that 'Mr Banks was not the true source of the £8m reported as loans' to the Leave.EU campaign.[11] Russian attempts to influence politics appear significant, but their mere presence gives no indication of their impact.

The pro-Brexit currents have not been seeded entirely by Russia. The shifting of responsibility towards Russia diverts attention from other pivotal domestic factors, such as long-standing trends towards racialized nationalism, and even in 2013 there were clear indications of rising Euroscepticism in the UK.[12] The British press, for example, has managed an excellent job of fomenting anti-migrant sentiment across the country, with Gary Jones, who assumed the role of *Daily Express* editor in March 2018, himself stating that some of the headlines that appeared in the past have nurtured an Islamophobic sentiment among readers 'which I find uncomfortable'.[13]

There are similar issues with pinning Trump's election victory on Putin. Putin explicitly wanted Trump to win, and even Republican senators like Lindsey Graham (SC) have noted there is plenty of evidence that Russia attempted to meddle in the 2016 elections, telling NBC's 'Meet the Press', 'I'm 1,000 per cent certain that the Russians interfered in our election'.[14] Fewer than 80,000 votes swung the result in Trump's favour. Russia may or may not have swung those votes, which were key across a handful of formerly Democratic states. However, in 2016 voter turnout also plummeted. Republican voter suppression laws (ID mandates, limits on early voting and a reduction in polling locations) saw a decline in turnout in areas such as Wisconsin. There, a margin of 27,000 separated the two political leaders, while '300,000 registered voters, according to a federal court, lacked strict forms of voter ID. Voter turnout in Wisconsin was at its lowest levels in twenty years'.[15] Overall turnout was only 56 per cent.[16] There is a real risk of overstating Putin's impact on other nations' domestic politics defined in part by the actions of the leaders. If the goal of Putin's government was to restore to Russia lost international prestige, the amount of significance the country's actions have been attributed in recent years has succeeded in that aim. Russia's position on the 'world stage' once again seems bolstered – a position disproportionate to its realistic capabilities. In short, Russia exaggerates its own power – but the 'west' similarly exaggerates Russia's reach.

The Baltic states are no stranger to this either, also amplifying Russian actions. However, as the threat seems potentially more immediate in the region, it is worth taking with a slightly higher degree of seriousness, especially given the significance of these countries' Russian-speaking populations.

Additionally, it is time for Russia to start focusing itself on domestic issues. After Putin was elected for a fourth term in March 2018 (and assumed the presidency once again in May the same year), his popularity started declining, and several Russia-watchers took to speculating about the possibilities of 'life after Putin'. He has stated that he would not seek to run again in the year 2024, and the Russian constitution stipulates that a president may not run for more than two consecutive terms. Putin, of course, circumvented this in the somewhat farcical 2008–12 period which saw him switch places with his slightly shorter prime minister, Dmitry Medvedev.

In this time (2008), presidential terms were extended from four to six years, allowing Putin to serve twelve consecutive years in his second epoch, under the guise of only two consecutive terms, and in March 2018, after the elections, Moscow correspondent Andrew Roth wrote in the *Guardian* that 'Putin has emerged from his third term far stronger than he was in 2012, shoring up his image as a generational leader who has cowed all but his most committed opposition.' But by the tail end of the year, his popularity (and that of Medvedev) was plummeting. The military patriotism that accompanied events in Ukraine and Syria stood in stark contrast to declining domestic conditions, and the sense of pride that accompanied events like the Winter Olympics in Sochi and the positive mood that came with the influx of World Cup fans had started to fade.

The sweeping pension reforms pushed through in 2018 were particularly unpopular. On 3 October 2018, Putin signed into law a bill raising the retirement ages by five years for both men and women, up from fifty-five to sixty for women, and sixty to sixty-five for men. However, average male life expectancy in the country at that point stood at sixty-seven, meaning many men may not live to see their retirement. Pollution and waste problems started plaguing localities, with a landfill in the north-western Moscow Oblast town of Volokolamsk emitting toxic fumes around election time, and bizarre black and green snow falling in the Siberian towns of Kiselyovsk and Pervouralsk respectively. Protests kicked off in scores of towns and cities in February 2019 ('Russia is not a dump') in the hopes of challenging an apparently increasing presence of rubbish piles, with plans in place for Moscow to start exporting its waste to the regions.[17] In short, Russia's projected image started to clash horribly with local realities. Domestically, the future of Russia remains to be seen.

The human factor

While the geopolitical intrigue of potential collaborations or confrontations between high-power figures continues to be a point of fascination, most important of all is to retain a sense of understanding as to why these leaders embody such a complicated multitude of factors and ideas. Much like the mural's eye-catching, almost meme-worthy presence on the Vilnius cafe wall, it's all too easy to forget the building's function, to become embroiled in navigating the sensational leadership relationships when ultimately the surrounding countries and people are still rebuilding themselves and developing. Older generations and younger generations overcome, observe, and adapt within their own varied contexts, defined by their own histories – but the younger generations only know relative peace.

Attitudes and stories and histories, public, real, imaginary alike, are still shaped by the misery of the Second World War which led these 'bloodlands' to particular devastation. And such beliefs still shape tensions in the present. A multi-faceted understanding of history is vital. These are the countries where Nazis clashed with Stalin on the ground, where Jews were exterminated, where Europe meets Russia, and where nations from around the world still deploy foot soldiers in case conflict erupts once again. The Baltic nations are a victim, in a way, of the superpowers' psychological need to manifest an 'east' versus 'west' polar mentality. But the Baltics are not simply peoples caught between, they have the right to establish their own paths. They have a lot to offer the world. European but still new and unencumbered by centuries of self-perpetuating structures. The future for the Baltics can be bright.

NOTES

Introduction

1 Sylvie Kauffmann, 'Le divorce Europe-Etats-Unis: la famille occidentale sous tension', *Le Monde* (9 November 2018), https://www.lemonde.fr/long-format/article/2018/11/09/europe-etats-unis-la-famille-occidentale-sous-tension_5380997_5345421.html.

2 Somewhat off-topic, but even the Soviet Union and South American states helped to shape the genocide convention, for example (see B. Van Schaak, (1996), https://digitalcommons.law.scu.edu/cgi/viewcontent.cgi?article=1418&context=facpubs. So international rules to which we adhere today were shaped by past governments, who did not want to be implicated, and Putin's Russian state doesn't necessarily feel the need to submit to rules from 'the west'.

3 *The Economist*, 'How the Baltics resist Russia', *The Economist* (2–8 February 2019), 32.

4 NATO, 'The North Atlantic Treaty', North Atlantic Treaty Organization (4 April 1949), https://www.nato.int/cps/ie/natohq/official_texts_17120.htm.

5 Tom Batchelor, 'The map that shows how many Nato troops are deployed along Russia's border', *Independent* (5 February 2017), https://www.independent.co.uk/news/world/europe/russia-nato-border-forces-map-where-are-they-positioned-a7562391.html.

6 US-CERT, 'Alert (TA18-074A): Russian Government Cyber Activity Targeting Energy and Other Critical Infrastructure Sectors', United States Computer Emergency Readiness Team (15 March 2018), https://www.us-cert.gov/ncas/alerts/TA18-074A.

7 Matthew Field and Mike Wright, 'Russian trolls sent thousands of pro-Leave messages on day of Brexit referendum, Twitter data reveals', *Daily Telegraph* (17 October 2018) https://www.telegraph.co.uk/technology/2018/10/17/russian-iranian-twitter-trolls-sent-10-million-tweets-fake-news/.

8 Latvian, Estonian and Lithuanian National Commissions for UNESCO, 'The Baltic Way – Human Chain Linking Three States in Their Drive for Freedom', http://www.balticway.net/uploads/Booklet%20BALTIC%20WAY%20en%20fr%20ru.pdf.

9 *Human Rights Watch*, 'Human Rights Developments', *Human Rights Watch* (1992), https://www.hrw.org/reports/1992/WR92/HSW-05.htm

10 Anda Boša, 'Izstādē aplūkojami barikāžu laikā izmantotie sakaru līdzekļi', Latvijas Sabiedriskie Mediji (LSM.LV) (14 May 2019), https://www.lsm.lv/raksts/dzive--stils/vesture/izstade-aplukojami-barikazu-laika-izmantotie-sakaru-lidzekli.a318990/

11 State Chancellery of Latvia, 'Towards the State of Latvia: Barricades of January 1991 and their role in restoring Latvia's independence', LV100 (2018), 5. https://www.mk.gov.lv/sites/default/files/editor/barikades_eng.pdf.

12 Latvian Public Broadcasting, 'Riga speaks more Russian than Latvian', *LSM. LV* (15 May 2015), https://eng.lsm.lv/article/society/society/riga-speaks-more-russian-than-latvian.a129764/.

13 *World Population Review*, 'Lithuania Population 2019 (Demographics, Maps, Graphs)' (2018), http://worldpopulationreview.com/countries/lithuania-population/.

14 Mira Kobuszynska, 'Wood Sector in Estonia', USDA GAIN Report (20 December 2016), https://gain.fas.usda.gov/Recent%20GAIN%20Publications/Wood%20Sector%20in%20Estonia_Warsaw_Estonia_12-20-2016.pdf. Margus Martin, 'Aburis raiuti püha his', Postimees (Virumaa Teataja) (13 June 2019) https://virumaateataja.postimees.ee/6706070/aburis-raiuti-puha-hiis.

15 Toivo V. Raun, 'Baltic Independence, 1917–1920 and 1988–1994: Comparative perspectives', The National Council for Soviet and East European Research (1994), https://www.ucis.pitt.edu/nceeer/1994-808-12-Raun.pdf.

16 Vello Pettai, 'The Baltic States: Staill a Single Political Model?' unpublished conference paper for 'The Fall of Communism: Ten Years On', Mayrock Center, Hebrew University Jerusalem (13–17 May 2001).

17 Gerald M. Easter, 'Preference for Presidentialism: Postcommunist Regime Change in Russia and the NIS', *World Politics*, 49:2 (January 1997), http://www.jstor.org/stable/pdf/25053997.pdf.

18 Mark S. Ellis, 'Purging the Past: The Current State of Lustration Laws in the Former Communist Bloc', *Law and Contemporary Problems* 59 (Fall 1996): 181–96.

19 Ieva Zake, 'Politicians Versus Intellectuals in the Lustration Debates in Transitional Latvia', *Memory and Pluralism in the Baltic States* (ed. Eva-Clarita Pettai). London: Routledge (2011), 111.

20 Jaan Masso, Kerly Espenberg, Anu Masso, Inta Mierina, Kaia Philips, 'Country Report for the Baltic States Estonia, Latvia, Lithuania', Growing Inequalities Impacts (GINI) (2012) 35, http://gini-research.org/system/uploads/437/original/Baltics.pdf?1370077200

21 Ibid., 36.

22 Ieva Gundare, email to Aliide Naylor (27 March 2018).

23 Dwight Garner, 'Review: In "Secondhand Time," Voices from a Lost Russia'. *New York Times*, 24 May 2016, sec. books, https://www.nytimes.com/2016/05/25/books/review-in-secondhand-time-voices-from-a-lost-russia.html.

24 Ibid.

1 The shadow of the past

1 Alfred Erich Senn, 'The Sovietization of the Baltic States', *The Annals of the American Academy of Political and Social Science*, 317 (May 1958): 123, https://doi.org/10.1177/000271625831700116.

2 Alexander Shtromas, Robert K. Faulkner, and Daniel J. Mahoney, *Totalitarianism and the Prospects for World Order: Closing the Door on the Twentieth Century* (Oxford: Lexington Books, 2003), 294.

3 Casimir Smogorzewski, 'The Russification of the Baltic States', *World Affairs*, 4 (1950): 168–81. Gil Loescher, *Calculated Kindness* (London: Collier Macmillan, 1986), 21.

4 Agate Nesaule, *A Woman in Amber: Healing the Trauma of War and Exile* (New York: Penguin, 1997).

5 Leena Kurvet-Käosaar, 'The Traumatic Impact of the Penal Frameworks of the Soviet Regime: Pathways of Female Remembering', *Teaching Empires. Gender and Transnational Citizenship in Europe* (eds. Mary Clancy and Andrea Pető). (Utrecht: Utrecht University, 2009), 76.

6 Alain Blum, Amandine Regamey, 'The hero, the martyr ad the erased rape (Lithuania 1944–2000)', *Gendered Laws of War*, 39 (2014): 103, 109.

7 Ibid., 114.

8 Tiina Kirss and Juri Kivimae, *Estonian Life Stories* (Budapest: Central European University Press, 2009), 47.

9 Māra Zālīte, *Five Fingers* (Champaign: Dalkey Archive, 2017), 65.

10 Jāzeps Bikše, interview with Aliide Naylor (24 July 2017).

11 Andrejs Plakans, *A Concise History of the Baltic States* (Cambridge: Cambridge University Press, 2011), 367.

12 Michael Weiss, 'Back in the USSR', *Foreign Policy* (11 December 2013), https://foreignpolicy.com/2013/12/11/back-in-the-ussr/.

13 Alexandra Ashbourne, *Lithuania: The Rebirth of a Nation, 1991–1994* (Maryland: Lexington Books, 1999), 41, 82.

14 Aleksandras Shtromas, 'The Baltic States as Soviet Republics: Tensions and Contradictions', in Graham Smith (ed.) *The Baltic States: The National Self-Determination of Estonia, Latvia and Lithuania* (Basingstoke: Palgrave Macmillan, 1996), 86.

15 Ibid.

16 Andres Küng, 'Communism and Crimes against Humanity in the Baltic states', *Report to the Jarl Hjalmarson Foundation* (seminar) (13 April 1999), https://web.archive.org/web/20010301223347/http://www.rel.ee/eng/communism_crimes.htm. ERR.ee, 'Enemies of the people: How the USSR had 90,000 deported in four days', Err.ee (24 March 2016), https://news.err.ee/117888/enemies-of-the-people-how-the-ussr-had-90-000-deported-in-four-days.

17 European Court of Human Rights (ECHR), 'Kolk and Kislyiy v. Estonia', Reports of Judgments and Decisions 2006-I (17 January 2006), http://hudoc. echr.coe.int/eng{"itemid":["001-72404"]}.

18 R.J. Rummel, *Lethal Politics: Soviet Genocide and Mass Murder Since 1917* (New York: Routledge, 2017), 193.

19 Raminta Biziuleviciute, 'Gendered Aspects of the Soviet deportations from Lithuania with the case study of the operation "Vesna", May 22–23, 1948' (2012), http://www.etd.ceu.hu/2012/biziuleviciute_raminta.pdf.

20 Tiina Kirss and Juri Kivimae, *Estonian Life Stories* (Budapest: Central European University Press, 2009), 13–14.

21 Ibid.

22 Valters Nollendorfs, interview with Aliide Naylor (25 July 2017).

23 J.T. Dykman, 'The Soviet Experience in World War Two', *Eisenhower Institute at Gettysburg College*, http://www.eisenhowerinstitute.org/about/living_history/wwii_soviet_experience.dot, accessed 14 November 2018.

24 Dov Levin, 'On the relations between the Baltic peoples and their Jewish neighbours before, during and after World War II', *Holocaust and Genocide Studies*, 5: 1 (1 January 1990): 53.

25 Ashbourne, *Lithuania*, 32. Ian Traynor, 'Patriots or Nazi collaborators? Latvians march to commemorate SS veterans', *Guardian* (16 March 2010), https://www.theguardian.com/world/2010/mar/16/latvians-march-commemorate-ss-veterans.

26 Traynor, 'Patriots or Nazi collaborators?'

27 Ieva Zake, '"The Secret Nazi Network" and Post-World War II Latvian Émigrés in the United States', *The Journal of Baltic Studies* 41:1 (2010): 91–2.

28 Ralph Blumenthal, 'Some Suspected of Nazi War Crimes Are Known as Model Citizens', *New York Times* (18 October 1976), http://www.nytimes.com/1976/10/18/archives/some-suspected-of-nazi-war-crimes-are-known-as-model-citizens.html?mcubz=0.

29 Valters Nollendorfs and Uldis Neiburgs, 'The Holocaust in German-Occupied Latvia', *Ministry of Foreign Affairs of the Republic of Latvia: Briefing papers of the Museum of the Occupation of Latvia* (16 August 2004), http://www.mfa.gov.lv/en/policy/information-on-the-history-of-latvia/briefing-papers-of-the-museum-of-the-occupation-of-latvia/the-holocaust-in-german-occupied-latvia.

30 Timothy Snyder and Simas Čelutka, 'Taking bad ideas seriously', *Eurozine* (28 August 2017), http://www.eurozine.com/taking-bad-ideas-seriously/.

31 Grant Arthur Gochin, interview with Aliide Naylor (15 October 2018).

32 Andrew Higgins, 'Nazi Collaborator or National Hero? A Test for Lithuania', *New York Times* (10 September 2018), https://www.nytimes.com/2018/09/10/world/europe/nazi-general-storm-lithuania.html.

33 Silvia Foti, 'My grandfather wasn't a Nazi-fighting war hero – he was a brutal collaborator', *Salon* (14 July 2018), https://www.salon.com/2018/07/14/my-grandfather-didnt-fight-the-nazis-as-family-lore-told-it-he-was-a-brutal-collaborator/.

34 Ibid.

35 Hanna Kuusi, 'Prison Experiences and Socialist Sculptures – Tourism and the Soviet Past in the Baltic States', *Touring the Past. Uses of History in Tourism. Discussion and Working Papers No. 6.* The Finnish University Network for Tourism Studies (FUNTS) (2008), 105–6.

36 *Like a Local*, Tallinn City Guide (2017).

37 Data on this front provide vague estimates as the figures are based on the language of the material requested.

38 Merilin Piipuu, interview with Aliide Naylor (14 August 2017).

39 LETA/TBT Staff, 'Lithuania to rename Museum of Genocide Victims after lengthy discussions', *Baltic Times* (8 September 2017), https://www.baltictimes.com/lithuania_to_rename_museum_of_genocide_victims_after_lengthy_discussions.

40 Ibid.

41 Traynor, 'Patriots or Nazi collaborators?'

42 Andres Kasekamp, *A History of the Baltic States* (Basingstoke: Palgrave Macmillan, 2010), 233.

43 Leigh Phillips, 'EU rejects eastern states' call to outlaw denial of crimes by communist regimes', *Guardian* (21 December 2010), https://www.theguardian.com/world/2010/dec/21/european-commission-communist-crimes-nazism.

44 Ibid.

45 Estonian MFA, email to Aliide Naylor (4 May 2018).

46 EER, "Patarei fortress could house planned center investigating communist crimes", ERR (6 June 2017), http://news.err.ee/600404/patarei-fortress-could-house-planned-center-investigating-communist-crimes.

47 Kuusi, 'Prison Experiences and Socialist Sculptures', 110, 112.

48 BBC, 'Tallinn tense after deadly riots', BBC (28 April 2007), http://news.bbc.co.uk/1/hi/world/europe/6602171.stm.

49 Damien McGuinness, 'How a cyber attack transformed Estonia', BBC News (27 April 2017), http://www.bbc.co.uk/news/39655415.

50 Baltic News Service, 'Lithuanian president supports removal of Soviet sculptures in Vilnius', Delfi.lt (24 July 2015), https://en.delfi.lt/lithuania/society/lithuanian-president-supports-removal-of-soviet-sculptures-in-vilnius.d?id=68567598.

51 Raimundas Karoblis, interview with Aliide Naylor (27 June 2017). The Commonwealth of Independent States was established after the Soviet Union collapsed as a federation of former Soviet states.

52 This is the cutoff number required – any more and OSCE observers would need to be present.

53 Svetlana Alexievich, *Second-Hand Time* (London: Fitzcarraldo Editions, 2016), 473–88.

54 Anton Troianovski, 'The Putin Generation', *The Washington Post* (9 March 2018), https://www.washingtonpost.com/news/world/wp/2018/03/09/feature/russias-young-people-are-putins-biggest-fans/?utm_term=.821eafd4898d.

55 Oneworld, 'I'm Going to Ruin Their Lives: Inside Putin's war on Russia's Opposition', Oneworld (25 February 2016), https://oneworld-publications.com/i-m-going-to-ruin-their-lives-pb.html.

56 Alberto Nardelli, Jennifer Rankin and George Arnett, 'Vladimir Putin's approval rating at record levels', *Guardian* (23 July 2015), https://www.theguardian.com/world/datablog/2015/jul/23/vladimir-putins-approval-rating-at-record-levels.

57 I posed the question of whether Russia should be feared to more than 100 across the Baltic states, and the majority cited Crimea as a turning point independently.

58 James Sherr, 'The Baltic States in Russian Military Strategy', *Security in the Baltic Sea Region: Realities and Prospects* (2017): 159–60, file:///C:/Users/bernard/Downloads/security-in-the-baltic-sea-region-realities-and-prospects-the-riga-conference-papers-2017-read-in-english.pdf.

59 BBC, 'Crimea referendum: Voters "back Russia union"', BBC (16 March 2014), http://www.bbc.co.uk/news/world-europe-26606097.

60 Erwin Oberländer, 'Soviet Genocide in Latvia? Conflicting Cultures of Remembrance of Stalin's Policy, 1940–1953', in Martyn Housden and David J. Smith (eds.), *Forgotten Pages in Baltic History: Diversity and Inclusion* (Amsterdam: Rodopi B.V., 2011), 240.

61 Katya Adler, 'Baltic States Shiver as Russia Flexes Muscles' BBC (6 March 2016), http://www.bbc.co.uk/news/world-europe-31759558; NBC News, 'Baltic States Fear Putin Amid Escalation in Ukraine', NBC (2 September 2014), https://www.nbcnews.com/storyline/ukraine-crisis/baltic-states-fear-putin-amid-escalation-ukraine-n193326.

62 NPR, 'Estonian President Says Russia's Show of Force Raises Issues Of "Transparency, Trust"', NPR (22 September 2017), http://www.npr.org/2017/09/22/552986956/estonian-president-says-russias-show-of-force-raises-issues-of-transparency-trus.

63 Ibid.

64 WBUR, 'Latvian President Raimonds Vējonis On Security and Russia Tensions', WBUR (21 September 2017), http://www.wbur.org/hereandnow/2017/09/21/latvia-raimonds-vejonis-russia.

65 Ibid.

66 Aliide Naylor, 'Trump, Russia and the new geopolitics of the Baltics', *New Eastern Europe* (30 January 2017), http://www.neweasterneurope.eu/interviews/2247-trump-russia-and-the-new-geopolitics-of-the-baltics.

67 Teabeamet (Estonian Information Board), 'International Security and Estonia', Estonian Information Board (2016), 6, https://www.valisluureamet.ee/pdf/2016-en.pdf.

68 Eugene Chausovsky, 'Russian Influence Fades in the Baltics', Stratfor (10 June 2016), https://worldview.stratfor.com/article/russian-influence-fades-baltics.

69 *New York Times*, 'Transcript: Donald Trump on NATO, Turkey's Coup Attempt and the World', *New York* Times (21 July 2016), https://www.nytimes.com/2016/07/22/us/politics/donald-trump-foreign-policy-interview.html.

70 Reena Flores, 'Newt Gingrich: NATO countries "ought to worry" about US commitment', CBS (21 July 2016), https://www.cbsnews.com/news/newt-gin-grich-trump-would-reconsider-his-obliga-tion-to-nato/. Richard Milne 'Baltics Fear for Any US Policy Changes to Nato', *Financial Times* (12 November 2016), https://www.ft.com/content/0036b09a-a825-11e6-8898-79a99e2a4de6?mhq5j=e7.

71 Linas Kojala, '"Brexit earthquake" and "stunning Trump win": the Baltic perspective', *Political State of the Region Report* (2017), 16.

72 Milne, 'Baltics fear for any US policy changes to Nato'.

73 Ian Bremmer, 'The Only 5 Countries That Meet NATO's Defense Spending Requirements', Time.com (24 February 2017), http://time.com/4680885/nato-defense-spending-budget-trump/. Leonid Bershidsky, 'Why NATO Wants Montenegro (Not for Its Military Might)', Bloomberg (1 May 2017), https://www.bloomberg.com/view/articles/2017-05-01/why-nato-wants-montenegro-not-for-its-military-might.

74 Andrius Sytas, Gederts Gelzis, 'Baltics keep fingers crossed that Trump won't keep his campaign pledges', Reuters (9 November 2016), http://www.reuters.com/article/usa-election-baltics/baltics-keep-fingers-crossed-that-trump-wont-keep-his-campaign-pledges-idUSL8N1DA597. LSM.LV, 'Baltics among 7 NATO countries that hit defense spending target in 2018', LSM.LV (14 March 2019), https://eng.lsm.lv/article/society/defense/baltics-among-7-nato-countries-that-hit-defense-spending-target-in-2018.a312737/.

75 Naylor, 'Trump, Russia and the new geopolitics of the Baltics'.

76 AFP, 'Russia Slams US Approval of Montenegro's NATO Accession', *NDTV* (13 April 2017), https://www.ndtv.com/world-news/russia-slams-us-approval-of-montenegros-nato-accession-1680990. Aliide Naylor, 'Russian Media Paint Dark Picture of Montenegro', *Balkan Insight* (19 April 2017), http://www.balkaninsight.com/en/article/russian-media-turn-hostile-gaze-on-montenegro-04-13-2017.

77 David Filipov, 'Putin says Russia planning "countermeasures" to NATO expansion', *Washington Post* (21 November 2016), https://www.

washingtonpost.com/world/putin-says-russia-planning-countermeasuresto-nato-expansion/2016/11/21/83f5673c-afe1-11e6-ab37-1b3940a0d30a_story.html?utm_term=.f2d0c09db969.

78 Adrian Blomfield and Mike Smith, 'Gorbachev: US could start new Cold War', *Daily Telegraph* (6 May 2008), http://www.telegraph.co.uk/news/worldnews/europe/russia/1933223/Gorbachev-US-could-start-new-Cold-War.html.

79 Maxim Kórshunov, 'Mikhail Gorbachev: I am against all walls', Russia Beyond the Headlines (RBTH) (16 October 2014), https://www.rbth.com/international/2014/10/16/mikhail_gorbachev_i_am_against_all_walls_40673.html.

80 Mark Kramer, 'The Myth of a No-NATO-Enlargement Pledge to Russia', *Washington Quarterly*, 32:2 (2009): 51, http://dialogueeurope.org/uploads/File/resources/TWQ%20article%20on%20Germany%20and%20NATO.pdf.

81 Alexander Lukin, *Pivot to Asia: Russia's Foreign Policy Enters the 21st Century* (Delhi: Vij Books India, 2017), https://books.google.co.uk/books?id=6RBtDQAAQBAJ&printsec=frontcover&source=gbs_ge_summary_r&cad=0#v=onepage&q&f=false.

82 Stephen J. Blank, *NATO Enlargement and the Baltic States: What Can the Great Powers Do?* (Collingdale PA: Diane Publishing, 1997), 20.

83 Ibid., 17.

84 Naylor, 'Trump, Russia and the new geopolitics of the Baltics'.

85 Vijai Maheshwari, 'In the Baltics, waiting for history to start up again', Politico Europe (27 January 2017), http://www.politico.eu/article/lithuania-russia-tension-baltics-waiting-for-history-to-start-again/.

86 Vanessa Gera, 'Lithuanians Are Preparing for a "Russian Invasion" in the Most Extreme Way Imaginable', *The Independent* (1 December 2016), http://www.independent.co.uk/news/world/europe/russia-eastern-europe-lithuania-vladimir-putin-estonia-latvia-a7449961.html and Andrew E. Kramer, 'Spooked by Russia, Tiny Estonia Trains a Nation of Insurgents', *The New York Times* (31 October 2016), https://www.nytimes.com/2016/11/01/world/europe/spooked-by-russia-tiny-estonia-trains-a-nation-of-insurgents.html.

87 DELFI, "Исследование: почти половина жителей Эстонии опасается военного конфликта на территории страны", rus.delfi.ee (4 July 2017), http://rus.delfi.ee/daily/estonia/issledovanie-pochti-polovina-zhitelej-estonii-opasaetsya-voennogo-konflikta-na-territorii-strany?id=78771916.

88 BNS, 'Survey: Less than half of Estonian residents fear military conflict', ERR (4 July 2017), http://news.err.ee/605662/survey-less-than-half-of-estonian-residents-fear-military-conflict.

89 https://www.nytimes.com/2016/11/18/world/europe/estonia-trump-baltics-putin.html?mcubz=0

90 Aliide Naylor, 'All Quiet on the Eastern Front', *Politico Europe* (12 September 2017), http://www.politico.eu/article/eastern-front-zapad-military-exercises-russia-lithuania-belarus/.

2 The threat from the East

1 Rokas Pukinskas, interview with Aliide Naylor (17 July 2017).

2 Rokas Pukinskas, interview with Aliide Naylor (17 July 2017).

3 Europol, 'European Migrant Smuggling Centre (EMSC): 3rd Annual Activity Report – 2018', EMSC (2019), www.europol.europa.eu/sites/default/documents/emsc_report_final_2019_2final.pdf.

4 Daina Bleiere and Rolands Henins, 'The Eastern Latvian Border: Potential for TransFrontier Co-operation with Russia', *Latvian Institute of Internal Affairs* (January 2004), http://liia.lv/site/attachments/17/01/2012/LatvianBorderfinal.pdf.

5 Angus Crawford, 'The town in Belarus from where cigarettes are smuggled to the UK', BBC News (1 December 2016) http://www.bbc.co.uk/news/uk-38170754.

6 Satversmes Aizsardzības Birojs (SAB), 'SAB 2015. Gada Darbības Pārskats', SAB, 5 (2015), http://www.sab.gov.lv/files/2015_parskats.pdf.

7 Mark Galeotti, 'Putin's Hydra: Inside Russia's Intelligence Services', European Council on Foreign Relations (ECFR) (May 2016): 5, http://www.ecfr.eu/page/-/ECFR_169_-_INSIDE_RUSSIAS_INTELLIGENCE_SERVICES_(WEB_AND_PRINT)_2.pdf.

8 Holger Roonemaa, 'These Cigarette Smugglers are on the Frontlines of Russia's Spy Wars', Buzzfeed (13 September 2017), https://www.buzzfeed.com/holgerroonemaa/these-cigarette-smugglers-are-on-the-frontlines-of-russias?utm_term=.fbNQM00A2#.hkQ4Pkk08.

9 Rashid Razaq, 'Pussy Riot Co-founder Nadya Tolokonnikova to Recreate Siberian Prison Camp at the Saatchi Gallery', *Evening Standard* (29 September 2017), https://www.standard.co.uk/goingout/arts/pussy-riot-cofounder-nadya-tolokonnikova-to-recreate-siberian-prison-camp-at-the-saatchi-gallery-a3646631.html.

10 Liis Velsker, 'Venemaa heaks luuranud Romanov juhtis salakaubaveo grupeeringut', *Postimees*, 23 February 2016, www.postimees.ee/3594319/venemaa-heaks-luuranud-romanov-juhtis-salakaubaveo-grupeeringut

11 Oliver Kund, 'Tartu ettevõtja teenis aastaid Vene sõjaväeluuret', *Postimees*, 12 April 2018 https://leht.postimees.ee/4469203/tartu-ettevotja-teenis-aastaid-vene-sojavaeluuret.

12 Kaitsepolitei (KAPO), 'Estonian Internal Security Service Annual Reviews', KAPO (2017), https://www.kapo.ee/en/content/annual-reviews.html.

13 Julius Barath and Marcel Harakal, 'Test Bed for Cyber-Attacks Mitigation', Brasov, Romania: Academiei Fortelor Aeriene (AFASES) (26–28 May 2011), http://www.afahc.ro/ro/afases/2011/math/BARATH_Harakal.pdf.

14 Chloe Arnold, 'Russia: Estonia Row Clouds Victory Day Ceremonies', RFE/RL (8 May 2007) https://www.rferl.org/a/1076345.html.

15 http://www.eesti.ca/the-tonismae-second-world-war-memorial/article16027.

16 http://www.spiegel.de/international/europe/spiegel-interview-with-estonian-president-toomas-hendrik-ilves-we-want-to-re-write-history-a-490811-2.html.

17 Damien McGuinness, 'How a Cyber Attack Transformed Estonia', BBC News (27 April 2017), http://www.bbc.co.uk/news/39655415. *The Economist*, 'A Cyber-Riot', *The Economist* (10 May 2007) http://www.economist.com/node/9163598.

18 Alison Lawlor Russell, *Cyber Blockades* (Washington DC: Georgetown University Press, 2014), 82.

19 Christian Lowe, 'Kremlin Loyalist Says Launched Estonia Cyber-Attack", Reuters (13 March 2009), https://www.reuters.com/article/us-russia-estonia-cyberspace/kremlin-loyalist-says-launched-estonia-cyber-attack-idUSTRE52B4D820090313.

20 ERR.ee, 'Ansip, Laaneots: Russian agents Present during Bronze Night Riots', ERR (26 April 2017), http://news.err.ee/592127/ansip-laaneots-russian-agents-present-during-bronze-night-riots.

21 Barath and Harakal, 'Test Bed For Cyber-Attacks Mitigation'.

22 *The Economist*, 'A Cyber-Riot', *The Economist* (10 May 2007), http://www.economist.com/node/9163598.

23 Peter Pomerantsev, 'Inside the Kremlin's hall of mirrors', *Guardian* (9 April 2015), https://www.theguardian.com/news/2015/apr/09/kremlin-hall-of-mirrors-military-information-psychology.

24 Center for European Policy Analysis (CEPA), 'Lithuania's Lonely Gambit', CEPA (15 May 2008), http://cepa.org/index/?id=d9b993256f4573d37b1cdc50ea3528d8.

25 William C. Ashmore, 'Impact of Alleged Russian Cyber Attacks', *Baltic Security & Defence Review*, 11 (2009): 11.

26 UN Security Council, 'Topic B: Cyberterrorism', *Cleveland Council on World Affairs* (March 2014): 13, https://www.ccwa.org/wp-content/uploads/2014/03/UNSC_Topic-B.docx.

27 Teri Schultz, 'Stealthy sleuths: Lithuania calls for "cyber Schengen" zone', Deutsche Welle (28 February 2018), https://www.dw.com/en/stealthy-sleuths-lithuania-calls-for-cyber-schengen-zone/a-42769925.

28 Second Investigation Department under the Ministry of National Defence, *National Security Threat Assessment* (Vilnius, 2017): 27.

29 GOV.UK, 'Overseas Business Risk – Lithuania', GOV.UK (28 March 2017), https://www.gov.uk/government/publications/overseas-business-risk-lithuania/overseas-business-risk-lithuania.

30 CISCO, 'Cisco 2017 Midyear Cybersecurity Report' (July 2017), https://www.cisco.com/c/dam/m/digital/elq-cmcglobal/witb/1456403/Cisco_2017_Midyear_Cybersecurity_Report.pdf?elqTrackId=f6ccd8439e9945639096a98 46044695a&elqaid=5897&elqat=2.

31 Stephen Jewkes and Oleg Vukmanovic, 'Suspected Russia-Backed hackers target Baltic energy networks', Reuters (11 May 2017), https://www.reuters.com/article/us-baltics-cyber-insight/suspected-russia-backed-hackers-target-baltic-energy-networks-idUSKBN1871W5.

32 Pomerantsev, 'Inside the Kremlin's hall of mirrors'.

33 Matt Burgess, 'Exposed: How One of Russia's Most Sophisticated Hacking Groups Operates', *Wired UK* (11 January 2017), http://www.wired.co.uk/article/how-russian-hackers-work.

34 Dmytro Shymkiv, deputy head of the Presidential Administration of Ukraine on Administrative, Social and Economic Reform, explained during the Future in Review conference in Park City, Utah, http://dailysignal.com/2017/10/27/russia-field-tested-hybrid-warfare-ukraine-cyberthreat-matters-us/.

35 Jaan Priisalu, interview with Aliide Naylor (15 August 2017).

36 BBC, 'A guided tour of the Cybercrime Underground', BBC News (23 February 2017), http://www.bbc.co.uk/news/technology-38755584.

37 Irina Borogan and Andrei Soldatov, 'The Kremlin and the Hackers: Partners in Crime?' openDemocracy (25 April 2012), https://www.opendemocracy.net/od-russia/irina-borogan-andrei-soldatov/kremlin-and-hackers-partners-in-crime.

38 Kapersky, *Kapersky Lab Security Bulletin* (2008), http://kasperskycontenthub.com/wp-content/uploads/sites/43/vlpdfs/kaspersky_security_bulletin_part_2_statistics_en.pdf.

39 defense-aerospace.com, 'Booz, Allen Escapes Spending Cuts on Consultants', defense-aerospace.com (14 May 2010), http://www.defense-aerospace.com/articles-view/release/3/114842/booz,-allen-escapes-spending-cuts-on-consultants.html.

40 Reuters 'Russia may have tested cyber warfare on Latvia, Western officials say', Reuters (5 October 2017), http://uk.reuters.com/article/us-russia-nato/russia-may-have-tested-cyber-warfare-on-latvia-western-officials-say-idUKKBN1CA142.

41 Thomas Grove, Julian E. Barnes and Drew Hinshaw, 'Russia Targets NATO Soldier Smartphones, Western Officials Say', *Wall Street Journal* (4 October 2017), https://www.wsj.com/articles/russia-targets-soldier-smartphones-western-officials-say-1507109402.

42 Jeff Daniels, 'Russian Rogue Cell Sites, Spy Drones Target NATO Troop Smartphones, Says Report'. CNBC (4 October 2017), https://www.cnbc.

com/2017/10/04/russian-rogue-cell-sites-drones-target-nato-troop-smartphones.html.

43 David A. Shlapak, Michael W. Johnson, 'Reinforcing Deterrence on NATO's Eastern Flank', RAND Corporation (2016), https://www.rand.org/content/dam/rand/pubs/research_reports/RR1200/RR1253/RAND_RR1253.pdf.

44 Dmitri Trenin, 'The Revival of the Russian Military: How Moscow Reloaded', *Foreign Affairs* 95 (2016): 24.

45 Julian E. Barnes and Anton Troianovski, 'NATO Allies Preparing to Put Four Battalions at Eastern Border With Russia', *Wall Street Journal* (29 April 2016), https://www.wsj.com/articles/nato-allies-preparing-to-put-four-battalions-at-eastern-border-with-russia-1461943315.

46 Alexander Lanoszka, 'Strategic Enabler or Point of Vulnerability: What Role for Belarus in Russia's Military Plans', Modern War Institute (21 March 2018), https://mwi.usma.edu/strategic-enabler-point-vulnerability-role-belarus-russias-military-plans/.

47 Elisabeth Sköns, 'Russian Military Expenditure, Reform and Restructuring SIPRI', Stockholm International Peace Research Institute (SIPRI): Oxford University Press (July 2013), https://www.sipri.org/yearbook/2013/03.

48 Dmitry Gorenburg, 'Russia's State Armaments Program 2020', PONARS Eurasia Policy Memo No. 125 (2010), http://www.ponarseurasia.org/sites/default/files/policy-memos-pdf/pepm_125.pdf.

49 Trenin, 'The Revival of the Russian Military', 23.

50 Vladimir Rasulov, 'Расходы на оборону вырастут', *Kommersant* (8 October 2017), https://www.kommersant.ru/doc/3433783.

51 Roland Oliphant, 'Photos Show Dramatic Near Miss of Russian and US Jets in "Dangerous" Interception Over Baltic Sea', *Daily Telegraph* (23 June 2017), http://www.telegraph.co.uk/news/2017/06/23/photos-show-dramatic-near-miss-russian-us-jets-dangerous-interception/.

52 Jaanus Piirsalu, 'Russian Warplanes Cannot Switch on Transponders', *Postimees* (6 September 2016), https://news.postimees.ee/3826371/russian-warplanes-cannot-switch-on-transponders.

53 Ibid.

54 Knut-Sverre Horn, 'Støy fra Russland slo ut GPS-signaler for norske fly', *NRK Finnmark* (5 October 2017), https://www.nrk.no/finnmark/stoy-fra-russland-slo-ut-gps-signaler-for-norske-fly-1.13720305.

55 Reuters, 'Lithuania Looking for Source of False Accusation of Rape by German Troops', Reuters (17 February 2017), http://www.reuters.com/article/us-lithuania-nato/lithuania-looking-for-source-of-false-accusation-of-rape-by-german-troops-idUSKBN15W1JO.

56 Andrew Higgins, 'Foot Soldiers in a Shadowy Battle Between Russia and the West', *New York Times* (28 May 2016), https://www.nytimes.com/2017/05/28/

world/europe/slovakia-czech-republic-hungary-poland-russia-agitation.
html.

57 Mustafa Nayyem and Svitlana Zalishchuk, 'Statement of Mustafa Nayyem and Svitlana Zalishchuk, Members of the Parliament of Ukraine before the Subcommittee on Department of State, Foreign Operations, and Related Programs of the Senate Committee on Appropriations', Senate Committee on Appropriations (29 March 2017), https://www.appropriations.senate. gov/imo/media/doc/032917-Nayyem-Zalishchuk-Outside-Witness-Testimony.pdf.

58 Chloe Farand, 'Swedish Teenagers Claim Russian TV Crew Offered to Bribe Them to Cause Trouble After Trump Comments', *Independent* (7 March 2017), http://www.independent.co.uk/news/world/europe/wedish-teenagers-russian-tv-name-of-channel-crew-money-action-camera-donald-trump-refugee-rape-a7615406.html.

59 Martin Kragh, 'Russia's Strategy for Influence Through Public Diplomacy and Active Measures: The Swedish Case', *Journal of Strategic Studies*, 40, 6 (5 January 2017): 773–816.

60 Ivan Lavrentjev, interview with Aliide Naylor (18 August 2017).

61 Felicity Capon, 'Baltic States Say Norway, UK and Finland Have Stolen Their Children', *Newsweek* (23 April 2015), http://www.newsweek.com/2015/05/01/baltic-states-say-norway-uk-and-finland-have-stolen-their-children-324031. html

62 Ben Knight, 'Teenage Girl Admits Making Up Migrant Rape Claim That Outraged Germany', *Guardian* (31 January 2016), https://www.theguardian. com/world/2016/jan/31/teenage-girl-made-up-migrant-claim-that-caused-uproar-in-germany.

63 Stefan Meister, 'The "Lisa case": Germany as a Target of Russian Disinformation', *NATO Review* (2016), http://www.nato.int/docu/review/2016/Also-in-2016/lisa-case-germany-target-russian-disinformation/EN/index.htm.

64 Deutsche Welle (AFP), 'Man Found Guilty of Abusing Russian-German Teenager Who Fabricated Rape Story', Deutsche Welle (20 June 2017), http:// www.dw.com/en/man-found-guilty-of-abusing-russian-german-teenager-who-fabricated-rape-story/a-39328894.

65 Chris Brown, 'Anti-Canada Propaganda Greets Troops in Latvia', CBC News (16 June 2017), http://www.cbc.ca/news/world/latvia-propaganda-1.4162612.

66 Ivan Lavrentjev, interview with Aliide Naylor (18 August 2017).

67 Propastop, 'A Child Removed from her Family is Used for Propaganda Accusations', Propastop (25 July 2017), https://www.propastop.org/eng/2017/07/25/a-child-removed-from-her-family-is-used-for-propaganda-accusations/.

68 Ibid.

69 Sputnik, 'Посольство РФ: В Ситуации с Беллой Михайловой Держим Руку На Пульсе'. Sputnik (17 July 2017). https://ru.sputnik-news.ee/

society/20170717/6481491/posoljstvo-eref-situatsija-bela-mihailova-derzhim-ruka-puljs.html.

70 David Robert Grimes, 'Russian Fake News Is Not New: Soviet Aids Propaganda Cost Countless Lives', *Guardian* (14 June 2017), https://www.theguardian.com/science/blog/2017/jun/14/russian-fake-news-is-not-new-soviet-aids-propaganda-cost-countless-lives.

71 Aliide Naylor, 'All Quiet on the Eastern Front'. *Politico Europe* (12 September 2017), https://www.politico.eu/article/eastern-front-zapad-military-exercises-russia-lithuania-belarus/.

72 ibid.

73 I drew this conclusion from a variety of interviews and informal conversations that took place over the summer of 2017, when I conducted fieldwork for the book.

74 Aliide Naylor, 'Estonian Foreign Minister Cautious but Calm on Relations with Russia', *Moscow Times* (18 October 2015), https://themoscowtimes.com/articles/estonian-foreign-minister-cautious-but-calm-on-relations-with-russia-50332.

75 ERR, 'ERR: Usefulness of Direct Interpretation into Estonian of ETV+ Live Broadcasts Questionable," ERR.ee (1 October 2017), http://news.err.ee/120299/err-usefulness-of-direct-interpretation-into-estonian-of-etv-live-broadcasts-questionable.

76 Ivars Belte, interview with Aliide Naylor (9 August 2017).

77 RT International, '"Medieval Barbarism": Riga Mayor Decries Fine for Use of Russian on Official Facebook Account', RT International (27 February 2017), https://www.rt.com/news/378811-riga-mayor-russian-language-facebook/.

78 Barbara Ālīte, 'Pētījums: Mediju telpas Latvijā ir nošķirtas', LA.LV (18 July 2017), http://www.la.lv/petijums-mediju-telpas-latvija-ir-noskirtas/.

79 Vytautas Bakas, interview with Aliide Naylor (10 July 2017).

80 Statista, 'TV Audience Market Share – Estonia 2013', Statista. https://www.statista.com/statistics/482903/tv-audience-market-share-in-estonia/ (accessed 11 May 2019).

The Baltic Course, 'In Latvia TV3 Remains Most Popular TV Channel'. The Baltic Course/Baltic States news & analytics (5 August 2014), http://www.baltic-course.com/eng/good_for_business/?doc=94707 (accessed 11 May 2019).

LSM.LV. 'Latvian Television the Most Watched TV Channel in June' (5 July 2016), http://eng.lsm.lv/article/society/society/latvian-television-the-most-watched-tv-channel-in-june.a190668/m.

81 *Baltic Times*. 'Russian-Language First Baltic Channel Most Fined TV Station in Latvia Last Year' (27 April 2015), https://www.baltictimes.com/russian-language_first_baltic_channel_most_fined_tv_station_in_latvia_last_year/.

The Baltic Course, 'PBK TV Channel Appeals EUR 10,000 Fine Imposed by Latvia's Broadcasting Watchdog', The Baltic Course/Baltic States news & analytics (23 February 2016) http://www.baltic-course.com/eng/markets_and_companies/?doc=117096

82 Lithuania MoD. 'National Security Threat Assessment', Second Investigation Department under the Ministry of National Defence, *National Security Threat Assessment* (Vilnius, 2017): 23.

83 Jenna Johnson, 'Trump on NATO: "I said it was obsolete. It's no longer obsolete", *Washington Post* (12 April 2017), https://www.washingtonpost.com/news/post-politics/wp/2017/04/12/trump-on-nato-i-said-it-was-obsolete-its-no-longer-obsolete/?utm_term=.314982534025.

84 David Mardiste and Andrius Sytas, 'VP Pence, in the Baltics, Voices Support for Mutual Defense in NATO', Reuters (31 July 2017), https://www.reuters.com/article/us-usa-pence-estonia/vp-pence-in-the-baltics-voices-support-for-mutual-defense-in-nato-idUSKBN1AG1G0.

85 Teri Schultz, 'NATO Says More Russian Buzzing of Baltic Airspace a Risk for Deadly Mistakes', Deutsche Welle (27 June 2017), http://www.dw.com/en/nato-says-more-russian-buzzing-of-baltic-airspace-a-risk-for-deadly-mistakes/a-39440788.

86 Roman Goncharenko, 'Zapad-2017: "Normal Military Business"'. DW.COM (27 September 2017), http://www.dw.com/en/zapad-2017-normal-military-business/a-40710010.

87 Mathieu Boulègue, 'Five Things to Know About the Zapad-2017 Military Exercise', Chatham House (25 September 2017), https://www.chathamhouse.org/expert/comment/five-things-know-about-zapad-2017-military-exercise.

3 The threat from the West

1 National Public Radio (NPR), 'If You Think Wealth Disparity Is Bad Here, Look At Russia', NPR.org (10 October 2013), https://www.npr.org/sections/parallels/2013/10/10/231446353/if-you-think-wealth-disparity-is-bad-here-look-at-russia.

2 http://dat abank.worldbank.org/data/reports.aspx?source=2&series=SI.POV.GINI&country=.

There isn't really enoug h available data for recent years. However, OECD data showing countries' Palma ratios (ratio of the richest 10 per cent of the population's share of gross national income (GNI) divided by the poorest 40 per cent's share) shows it to be on a par with Uganda, El Salvador and Uruguay. http://hdr.undp.org/en/composite/IHDI.

3 *Moscow Times*, 'Highest Average Salary in Russia Is in Gas-Rich Siberian Town', *Moscow Times* (13 April 2015), http://www.themoscowtimes.com/

news/article/highest-average-salary-in-russia-is-in-gas-rich-siberian-town/519044.html.

4   http://users.humboldt.edu/ogayle/hist111/WWII_EasternFront.html.

5   Mark Davis, 'How World War II Shaped Modern Russia', Euronews (4 May 2015), http://www.euronews.com/2015/05/04/how-world-war-ii-shaped-modern-russia.

6   M.J. Broekmeyer, *Stalin, the Russians, and Their War* (Madison: University of Wisconsin, 2000), 184, 186. Some modern-day continuity of this kind of atmosphere can be found in both Arkady Babchenko's *One Soldier's War in Chechnya* and the late Anna Politkovskaya's *A Small Corner of Hell: Dispatches From Chechnya.*

7   Jonathan Mirsky, 'The Full Horror of the Siege of Leningrad Is Finally Revealed', *Spectator* (31 December 2016), https://www.spectator.co.uk/2016/12/the-full-horror-of-the-siege-of-leningrad-is-finally-revealed/.

8   Ilia Utekhin, 'Memories of Leningrad's Blockade: Testimonies from Two Generations', Generations in Europe (n.d.): 292–3, 304–5, http://anthropologie.kunstkamera.ru/files/pdf/eng004/eng4_utekhin.pdf.

9   Anna Reid, 'Myth and Tragedy at the Siege of Leningrad – Gallery'. *Guardian* (15 September 2011), https://www.theguardian.com/books/gallery/2011/sep/15/siege-leningrad-history-anna-reid.

10 Yvonne Pörzgen, 'Siege Memory – Besieged Memory? Heroism and Suffering in St Petersburg Museums dedicated to the Siege of Leningrad', Museums and Society, 14:3 (2016): 417–18, https://www2.le.ac.uk/departments/museumstudies/museumsociety/documents/volumes/porzgen.

11 For a Russian counterpart to Felicia's story, the tale of Bella Markaryan can be found at the *Calvert Journal*. She was a five-year-old during World War Two. 'What remains from my childhood is a fear not of bombs, not of explosions, but a fear of panic, of screams and of weeping', https://www.calvertjournal.com/features/show/9624/letter-from-stalingrad-volgograd-second-world-war.

12 Ishaan Tharoor, 'Don't Forget How the Soviet Union Saved the World from Hitler', *Washington Post* (8 May 2015), https://www.washingtonpost.com/news/worldviews/wp/2015/05/08/dont-forget-how-the-soviet-union-saved-the-world-from-hitler/.

13 *Moscow Times*, 'Ira', *Moscow Times*: 'Generation P' (2018), https://generationp.themoscowtimes.com/ira/.

14 Aliide Naylor, 'Russia's Reaction to The Death of Stalin Shows Its Changing Attitudes towards Him', *New Statesman* (23 October 2017), https://www.newstatesman.com/culture/film/2017/10/russia-s-reaction-death-stalin-shows-its-changing-attitudes-towards-him.

15 Levada, 'СТАЛИН В ОБЩЕСТВЕННОМ МНЕНИИ' (10 April 2018), https://www.levada.ru/2018/04/10/17896/.

16 Elena Radcheva, Viktoria Odissonova, 'Обиды ненайденных дедов', Новая газета (17 May 2017), https://www.novayagazeta.ru/articles/2017/05/17/72469-obidy-nenaydennyh-dedov.

17 Ibid.

18 Polina Efimova and Katerina Patin, 'Who Were the 27,000 Victims of Russia's Worst Holocaust-era Crime?' Coda Story (25 January 2019), https://codastory.com/disinformation-crisis/rewriting-history/who-victims-russia-worst-holocaust.

19 Lilya Palveleva, 'Russian Museum Celebrating Stalin Slated to Open for Victory Day', RFE/RL (18 March 2015), https://www.rferl.org/a/russia-stalin-museum/26907807.html.

20 Ibid.

21 I have no evidence to verify the accuracy of these statistics but this quote is used to convey more popular beliefs among locals, and they are backed up by some newspaper reports and around 500/50 people either way.

22 Interviews with residents, Aliide Naylor (May 2015).

23 Radcheva and Odissonova, 'Обиды ненайденных дедов'.

24 Vladimir Kara-Murza, 'Putin's Russia Is Becoming More Soviet by the Day', *Washington Post* (26 February 2018), https://www.washingtonpost.com/news/democracy-post/wp/2018/02/26/putins-russia-is-becoming-more-soviet-by-the-day/?utm_term=.ba0570cc89ec.

25 Neil MacFarquhar, 'A Russian Master of the "Dark Side" in Film', *New York Times* (23 February 2018), https://www.nytimes.com/2018/02/23/world/europe/andrey-zvyagintsev-russia-loveless.html.

26 Blake Hounshell, 'Putin Uses Dog to Intimidate Merkel'. Foreign Policy (blog) (14 June 2007), http://foreignpolicy.com/2007/06/14/putin-uses-dog-to-intimidate-merkel/.

27 *The Economist*, 'The View from the Kremlin: Putin's War on the West', *The Economist* (12 February 2015), https://www.economist.com/news/leaders/21643189-ukraine-suffers-it-time-recognise-gravity-russian-threatand-counter.

28 Fort Ross, 'Putin knew what to do! His first interview, 2000', YouTube (5 September 2016), https://www.youtube.com/watch?v=EjU8Fg3NFmo.

29 Michael Birnbaum, 'How to Understand Putin's Jaw-Dropping High Approval Ratings', *Washington Post* (6 March 2016), https://www.washingtonpost.com/world/europe/how-to-understand-putins-jaw-dropping-high-approval-ratings/2016/03/05/17f5d8f2-d5ba-11e5-a65b-587e721fb231_story.html?utm_term=.f801726f5f06.

30 Levada, 'Более половины россиян не видят альтернативы Путину' (10 October 2017), https://www.levada.ru/2017/10/10/bolee-poloviny-rossiyan-ne-vidyat-alternativy-putinu/.

31 Ibid.

32 *Moscow Times.* 'Generation P'.

33 Дергачев, Владимир. 'Россияне Стали Лучше Относиться к ВЧК и КГБ'. РБК (21 February 2018), https://www.rbc.ru/politics/21/02/2018/5a8d59f49a 79471a70e186ba?from=main.

34 Levada. 'Левада-центр: президентский рейтинг Путина составляет 37%, за месяц изменился в рамках погрешности' (25 January 2012), https:// www.levada.ru/2012/01/25/levada-tsentr-prezidentskij-rejting-putina-sostavlyaet-37-za-mesyats-izmenilsya-v-ramkah-pogreshnosti/.

35 Ellen Barry, 'Tens of Thousands Protest in Moscow, Russia, in Defiance of Putin', *New York Times* (10 December 2011), http://www.nytimes. com/2011/12/11/world/europe/thousands-protest-in-moscow-russia-in-defiance-of-putin.html.

While official police figures said the number of attendees was closer to 25,000, they frequently underestimate turnouts for opposition rallies – this has been widely recorded in media and I have seen it with my own eyes.

36 Individual agents of change and state response: Performance art and its impact in contemporary Russia, presented at Central European University (Budapest), 10th Graduate Conference in European History (April 21–23, 2016).

37 https://eeas.europa.eu/headquarters/headquarters-homepage_en/9497/%20 Inclusion%20of%20the%20Levada%20Centre%20in%20the%20 %22Foreign%20Agents%20Registry%22%20of%20the%20Russian%20 Federation

38 Robert Baryshnikov and Valentin Coalson. 'Just How Fraudulent Were Russia's Elections?' *The Atlantic*, 21 September 2016, https://www.theatlantic. com/international/archive/2016/09/russia-putin-election-fraud/500867/.

39 Reuters, 'Phantom Voters, Smuggled Ballots Hint at Foul Play in Russian Vote', Reuters. http://cc.bingj.com/cache.aspx?q=alexander+winning+reuters +ballott+stuffing%5c&d=4775919480803092&mkt=en-GB&setlang=en-US&w=5CPuY3H7eVB71nSg1k863ijzOui1fuBT.

40 Timothy Frye, Ora John Reuter and David Szakonyi, 'Hitting Them with Carrots: Voter Intimidation and Vote Buying in Russia', *British Journal of Political Science* (5 February 2018): 1–25, https://doi.org/10.1017/ S0007123416000752.

41 ZNAK, 'Источник: Московских Студентов Сгоняют На Митинг-Концерт в 'Лужниках' в Поддержку Путина'. ZNAK (26 February 2018), https://www.znak.com/2018-02-26/istochnik_moskovskih_studentov_sgonyayut_na_miting_koncert_v_luzhnikah_v_podderzhku_putina and https://themoscowtimes.com/news/the-kremlin-is-launching-a-news-site-for-teenagers-59508.

42 Эхо Москвы, "Москвичам предложили поучаствовать в митинге-концерте в поддержку Владимира Путина за деньги", Эхо Москвы (28 February 2018), https://echo.msk.ru/news/2156366-echo.html.

43 *Kommersant*, "Избирателей зазывают на выборы квартирами и машинами", *Kommersant* (8 September 2017) https://www.kommersant.ru/doc/3404345?tw.

44 https://www.rferl.org/a/1079601.html.

45 Ruben Enikolopov, Vasily Korovkin, Maria Petrova, Konstantin Sonin and Alexei Zakharov, 'Field Experiment Estimate of Electoral Fraud in Russian Parliamentary Elections'. Proceedings of the National Academy of Sciences (PNAS) 110, no. 2 (8 January 2013): 448–52, http://www.pnas.org/content/110/2/448.

For extensive insights into the inner workings of Russia's upper echelons of power, I highly recommend Alena V. Ledeneva's *Can Russia Modernise? Sistema, Power Networks and Informal Governance* (Cambridge: Cambridge University Press, 2013), and for insights into Putin's post-2012 crackdowns, Marc Bennetts' *I'm Going to Ruin Their Lives: Inside Putin's War on Russia's Opposition* (London: Oneworld, 2016).

46 Associated Press, 'Putin: Soviet Collapse a "genuine tragedy", NBC News (25 April 2005), http://www.nbcnews.com/id/7632057/ns/world_news/t/putin-soviet-collapse-genuine-tragedy/#.WpcWILMQ9dg.

47 TASS, 'Putin Confesses He Would Like To Prevent USSR Breakup If He Could', TASS (3 March 2018), http://tass.com/politics/992609.

48 NATO, 'Bucharest Summit Declaration', NATO Official Texts (3 April 2008), https://www.nato.int/cps/ua/natohq/official_texts_8443.htm.

49 Robin Emmott and Sabine Sebold, 'NATO Split on Message to Send Georgia on Membership Hopes', Reuters (27 November 2015), https://www.reuters.com/article/us-nato-georgia/nato-split-on-message-to-send-georgia-on-membership-hopes-idUSKBN0TG1HP20151127. However, NATO coordinators have stated there are elements of discretion and case-by-case decision making. For more on the 'myth' of NATO accession under occupation see Ira Louis Straus http://www.atlantic-community.org/-/the-myth-that-ukraine-cannot-join-nato-while-russia-occupies-some-of-its-territo-1.

50 Lauren Carroll, 'Obama: US Spends More on Military than next 8 Nations Combined', Politifact (Poynter Institute) (13 January 2016), http://www.politifact.com/truth-o-meter/statements/2016/jan/13/barack-obama/obama-us-spends-more-military-next-8-nations-combi/.

51 https://data.worldbank.org/indicator/MS.MIL.XPND.GD.ZS?end=2016&start=2016&view=bar.

52 Olga Dzyubenko, '"Mission Accomplished" for U.S. Air Base in pro-Moscow Kyrgyzstan', Reuters (6 March 2014), https://www.reuters.com/article/us-kyrgyzstan-usa-base/mission-accomplished-for-u-s-air-base-in-pro-moscow-kyrgyzstan-idUSBREA251SA20140306. Former US Ambassador to Russia Michael McFaul suggested that money had changed hands between Russian and Kyrgyz politicians. However, in the article in question he perhaps mistakenly referred to an old president ousted in 2010, as opposed to the current president (who left office in 2017), https://www.foreignaffairs.com/articles/eastern-europe-caucasus/2014-10-17/faulty-powers.

53 Svetlana Savranskaya and Tom Blanton, 'NATO Expansion: What Gorbachev Heard' (12 December 2017), https://nsarchive.gwu.edu/briefing-book/russia-programs/2017-12-12/nato-expansion-what-gorbachev-heard-western-leaders-early.

54 https://www.unian.info/politics/10012331-lavrov-blames-nato-for-russian-aggression-in-ukraine.html.

55 Pavel Palazhchenko, Facebook post (9 March 2018), https://www.facebook.com/pavel.palazhchenko/posts/1599564853496784.

56 Daniel Treisman, 'Why Putin Took Crimea: The Gambler in the Kremlin', *Foreign Affairs*, 95:47 (2016): 47.

57 John J. Mearsheimer, 'Why the Ukraine Crisis is the West's Fault: The Liberal Delusions That Provoked Putin', *Foreign Affairs* (September/October 2014), https://www.foreignaffairs.com/articles/russia-fsu/2014-08-18/why-ukraine-crisis-west-s-fault.

58 TASS, 'Russia's Top Brass Sets Up Heliport in Gulf of Finland', TASS (7 August 2019), https://tass.com/defense/1072318.

59 Shaun Walker, 'Ukraine's EU Trade Deal Will Be Catastrophic, Says Russia', *Guardian* (22 September 2013), https://www.theguardian.com/world/2013/sep/22/ukraine-european-union-trade-russia.

60 Roland Oliphant, 'Viktor Yanukovych leaves behind palace monument to greed and corruption', *Daily Telegraph* (23 February 2014), https://www.telegraph.co.uk/news/worldnews/europe/ukraine/10657109/Viktor-Yanukovych-leaves-behind-palace-monument-to-greed-and-corruption.html.

61 https://www.svoboda.org/a/27483054.html; Фон Эггерт, Константин, 'Провидец Из Вильнюса'. *New Times* (17 October 2016), https://newtimes.ru/articles/detail/116605/.

62 http://lurkmore.to/%D0%9F%D1%80%D0%B8%D0%B1%D0%B0%D0%BB%D1%82%D0%B8%D0%BA%D0%B0.

63 TASS, 'About 1,000 in Central Riga Rally Against Reform of Russian-language Schools', TASS (24 February 2018), http://tass.com/society/991446.

64 Victor Mizin, phone call with Aliide Naylor (15 February 2018).

65 Levada, 'в основном хорошо, Эстония, ЛАТВИЯ И ЛИТВА', Levada (16 September 2007) ЛАТВИЯ И ЛИТВА.

66 Anastasia Mironova, 'Они постоянно говорят о еде', Gazeta.ru (8 September 2017), https://www.gazeta.ru/comments/column/mironova/10874966.shtml?updated.

67 Aliide Naylor, survey (7 February 2018).

68 Aliide Naylor, survey respondents #10 and #11 (2017).

69 Email to Aliide Naylor (7 January 2018).

70 Aliide Naylor, survey respondent #10 (12 February 2018).

71 Носович, Александр, 'Директор ВЦИОМ: в странах Балтии боятся говорить о советском прошлом'. RuBaltic.Ru (28 January 2014), https://www.rubaltic.ru/article/obrazovanie-i-nayka/direktor-vtsiom-v-stranakh-baltii-boyatsya-govorit-o-sovetskom-proshlom28012014/.

72 Nikolai Mezhevich, 'Russia and the Baltic States: Some Results and a Few Perspectives', *Baltic Region* 2:24 (2015), https://cyberleninka.ru/article/n/russia-and-the-baltic-states-some-results-and-a-few-perspectives.

73 Aliide Naylor, survey respondent #19 (February 2018).

74 Aliide Naylor, survey respondents #10, #6, #3 (February 2018).

75 Aliide Naylor, survey Q7, all respondents (February 2018).

76 Tamara Guzenkova et al., "Политика Евросоюза в отношении стран постсоветского пространства в контексте евразийской интеграции", *Perspektivy* (8 July 2015), http://www.perspektivy.info/rus/desk/politika_jevrosojuza_v_otnoshenii_stran_postsovetskogo_prostranstva_v_kontekste_jevrazijskoj_integracii_2015-07-08.htm.

77 Алексей Гусев, 'Историк: стать независимой Литве подсказали в Москве', RuBaltic.ru (12 March 2018), https://www.rubaltic.ru/article/politika-i-obshchestvo/05022018-litva-vmeshivaetsya-v-rossiyskie-vybory/.

78 Oleg Matsnev, 'Aides to Russian Opposition Leader Sentenced to Jail', *New York Times* (31 January 2018), https://www.nytimes.com/2018/01/31/world/europe/navalny-russia-aides-jail.html.

Александр Носович, 'Литва вмешивается в российские выборы'. RuBaltic.Ru (5 February 2018), https://www.rubaltic.ru/article/politika-i-obshchestvo/05022018-litva-vmeshivaetsya-v-rossiyskie-vybory/.

79 Masha Lipman, 'Constrained or Irrelevant: The Media in Putin's Russia', *Current History* (October 2005), http://carnegieendowment.org/files/CurHistLipman.pdf.

80 Georgy Bovt, 'After Surkov', *Moscow Times* (15 May 2013), https://themoscowtimes.com/articles/after-surkov-24031.

81 Tim Hains, 'BBC's Adam Curtis On The "Contradictory Vaudeville" of Post-Modern Politics', RealClear Politics (31 December 2014), https://www.realclearpolitics.com/video/2016/10/12/bbcs_adam_curtis_how_propaganda_turned_russian_politics_into_a_circus.html.

82 Zoya Svetova, 'Политтехнолог всея Руси: Владислав Сурков – человек с тысячью лиц', *New Times* (7 March 2011), https://newtimes.ru/articles/detail/35589.

83 https://generationp.themoscowtimes.com/kirill/.

84 Maxim Ivanov, 'Телевидение выходит из поля зрения' Kommersant (16 December 2015), http://www.kommersant.ru/doc/2878258.

85 Victor Mizin, phone call with Aliide Naylor (15 February 2018).

86 Россия 24, 'Russian Forecaster Says Weather is "excellent" for Bombing Syria – Video', *Guardian* (5 October 2015), https://www.theguardian.com/world/video/2015/oct/05/russian-forecaster-says-weather-is-excellent-for-bombing-syria-video.

87 Andrei Arkhangelsky, "Роднее некуда", Colta.ru (15 April 2015), http://www.colta.ru/articles/media/7020.

88 European Endowment for Democracy (EED), 'Bringing Plurality and Balance to the Russian Language Media – Final Recommendation' (EED) (n.d.), https://www.democracyendowment.eu/news/bringing-plurality-1/.

89 https://www.rubaltic.ru/article/politika-i-obshchestvo/01032018-istoriya-uspekha-pribaltiki-evropeyskoe-liderstvo-po-ubiystvam/.

90 Alexey Gusev, 'сторик: стать независимой Литве подсказали в Москве', RuBaltic (12 March 2018), https://www.rubaltic.ru/article/politika-i-obshchestvo/12032018-istorik-za-postsovetskoe-vremya-u-litvy-ne-bylo-printsipialnogo-ryvka/.

91 Valerie Sperling, *Sex, Politics, and Putin: Political Legitimacy in Russia* (Oxford: Oxford University Press, 2015), 192.

92 Paul Saunders, 'Sergey Lavrov: The Interview', *The National Interest* (29 March 2017), http://nationalinterest.org/feature/sergey-lavrov-the-interview-19940?page=show.

93 Ibid.

94 Interfax.ru, 'Генпрокуратура РФ проверит законность признания независимости республик Прибалтики', Interfax.ru (30 June 2015), http://www.interfax.ru/russia/450574.

95 Aliide Naylor, survey response #6 (8 February 2018).

96 Sergey Rekeda, email to Aliide Naylor (8 February 2018).

97 Viktor Denisenko, 'The Basic Concepts of the Baltic States Image in the Russian Periodical Press after the Collapse of the Soviet Union (1991–2009), *Journalism and Research*, 8 (7 December 2015): 119.

98 Ibid., 122–4.

99 https://www.youtube.com/watch?v=YRLAjR3-Ax4.

100 https://twitter.com/Alexey__Kovalev/status/914782525502914560.

101 Aliide Naylor, survey respondent #5 (7 February 2018).

102 Generation P project (The Moscow Times, 'Ira', The Moscow Times: 'Generation P' (2018), https://generationp.themoscowtimes.com/ira/)

4 Baltic Russians

1 Editors and staff, 'Дорогим Читателям От Дорогой Редакции (Group Statement)', Lenta.ru (12 March 2014), https://lenta.ru/info/posts/statement/.

2   Ibid.

3   Meduza, 'Welcome to Meduza Russia's Top News and Reporting, in English', Meduza (2 February 2015), https://meduza.io/en/feature/2015/02/02/welcome-to-meduza. Даниил Туровский, 'Грузить по полной программе Зачем госкорпорации понадобилась система для организации DDoS-атак. Репортаж Даниила Туровского', Meduza (3 September 2015), https://meduza.io/feature/2015/09/03/gruzit-po-polnoy-programme.

4   Ivan Kolpakov, interview with Aliide Naylor (20 July 2017).

5   Vsevolod Chernozub, interview with Aliide Naylor (13 July 2017).

6   Vitaly Mansky, interview with Aliide Naylor (2 August 2017). Russian use of armed forces abroad only needs approval from the Federation Council.

7   TASS, 'СМИ: у семьи Грудинина имеется недвижимость в Латвии", TASS (20 February 2018), http://tass.ru/politika/4974577 (also https://vk-smi.ru/politika/pavel-grudinin-podtverdil-chto-ego-syn-imeet-nedvijimost-v-latvii/).

8   Associated Press, 'Russia's leading environmentalist flees to Estonia', *Guardian* (20 April 2015), https://www.theguardian.com/environment/2015/apr/20/russias-leading-environmentalist-flees-to-estonia.

9   Richard Martyn-Hemphill, 'Russia's Dissident Poets Society'. Politico Europe (26 December 2015), https://www.politico.eu/article/russias-dissident-poets-society-latvia-russian-culture/.

10   Татьяна Вольтская, 'В Санкт-Петербурге журналиста Романа Захарова не отключат от "прослушки"', Радио Свобода (19 August 2016), https://www.svoboda.org/a/27933969.html.

11   Aleksandr Morozov, correspondence with Aliide Naylor (26 January 2019).

12   Rémy Rouillard, 'Between East and West is North: The Loyalties and Allegiances of Russian Authors and Painters Living in EU Estonia', *Journal of Multilingual and Multicultural Development*, 26:5 (2005): 397.

13   Ilya Varmalov, 'Ивангород – Нарва: Евросоюз На Том Берегу'. Varlamov.ru (21 June 2017), https://varlamov.ru/2434012.html.

14   Calculations from Statistics Estonia: http://pub.stat.ee/px-web.2001/Dialog/varval.asp?ma=PO0222&path=../I_Databas/Population/01Population_indicators_and_composition/04Population_figure_and_composition/&lang=1.

15   Ivan Lavrentiev, 'Discussions about Narva's Autonomy are Dangerous', Rus.Postimees.ee (29 June 2017), https://rus.postimees.ee/4162273/ivan-lavrentev-mihkelyu-muttyu-razgovory-ob-avtonomii-narvy-opasny.

16   Sergei Stepanov, 'Krenholm Plans More Layoffs', *Baltic Times* (12 February 2004), https://www.baltictimes.com/news/articles/9459/.

17   Helen Wright, 'Narva is Aiming to Become European Capital of Culture in 2024'. *Estonian World* (1 February 2018), http://estonianworld.com/culture/narva-aiming-become-european-capital-culture-2024/.

18 Tacita Vero, 'Many Ethnic Russians in Estonia Are Still Living in Post-Soviet Limbo', *Slate Magazine* (13 March 2017), http://www.slate.com/articles/news_and_politics/roads/2017/03/many_ethnic_russians_in_estonia_have_gray_passports_live_in_legal_limbo.html.

19 Novaya Gazeta, Чемодан, вокзал, и обратно, https://www.novayagazeta.ru/articles/2015/02/06/62945-chemodan-151-vokzal-133-i-obratno.

20 SARGS.LV, 'Drošības un stratēģiskās pētniecības centrs: Krievijas ietekme Latvijā ir ierobežota', SARGS (10 June 2016), http://www.sargs.lv/Viedokli/2016/06/20-01.

21 Reuters, 'Disquiet in Baltics Over Sympathies of Russian Speakers', Reuters (24 March 2014), https://www.reuters.com/article/us-ukraine-crisis-russia-insight/disquiet-in-baltics-over-sympathies-of-russian-speakers-idUSBREA2K07S20140324.

22 Ammon Cheskin, 'Identity and Integration of Russian Speakers in the Baltic States: A Framework for Analysis', *Ethnopolitics* 14:1 (January 2015): 3, http://eprints.gla.ac.uk/95091/1/95091.pdf.

23 International Centre for Defence and Security, 'Estonia's "Virtual Russian World"': The Influence of Russian Media on Estonia's Russian Speakers', *Eesti* (October 2015): 6.

24 Reuters, 'Disquiet in Baltics over sympathies of Russian speakers'.

25 Ibid.

26 EurAsia Daily (EAD), 'By denying visa-free entry to Baltic non-citizens, Russia is narrowing the Russian world', EurAsia Daily (1 September 2016), https://eadaily.com/en/news/2016/09/01/by-denying-visa-free-entry-to-baltic-non-citizens-russia-is-narrowing-the-russian-world.

27 Leonid Rybakovsky and Sergey Ryazantsev, 'International Migration in the Russian Federation', United Nations Expert Group Meeting on International Migration and Development (5 July 2005): 7, http://www.un.org/en/development/desa/population/events/pdf/expert/8/P11_Rybakovsky&Ryazantsev.pdf.

28 Lydia Lamberty, 'Explaining Baltic Migration After EU Accession: Determinants and Consequences', Lunds Universitet (December 2015): 13, https://www.ehl.lu.se/media/ehl/snee/papers/lamberty.pdf.

29 Minorities at Risk Project, 'Assessment for Russians in Lithuania', University of Maryland (31 December 2006), http://www.mar.umd.edu/assessment.asp?groupId=36802.

30 Stanisław Tarasiewicz, 'Rosjanie Kłajpedy również chcą podwójnych nazw ulic', *Kurier Wilenski* (30 January 2013), http://kurierwilenski.lt/2013/01/30/rosjanie-klajpedy-rowniez-chca-podwojnych-nazw-ulic/.

31 Luke Harding, 'Latvia: Russia's Playground for Business, Politics – and Crime', *The Guardian* (23 January 2013), https://www.theguardian.com/world/2013/jan/23/latvia-russian-playground. Jakobsons has interesting history himself kompromat.lv published private correspondence between Nils Ushakov and RU embassy, litigation ensued. He was cleared in 2016. LETA, 'Jakobsons is Cleared of All Charges in Criminal Case about Ushakov's e-Mail Correspondence', *Baltic News Network – News from Latvia, Lithuania, Estonia* (20 September 2016), http://bnn-news.com/jakobsons-is-cleared-of-all-charges-in-criminal-case-about-ushakov-s-e-mail-correspondence-151485.

32 Inga Springe and Sanita Jemberga, 'Russians Moving to Latvia: Dream or Nightmare?' OCCRP (12 March 2015), https://www.occrp.org/en/investigations/3754-russians-moving-to-latvia-dream-or-nightmare.

33 David Crouch, 'Russian buyers have deserted Latvia's high-end property market', *The Financial Times* (13 April 2015), https://www.ft.com/content/6b06883c-d932-11e4-a8f1-00144feab7de.

34 Bernhard Loew, interview Aliide Naylor (21 July 2017).

35 Re:Baltica, 'Who Has a Second Base in Latvia', Re:Baltica (22 February 2015), https://en.rebaltica.lv/2015/02/who-has-a-second-base-in-latvia/.

36 RBC, 'В Лондоне Исчезла Жена Леонида Рожецкина', RBC (23 September 2008), https://www.rbc.ru/society/23/09/2008/5703cf1c9a79473dc814923c.

37 Ibid.

38 Max Delany, 'Latvia Police Say Blood Is Rozhetskin's', *The Moscow Times* (26 March 2008), http://old.themoscowtimes.com/sitemap/free/2008/3/article/latvia-police-say-blood-is-rozhetskins/361426.html.

39 Kirill Galetski, 'Russian-American media investor missing', *Hollywood Reporter* (27 March 2008), https://www.hollywoodreporter.com/news/russian-american-media-investor-missing-108022.

40 Talis Saule Archdeacon, 'Intrigue Surrounding Missing Businessman Deepens', *Baltic Times* (3 April 2008), https://www.baltictimes.com/news/articles/20131/.

41 Martin Tomkinson and Cole Moreton, 'The Missing Multi-Millionaire: A Cut-Throat Mystery for the New Cold War', *Independent* (10 May 2008), http://www.independent.co.uk/news/world/europe/the-missing-multi-millionaire-a-cut-throat-mystery-for-the-new-cold-war-825920.html.

42 Mark Galeotti, 'Crimintern: How the Kremlin Uses Russia's Criminal Networks in Europe', ECR Policy Brief (April 2017), http://www.ecfr.eu/page/-/ECFR208_-_CRIMINTERM_-_HOW_RUSSIAN_ORGANISED_CRIME_OPERATES_IN_EUROPE02.pdf.

43 OCCRP, 'Latvian Bank Was Laundering Tool' https://www.reportingproject.net/therussianlaundromat/latvian-bank-was-laundering-tool.php.

44 OCCRP, "The Russian Laundromat Exposed", https://www.occrp.org/en/laundromat/the-russian-laundromat-exposed/.

45 https://www.occrp.org/assets/laundromat/laundromat-infographic.png.

46 Amnesty International, 'Estonia. Linguistic minorities in Estonia: Discrimination must end', 18. https://www.amnesty.org/download/Documents/76000/eur510022006en.pdf.

47 Ibid.

48 Mart Rannut, 'Estonianization Efforts Post-Independence', in *Multilingualism in Post-Soviet Countries*, ed. Aneta Pavlenko, (Bristol: Multilingual Matters, 2008), 149.

49 Merli Tamtik and Soon Young Jang, 'Administering Higher Education Policies in the Baltic States: Balancing the Language Demands in Multilingual Society', *Journal of Multilingual and Multicultural Development* (2018): 3.

50 Ibid., 4.

51 Ibid., 3.

52 Meduza, 'Riga Mayor is Fined for Using Russian on Social Media', Meduza (27 July 2016), https://meduza.io/en/news/2016/07/27/latvian-mayor-is-fined-for-using-russian-on-social-media.

53 Ibid.

54 Aneta Pavlenko (ed), *Multilingualism in Post-Soviet Countries*, Bristol: Multilingual Matters (2008), 144.

55 Асадова Наргиз, 'Интервью / Жизнь русских в Литве/Наргиз Асадова', Эхо Москвы (20 August 2013), https://echo.msk.ru/programs/linguafranca/1139146-echo/.

56 Linas Jegelevičius, 'Lithuanian-Russian School Teachers Say Their Schools Are Not Vehicles for Moscow Propaganda', *LT Daily*, DELFI (18 December 2015), http://www.lrt.lt/en/news-in-english/29/122970/lithuanian-russian-school-teachers-say-their-schools-are-not-vehicles-for-moscow-propaganda.

57 Tamtik and Soon Young Jang, 'Administering Higher Education Policies in the Baltic States', 3.

58 Ibid. 10.

59 TASS, 'Latvian Government Endorses Reform of Russian-Language Schools', TASS (23 January 2018), http://tass.com/society/986468.

60 TASS, 'Bill Against Russian Language in Latvian Schools Passed in Second Reading', TASS (9 March 2018), http://tass.com/society/993327.

61 Ammon Cheskin, 'The Discursive Construction of "Russian-speakers": The Russian-Language Media and Demarcated Political Identities in Latvia', in M. Golubeva and R. Gould (eds.), *Shrinking Citizenship: Discursive Practices that Limit Democratic Participation in Latvian Politics* (Amsterdam: Rodopi, 2010), 133–54.

62 Pavlenko (ed.), *Multilingualism in Post-Soviet Countries*, 13.

63 Ammon Cheskin, 'Identity and Integration of Russian speakers in the Baltic States: A framework for analysis', *Ethnopolitics* 14:1 (January 2015): 72–93, https://www.tandfonline.com/doi/abs/10.1080/17449057.2014.933051.

5 The Baltic future

1 Little Big, 'Give Me Your Money' (feat. Tommy Cash), YouTube (9September 2015), https://www.youtube.com/watch?v=2uTMTyqQxl4.

2 Madis Nestor, 'Uus Eesti Biit: Tommy Cash', Müürileht (6 June 2013), http://www.muurileht.ee/uus-eesti-biit-tommy-cash/.

3 Ibid.

4 Joe Zadeh, '"Is this for real?" Meet Tommy Cash, the surreal, post-Soviet rap sensation', *Guardian* (19 June 2017), https://www.theguardian.com/music/2017/jun/19/tommy-cash-surreal-post-soviet-rap-sensation.

5 Whitney Wei, 'Meet "Kanye East," the Estonian Rapper Who Spoofs American Pop Culture', *Vogue* (24 January 2018), https://www.vogue.com/article/tommy-cash-kanye-east-west-estonia-rapper-pussy-money-weed-merch-yeezy-off-white-virgil-abloh-vetements-life-of-pablo-pavel.

6 Aleks Eror, 'Is Post-Soviet Fashion Ethically Problematic?', HighSnobiety (1 February 2017), https://www.highsnobiety.com/2017/02/01/post-soviet-fashion-trend/.

7 LETA/TBT Staff, 'Ambassadors of Baltic States ask French *Le Monde* Paper to Stop Calling Them "Former Soviet republics"', *Baltic Times* (10 September 2017), https://www.baltictimes.com/ambassadors_of_baltic_states_ask_french_le_monde_paper_to_stop_calling_them__former_soviet_republics_/.

8 Rusif Huseynov, 'Baltic States are no longer ex-Soviet', Modern Diplomacy (20 January 2017). *Estonian World*, 'The UN Classifies Estonia as Northern European country', *Estonian World* (8 January 2018).

9 Joe Zadeh, '"Is this for real?" Meet Tommy Cash, the Surreal, Post-Soviet Rap Sensation', *Guardian* (June 19, 2017), https://www.theguardian.com/music/2017/jun/19/tommy-cash-surreal-post-soviet-rap-sensation.

10 Aliide Naylor, 'Tommy Cash's new collaboration with Rick Owens is as horrifying as it is fascinating', i-D (May 30, 2019) https://i-d.vice.com/en_uk/article/nea43q/tommy-cashs-new-collaboration-with-rick-owens-is-as-horrifying-as-it-is-fascinating

11 ERR, 'Security Guards Severely Injured in Shooting in Tallinn's Kopli District', Err.ee (3 July 2017), https://news.err.ee/605421/security-guards-severely-injured-in-shooting-in-tallinn-s-kopli-district.

12 Museum of Estonian Architecture, 'Kopli Sonata. The Russo-Baltic Shipyard', Arhitektuurimuuseum (6 May 2017), http://www.arhitektuurimuuseum.ee/en/naitus/kopli-sonata-the-russo-baltic-shipyard/.

13 Susanna Mett, interview with Aliide Naylor (28 August 2017).

14 Taavi Rokka, interview with Aliide Naylor (28 August 2017).

15 ERR, 'Kopli €60 million development finally on', ERR (26 August 2015), https://news.err.ee/116583/kopli-60-million-development-finally-on.

16 Tiit Tammaru, Kadri Leetmaa, Siiri Silm and Rein Ahas, 'Temporal and Spatial Dynamics of the New Residential Areas around Tallinn', *European Planning Studies*, 17:3 (n.d.): 423–39; Kalev Sepp, *The Estonian Green Belt*, Tallinn: The Estonian University of Life Sciences (2011): 13, http://citeseerx. ist.psu.edu/viewdoc/download?doi=10.1.1.465.5277&rep=rep1&type=pdf.

17 Anna Semjonova and Mihkel Kõrvits, interview with Aliide Naylor (28 August 2017). Kõrvits recommended consulting the City of Tallinn who were likely responsible for allocating municipal housing.

18 Sasha Rospopina, 'How Space Exploration Replaced Religion in the USSR', *Calvert Journal* via *Guardian* (17 September 2015), https://www.theguardian. com/world/2015/sep/17/ussr-space-exploration-religion-russia.

19 Aliide Naylor, 'Latvia's Kuš! Comics Turns Ten', *New Eastern Europe* (12 December 2017), http://neweasterneurope.eu/2017/12/12/latvias-kus-comics-turns-ten/.

20 Viktorija Prilenska and Roode Liias, 'Challenges of Recent Participatory Urban Design Practices in Riga', *Procedia Economics and Finance* 21 (1 January 2015): 88–96, https://ac.els-cdn.com/S2212567115001549/1-s2.0-S2212567115001549-main.pdf?_tid=4a5781e3-5199-4ff0-87c7-de2350e9549 b&acdnat=1520264675_8cc0870792d509fe7a20cbfce5f0c7cd.

21 Latvian Ministry of Finance, *Tax System in Latvia* (17 January 2018), http:// www.fm.gov.lv/en/s/taxes/.

22 Jāzeps Bikše, interview with Aliide Naylor (24 July 2017).

23 Andrejs Plakans, 'From a Regional Vernacular to the Language of a State: The Case of Latvian', *International Journal of the Sociology of Language*, 100:101 (1993), http://home.lu.lv/~pva/Sociolingvistika/Plakans_From%20a%20 regional%20vernacular_1993.pdf.

24 Marek Tamm, Linda Kaljundi and Carsten Selch Jensen (eds.), *Crusading and Chronicle Writing on the Medieval Baltic Frontier: A Companion to the Chronicle of Henry of Livonia* (Farnham: Ashgate, 2011), 419–23.

25 Rowena Smith, 'Tabula Rasa review – ambitious staged work suffused with Arvo Pärt's mystical music', *Guardian* (10 November 2017), https://www. theguardian.com/music/2017/nov/10/tabula-rasa-review-arvo-part-traverse-theatre.

26 Elisabeth Braw, 'Latvian Singers, Conductors Stealing Global Spotlight, Thanks To Soviet Legacy' *RFE/RL* (16 August 2015), https://www.rferl.org/a/ latvia-music-education-spotlight-singers-conductors/27191520.html.

27 Kristine Opolais, interview with Aliide Naylor (27 July 2017).

28 Katharine Schwab, 'A Country Created Through Music', *The Atlantic* (12 November 2015), https://www.theatlantic.com/international/archive/2015/11/ estonia-music-singing-revolution/415464/. This is a stupid headline though – the country already existed, and the 'west' never recognized the Baltics as part of the USSR so I wouldn't take these headline / blurb claims particularly seriously.

29 Kristine Opolais, interview with Aliide Naylor (27 July 2017).

30 Urve Lippus, 'Transformation of an Institution – the First Soviet Estonian Song Festival', *Musik in Diktaturen des 20. Jahrhunderts* – Internationales Symposium an der Bergischen Universität Wupperta (2006): 1–5.

31 Ibid., 11, 13.

32 Lennart Meri, 'President of the Republic at the XXIII All-Estonian Song Festival on July 3, 1999', *Speeches of the President of the Republic, 1992–2001* (3 July 1999), https://vp1992-2001.president.ee/eng/k6ned/K6ne.asp?ID=4285.

33 Hilary Davidson and Ieva Pīgozne, 'Archaeological Dress and Textiles in Latvia from the Seventh to Thirteenth Centuries: Research, Results, and Reconstructions', *Medieval Clothing and Textiles* (2010): 32.

34 Michael Strmiska, 'The Music of the Past in Modern Baltic Paganism', *Nova Religio: The Journal of Alternative and Emergent Religions*, 8:3 (March 2005), https://doi.org/10.1525/nr.2005.8.3.39.

35 Davidson and Pīgozne, 'Archaeological Dress and Textiles in Latvia': 5.

36 Strmiska, 'The Music of the Past in Modern Baltic Paganism'.

37 Epp Annus, 'Layers of Colonial Rule in the Baltics: Nation-Building, the Soviet Rule and the Affectivity of a Nation' (2013), http://www.eki.ee/km/annus/2013%20Bremen%20Layers%20of%20Colonial%20Rule%20in%20the%20Baltics%20Feb11.pdf.

38 Arturas Bumšteinas, Skype interview with Aliide Naylor (6 March 2018).

39 *Kauno Diena*, '"Chorų karus" laimėjo Lietuvos aklųjų chora', *Kaunu Diena* (5 March 2015), http://kauno.diena.lt/naujienos/laisvalaikis-ir-kultura/zvaigzdes-ir-pramogos/choru-karus-laimejo-lietuvos-akluju-choras-688912.

40 Aliide Naylor, 'Soviet power gone, Baltic countries' historic pagan past re-emerges', Religion News Service (31 May 2019), https://religionnews.com/2019/05/31/with-soviet-power-gone-baltic-countries-historic-pagan-past-re-emerges/.

41 Janis Cepītis and Lilija Jakubenoka, 'Mythical Creatures, The Making of Wearing Apparel and the Landscape', *Archaeological Baltica* (12 June 2013): 24–44, http://journals.ku.lt/index.php/AB/article/view/17/pdf.

42 Juris Urtāns and Guntis Eniņš, 'Latvian sandstone caves as cultural phenomena', *JBS* 32:1 (Spring 2001): 95.

43 Aija Austruma, 'Zinību pilni meži: Pokaiņu gadatirgus fotomirkļos', delfi.lv (18 September 2017), http://www.delfi.lv/orakuls/biblioteka/49249359_zinibu-pilni-mezi-pokainu-gadatirgus-fotomirklos.

44 Kevin O'Connor, *Culture and Customs of the Baltic States* (Westport: Greenwood Publishing Group), 38.

45 Aldis Pūtelis, interview with Aliide Naylor (20 May 2019).

46 *Estonian World*, 'Estonian beliefs and rituals carried on by Jaanipäev', *Estonian World* (23 June 2013), http://estonianworld.com/life/it-is-this-time-of-the-year-again-jaanipaev/.

47 Ergo-Hart Västrik, 'In Search of Genuine Religion: The Contemporary Estonian Maausulised Movement and Nationalist Discourse', in *Contemporary Pagan and Native Faith Movements in Europe: Colonialist and Nationalist Impulses,* Kathryn Rountree (ed), EASA Series, vol. 26. New York: Berghahn, 2015.

48 Monika Hanley, 'Baltic diaspora and the rise of Neo-Paganism', *Baltic Times* (28 October 2010), https://www.baltictimes.com/news/articles/27265/.

49 Fiona Zublin, 'Why Folk Religions are Booming in Lithuania', OZY (14 February 2018), https://www.ozy.com/fast-forward/why-folk-religions-are-booming-in-lithuania/83397.

50 Hanley, 'Baltic diaspora and the rise of Neo-Paganism'.

51 Kaarina Aitamurto and Scott Simpson, 'The Dievturi Movement in Latvia as Invention of Tradition' in *Modern Pagan and Native Faith Movements in Central and Eastern Europe* (London: Routledge, 2013), 94–6.

52 Andrus Kivirähk, *The Man Who Spoke Snakish* (London: Grove Press UK), 25.

53 Ibid., 341.

54 White Guide, 'There is no better time than NOW to visit Baltic restaurants', White Guide Nordic (29 November 2017) http://whiteguide-nordic.com/nyheter/there-is-no-better-time-than-now-to-visit-baltic-restaurants.

55 Ibid.

56 http://www.livingit.euronews.com/2017/12/18/the-new-latvian-cuisine-heroes.

57 Anders Husa, 'Meet the Future of Estonian Cooking', Andershusa (blog) (13 October 2017), https://andershusa.com/chef-orm-oja-noa-chefs-hall-tallinn-estonia-meet-the-future-of-estonian-cooking.

58 Reuters, 'Chef Martins Ritins Brings Top Cuisine to Small Latvia', Reuters (9 December 2008), https://uk.reuters.com/article/us-food-chefs-ritins/chef-martins-ritins-brings-top-cuisine-to-small-latvia-idUKTRE4B82BY20081209; http://www.livingit.euronews.com/2017/12/18/the-new-latvian-cuisine-heroes.

59 Aija Kaukule, 'Mārtiņš Rītiņš: "Joprojām neesmu piepildījis visu, ko vēlējos, kad atbraucu uz Latviju!"', LA.LV (15 November 2018), http://kokteilis.la.lv/martins-ritins-joprojam-neesmu-piepildijis-visu-ko-velejos-kad-atbraucu-uz-latviju.

60 InterNations, 'Digital Life Abroad', The Expat Insider 2018 survey report (May 2019), https://cms-internationsgmbh.netdna-ssl.com/sites/default/files/2019-05/2019-05-22_Digital_Life_Abroad_Report_by_InterNations.pdf.

61 Matt Simon, 'San Francisco Tries to Ban Delivery Robots Before They Flatten Someone's Toes'. *Wired* (17 May 2017), https://www.wired.com/2017/05/san-francisco-wants-ban-delivery-robots-squash-someones-toes/.

62 Michael Laris, 'Driverless delivery robots could be hitting D.C. sidewalks soon', *Washington Post* (23 March 2016), https://www.washingtonpost.com/

news/dr-gridlock/wp/2016/03/23/driverless-delivery-robots-could-be-hitting-d-c-sidewalks-soon.

63 *Mercury News*, 'Sidewalk Robots Smacked down in S.F. Coming to San Jose', *Mercury News* (blog) (16 April 2018), https://www.mercurynews.com/2018/04/16/sidewalk-robots-smacked-down-in-s-f-coming-to-san-jose-company/.

64 Jill Duffy, 'Toggl', *PC Mag UK* (7 February 2018), http://uk.pcmag.com/software/93243/review/toggl.

65 Iris Leung, 'This Tech Company Uses Remote Work To Win The War For Talent', *Forbes* (20 July 2017), https://www.forbes.com/sites/irisleung/2017/07/20/this-tech-company-uses-remote-work-to-win-the-war-for-talent/#78b3cbd23624.

66 Zach Marzouk, 'Ex-Estonian president: Other countries staying silent over digital ID flaws', *ITPRO* (14 November 2017), http://www.itpro.co.uk/security/29898/ex-estonian-president-other-countries-staying-silent-over-digital-id-flaws.

67 Dan Peleschuk, 'The Migrant Leading Lithuania's Fintech Sector', OZY (24 November 2017), http://www.ozy.com/rising-stars/the-migrant-leading-lithuanias-fintech-sector/81467.

68 Invest Lithuania, 'Lithuania Clocks 35 New Fintech Companies in 2017', Invest Lithuania (blog) (2018), https://investlithuania.com/wp-content/uploads/2018/02/Lithuanian-Fintech-Report-2017.pdf.

69 Ibid.

70 The Baltic Course, 'Cheaper business opportunities probably lead to Barclays' decision in Lithuania', The Baltic Course (23 April 2018), http://www.baltic-course.com/eng/Technology/?doc=139500.

71 Pew Research Center, 'Eastern and Western Europeans Differ on Importance of Religion, Views of Minorities, and Key Social Issues' (29 October 2018), http://www.pewforum.org/2018/10/29/eastern-and-western-europeans-differ-on-importance-of-religion-views-of-minorities-and-key-social-issues/.

72 Eurostat, 'Household spending on alcohol close to €130 billion', Eurostat (4 December 2017), http://ec.europa.eu/eurostat/web/products-eurostat-news/-/DDN-20171204-1.

73 Ugnė Grigaitė and Mažvydas Karalius, 'Intymaus partnerio smurtavimo apraiškos Lietuvoje – moterų perspektyva', Žmogaus teisių stebėjimo institutas (2018), https://hrmi.lt/wp-content/uploads/2018/10/Intymaus-partnerio-smurtavimo-aprai%C5%A1kos_%C5%BDTSI.pdf.

74 *Passport Magazine*, 'Baltic Seeing: Estonia, Latvia, Lithuania' (n.d.), https://passportmagazine.com/baltic-seeing-estonia-latvia-lithuania/.

75 J. Lester Feder, 'Estonia Becomes First Former Soviet Country To Recognize Same-Sex Partnerships', Buzzfeed News (9 October 2014), https://www.

buzzfeed.com/lesterfeder/estonia-poised-to-become-first-former-soviet-country-to-reco?utm_term=.ynbVb31OE#.me16NV95a.

76 *Estonian World*, 'Estonian drinks maker stands up for LGBTQ rights', *Estonian World* (6 October 2017), http://estonianworld.com/business/estonian-drinks-maker-stands-lgbtq-rights/.

77 Dan Allen, 'Bold Art Helps Move the Needle on LGBTQ Acceptance in the Baltics', NBC Out (29 September 2016), https://www.nbcnews.com/feature/nbc-out/bold-art-helps-move-needle-lgbtq-acceptance-baltics-n654456.

78 *The Economist*, 'A Minister Comes Out' *The Economist* (12 November 2014), https://www.economist.com/blogs/easternapproaches/2014/11/latvia-and-gay-rights.

79 Aušra Kaziliūnaitė 'Holiday makeup' in *The Moon is a Pill* (translated by Rimas Uzgiris), (Swansea: Parthian Books, 2018), 24.

80 Natalia Antelava, 'On the Frontiers of the "Russian World"', Coda Story (blog) (17 January 2016), https://codastory.com/lgbt-crisis/frontiers-of-the-russian-world.

6 The Baltics in Europe

1 Katrina Manson, 'Why does Donald Trump treat Iran differently to North Korea?' *Financial Times* (14 June 2018), https://www.ft.com/content/dac14fb4-6f47-11e8-92d3-6c13e5c92914.

2 Tim Shipman, *Fall Out: A Year of Political Mayhem* (London: William Collins, 2017), 107–8.

3 Uri Friedman, 'Can America and Russia Both Be Great Again?' *The Atlantic* (20 November 2016), https://www.theatlantic.com/international/archive/2016/11/trump-russia-policy/507587/.

4 Carol Morello, 'Top diplomat for European affairs resigns from State Department', *Washington Post* (22 January 2019), https://www.washingtonpost.com/world/national-security/top-diplomat-for-european-affairs-resigns-from-state-department/2019/01/22/ada80048-1e3f-11e9-8b59-0a28f2191131_story.html?noredirect=on&utm_term=.0e4e72f0121c.

5 Harry Webers, 'Van Hanzepaper naar Hanzepep[p]er', *Die Evolutie Gids* (29 December 2018), https://evolutiegids.nl/harry-webers-hanzepaper/.

6 Caroline de Gruyter, 'Waarom Brexit tot meer cohesie leidt', NRC (26 December 2018), https://www.nrc.nl/nieuws/2018/12/26/waarom-brexit-tot-meer-cohesie-leidt-a3127047.

7 Natalie Righton, 'Sie Dhian Ho: "Rutte heeft meer nodig dan de zeven dwergen"', *de Volkskrant* (7 September 2018), https://www.volkskrant.nl/nieuws-achtergrond/sie-dhian-ho-rutte-heeft-meer-nodig-dan-de-zeven-dwergen-~bea8ddb3/.

8 Andreas Noll and Ralf Bosen, 'Merkel and Macron Sign Treaty of Aachen to Revive EU', dw.com (22 January 2019), https://www.dw.com/en/merkel-and-macron-sign-treaty-of-aachen-to-revive-eu/a-47172186; Oliver Moody, 'Merkel and Macron sign Aachen treaty to protect ideals of Europe', *The Times* (22 January 2019), https://www.thetimes.co.uk/edition/news/merkel-and-macron-sign-aachen-treaty-to-protect-ideals-of-europe-md902t2kq.

9 Celestine Bohlen, 'Russia Cuts Gas Supply to Estonia in a Protest', *The New York Times* (26 June 1993), http://www.nytimes.com/1993/06/26/world/russia-cuts-gas-supply-to-estonia-in-a-protest.html.

10 Andrius Sytas, 'Baltic States Agree to Link Their Power Grids to EU Via Poland', VOA (8 May 2017), https://af.reuters.com/article/worldNews/idAFKBN1841T4.

11 Gazprom, 'Underground Gas Storage', Gazprom (2003–19), http://www.gazprom.com/about/production/underground-storage/.

12 BNN, 'EC Finances Synchronization of Baltic and European Power Grids', *Baltic News Network* (24 January 2019), https://bnn-news.com/ec-finances-synchronization-of-baltic-and-european-power-grids-196468.

13 Isabel Gorst and Nina Poussenkova, 'Unlocking the assets: energy and the future of central Asia and the Caucasus', Center for International Political Economy and the James A. Baker III Institute for Public Policy Rice University (April 1998), https://www.bakerinstitute.org/media/files/Research/44988762/petroleum-ambassadors-of-russia-state-versus-corporate-policy-in-the-caspian-region.pdf.

14 ERR, 'Gazprom Sells Eesti Gaas Stake to Infortar Subsidiary', ERR (16 May 2016), http://news.err.ee/118163/gazprom-sells-eesti-gaas-stake-to-infortar-subsidiary.

15 The Baltic Course, 'Gazprom regains half of Lithuania's gas market', The Baltic Course (3 January 2017), http://www.baltic-course.com/eng/good_for_business/?doc=126571.

16 Arunas Molis, 'Towards a regional gas market in the Baltic states: Political, economic and legal aspects', *Humanities and Social Sciences Latvia*, 24:1 (Spring–Summer 2016): 92.

17 Reuters, 'Lithuania Receives First LNG from the United States', Reuters (21 August 2017), https://www.reuters.com/article/us-lithuania-lng/lithuania-receives-first-lng-from-the-united-states-idUSKCN1B11BW.

18 Tatiana Romanova, 'LNG in the Baltic sea region in the context of EU-Russian relations', *BSR Policy Briefing* 1 (2015): 24–5.

19 Martin Jirušek and Tomáš Vlček, *Energy Security in Central and Eastern Europe and the Operations of Russian State-Owned Energy Enterprises* (Brno: Masaryk University, 2015).

20 Marcin Goettig and Lidia Kelly, 'U.S. says planned Russian pipeline would threaten European energy security', Reuters (27 January 2018), https://uk.

reuters.com/article/uk-europe-nordstream-usa/u-s-says-planned-russian-pipeline-would-threaten-european-energy-security-idUKKBN1FG0ST.

21 Claudia von Salzen, 'Estonia urges caution on Nord Stream 2 pipeline', *Der Tagesspiegel*, via Euractiv (18 July 2017), https://www.euractiv.com/section/energy/news/estonia-urges-caution-on-nord-stream-2-pipeline/.

22 Goettig and Kelly, 'U.S. says planned Russian pipeline would threaten European energy security'.

23 VOA, 'Opposition to Russia's Nord Stream Pipeline Growing In Eastern Europe', RFE/RL (9 March 2018), https://www.rferl.org/a/opposition-growth-eastern-europe-russia-nord-stream-2-pipeline-germany-baltic-sea-lithuania-estonia-latvia/29087938.html.

24 Andreas Goldthau, 'Assessing Nord Stream 2: regulation, geopolitics and energy security in the EU, Central Eastern Europe and the UK' (July 2016): 6.

25 Olena Zerkal, 'NordStream 2 and Ukraine's and Europe's Interests', 15th YES Annual Meeting (15 September 2018).

26 Sean O'Neill, 'Putin Crony Arkady Rotenberg Loses Right to Secrecy in Britain', *The Times* (24 February 2018), https://www.thetimes.co.uk/article/putin-crony-arkady-rotenberg-loses-right-to-secrecy-in-britain-9gbl8x8rg.

27 Hayla Coynash, 'Putin's New Bridge to Crimea Is Doomed to Collapse', *Newsweek* (13 January 2017), https://www.newsweek.com/putin-bridge-crimea-doomed-collapse-541578. Aleksey Ramm, "Боевые дайверы Росгвардии защитят мост в Крым", *Izvestia* (9 September 2016) https://iz.ru/news/631455.

28 Fraunhofer-Gesellschaft, 'Hazardous Contaminated Sites in the North and the Baltic Sea', phys.org (1 August 2018), https://phys.org/news/2018-08-hazardous-contaminated-sites-north-baltic.html. Espoo, 'ESPOO Report Nord Stream 2', Nord Stream 2 (2017) http://www.envir.ee/sites/default/files/ns2_aruanne_en.pdf).

29 DPA, AFP, Reuters, 'Nord Stream 2: German Environmentalists Sue to Halt Construction of Controversial Gas Pipeline', *Deutsche Welle* (3 July 2018), https://www.dw.com/en/nord-stream-2-german-environmentalists-sue-to-halt-construction-of-controversial-gas-pipeline/a-44507377.

30 Olesya Astakhova and Vera Eckert, 'Nord Stream 2 Pipeline on Track despite Sanctions Risk, Operator Says', Reuters (31 August 2018), https://uk.reuters.com/article/uk-russia-gazprom-nordstream/nord-stream-2-pipeline-on-track-despite-sanctions-risk-operator-says-idUKKCN1LG178.

31 TASS, 'Shell May Invest in Nord Stream-2 to Improve Europe's Energy Security', TASS (2 February 2017), http://tass.com/economy/928641.

32 Stratfor, 'Despite Looming U.S. Sanctions, the Nord Stream 2 Pipeline Will Likely Proceed', Stratfor (17 July 2019), https://worldview.stratfor.com/article/despite-looming-us-sanctions-nord-stream-2-pipeline-will-likely-proceed.

33 Olga Černovaitè, 'Butterfly City: Short Trailer', Vidopress (2016), https://videopress.com/v/WNAZ9B5w.

34 BBC News, 'Chernobyl's Continuing Hazards', BBC (25 April 2006), http://news.bbc.co.uk/1/hi/world/europe/4942828.stm.

35 World Nuclear News, 'Ignalina 2 free of used fuel', WNN (27 February 2018), http://www.world-nuclear-news.org/WR-Ignalina-2-free-of-used-fuel-27021802.html.

36 Interview with anonymous local, Aliide Naylor (July 2017).

37 Rasa Baločkaitė, 'Post-Soviet Transitions of the Planned Socialist Towns: Visaginas, Lithuania', Vytautas Magnus University (n.d.), https://iweb.cerge-ei.cz/pdf/gdn/IRP-cities-post-soviet-transitions-visaginas-balockaite.pdf.

38 Lithuania's Ignalina nuclear power plant passes decommissioning milestone (n.d.), https://www.finchannel.com/business/60005-lithuania-s-ignalina-nuclear-power-plant-passes-decommissioning-milestone.

39 Alexander Grebenkin, and Tatiana Kalinovskaya, 'Belarus nuclear power plant stirs fears in Lithuania', AFP (26 November 2017), https://www.kyivpost.com/world/afp-belarus-nuclear-power-plant-stirs-fears-lithuania.html.

40 Richard Milne and Henry Foy, 'Russian-built nuclear plant revives Chernobyl fears', *Financial Times* (18 September 2017), https://www.ft.com/content/a98322de-96f7-11e7-b83c-9588e51488a0.

41 Grebenkin and Kalinovskaya, 'Belarus nuclear power plant stirs fears in Lithuania'.

42 Aurélien Poissonnier, 'The Baltics: Three Countries, One Economy?' European Commission: Economic Brief 024 (April 2017): 2; 5–6; 7–9.

43 Aldona Jočienė, 'Scandinavian bank subsidiaries in the Baltics: Have they all behaved in a similar way?'', *Intellectual Economics*, 9: 1, (April 2015): 43–54, https://doi.org/10.1016/j.intele.2015.09.002.

44 EWR, 'Remediation of Sillamäe's radioactive tailings pond completed', *Estonian World Review* (11 November 2008), http://www.eesti.ca/remediation-of-sillamaes-radioactive-tailings-pond-completed/print21671.

45 Ibid. More details of the pilot projects can be found here http://www.iaea.org/inis/collection/NCLCollectionStore/_Public/33/032/33032893.pdf#page=363.

46 Ministry of Foreign Affairs of Denmark, 'Baltic Sea Cooperation', Ministry of Foreign Affairs of Denmark, http://um.dk/en/foreign-policy/baltic-sea-cooperation/

47 Swedish Agency for Economic and Regional Growth, 'The Baltic sea region strategy for beginners', Swedish Agency for Economic and Regional Growth (2016), https://www.balticsea-region-strategy.eu/news-room/documents-materials?task=document.viewdoc&id=26.

48 Ilze Šteinfelde, 'Saldā cukura rūgtā cena – ko maksājusi mums ES cukura reforma?' nra.lv (4 October 2017), http://nra.lv/latvija/224383-salda-cukura-rugta-cena-ko-maksajusi-mums-es-cukura-reforma.htm.

49 Isabelle de Pommereau, 'Estonia reaches out to its very own Russians at long last', *Deutsche Welle* (24 February 2018), http://www.dw.com/en/estonia-reaches-out-to-its-very-own-russians-at-long-last/a-42680725.

50 Michael Bröning, 'The Rise of Populism in Europe', *Foreign Affairs* (3 June 2016), https://www.foreignaffairs.com/articles/europe/2016-06-03/rise-populism-europe.

51 http://www.dw.com/en/putins-friends-in-austrias-right-wing-fp%C3%B6-achieve-strong-election-result/a-40960928; https://www.theatlantic.com/international/archive/2017/01/putin-trump-le-pen-hungary-france-populist-bannon/512303/; https://www.theatlantic.com/international/archive/2016/10/trump-putin-alt-right-comintern/506015/; https://www.nbcnews.com/news/world/europe-s-far-right-enjoys-backing-russia-s-putin-n718926.

52 Ilze Balcere, 'Comparing Populist Political Parties in the Baltic States and Western Europe', Paper prepared for the 6th ECPR General Conference in Reykjavik (25–7 August 2011), https://pdfs.semanticscholar.org/8c70/f438122a78d309246930593d40d6ee017053.pdf.

53 *Baltic Times*, 'Incumbent Reform Party wins Estonian parliamentary elections', *Baltic Times* (2 March 2015), https://www.baltictimes.com/incumbent_reform_party_wins_estonian_parliamentary_elections/.

54 Vassilis Petsinis and Stefano Braghiroli, 'Estonia's Populist and Radical Right: How Radical Are They?' openDemocracy (18 December 2018), https://www.opendemocracy.net/can-europe-make-it/vassilis-petsinis-stefano-braghiroli/estonia-s-populist-and-radical-right-how-rad.

55 Vassilis Petsinis, 'Contentious politics in the Baltics: the "new" wave of right-wing populism in Estonia', openDemocracy (28 April 2016), https://www.opendemocracy.net/can-europe-make-it/vassilis-petsinis/contentious-politics-in-baltics-new-wave-of-right-wing-populism.

56 Kristi Raik, 'The Rise of Estonia's Radical Right: To Engage or Not to Engage?' ECFR (15 October 2018), https://www.ecfr.eu/article/commentary_the_rise_of_estonias_radical_right_to_engage_or_not_to_engage.

57 Oxana Antonenko, 'Refugees frustrated and trapped in chilly Baltic states', BBC (4 July 2017), http://www.bbc.co.uk/news/world-europe-40479224.

58 Andrius Sytas and Gederts Gelzis, 'Resettled in the Baltics, refugees flee for wealthier lands', Reuters (28 November 2016), https://www.reuters.com/article/us-europe-migrants-baltics/resettled-in-the-baltics-refugees-flee-for-wealthier-lands-idUSKBN13N0RY.

59 Antonenko, 'Refugees frustrated and trapped in chilly Baltic states'.

60 European Commission. Member States' Support to Emergency Relocation Mechanism (as of 16 February 2018),, https://ec.europa.eu/home-affairs/sites/homeaffairs/files/what-we-do/policies/european-agenda-migration/press-material/docs/state_of_play_-_relocation_en.pdf.

61 LETA/TBT Staff, '17 refugees sent back to Lithuania from other EU countries' (5 March 2018), https://www.baltictimes.com/17_refugees_sent_back_to_lithuania_from_other_eu_countries/.

62 Eero Janson, email to Aliide Naylor (17 September 2015).

63 Tharik Hussain, 'The Amazing Survival of the Baltic Muslims', BBC Magazine (1 January 2016), http://www.bbc.com/news/magazine-35170834.

64 Statistics Latvia, 'ISG01. Area, population density and resident population by statistical region, city and county', http://data.csb.gov.lv/pxweb/en/Sociala/Sociala__ikgad__iedz__iedzskaits/IS0010.px/table/tableViewLayout2/?rxid=a79839fe-11ba-4ecd-8cc3-4035692c5fc8.

65 Statistics Latvia, 'IBG04. International long-term migrants by age and sex', http://data.csb.gov.lv/pxweb/en/Sociala/Sociala__ikgad__iedz__migr/IB0010.px/table/tableViewLayout2/?rxid=a79839fe-11ba-4ecd-8cc3-4035692c5fc8.

66 Gordon F. Sander, 'Latvia, a disappearing nation', *Politico Europe* (5 January 2018), https://www.politico.eu/article/latvia-a-disappearing-nation-migration-population-decline/.

67 Statistics Latvia, 'IBG04. International long-term migrants by age and sex'.

68 Li Ping Luo, 'Demographic Divergence', RFE/RL (2016), https://www.rferl.org/a/27927989.html#tabs-migration-2.

79 United Nations, Department of Economic and Social Affairs (2015), 'Trends in International Migrant Stock: Migrants by Destination and Origin', United Nations database, POP/DB/MIG/Stock/Rev.2015.

70 Freedom House, 'Nations in Transit: Latvia', Freedom House Report (2006), https://freedomhouse.org/report/nations-transit/2006/latvia.

71 Freedom House, 'Nations in Transit: Latvia', Freedom House Report (2017), https://freedomhouse.org/report/nations-transit/2017/latvia.

72 Nils Muiznieks, Juris Rozenvalds and Ieva Birka, 'Ethnicity and social cohesion in the post-Soviet Baltic states', Patterns of Prejudice, 47:3 (2013), https://www.tandfonline.com/doi/full/10.1080/0031322X.2013.812349?scroll=top&needAccess=true.

73 GINI, 'Country Report for the Baltic States Estonia, Latvia, Lithuania', Growing Inequalities and its Impacts in the Baltics (2012), http://www.gini-research.org/system/uploads/606/original/CR-Baltics-v2.pdf?1400771099.

Conclusion

1 Alexander Lanoszka and Michael A. Hunzeker, 'Conventional Deterrence and Landpower in northeastern Europe', Executive Summary: Strategic Studies Institute and US Army War College Press https://ssi.armywarcollege.edu/files/1404-summary.pdf.

2 Välisluureamet, 'International Security and Estonia 2019', Välisluureamet (2019): 7.

3 George Allison, 'NATO working on cyber attack trigger for Article 5', *UK Defence Journal* (19 March 2018) https://ukdefencejournal.org.uk/nato-working-on-cyber-attack-trigger-for-article-5/>.

4 NATO Strategic Communications Centre of Excellence, 'Robotrolling', *Robotrolling*, 1 (2019): 1.

5 Gatis Krumiņš, 'Soviet Economic Gaslighting of Latvia and the Baltic States', *Defence Strategic Communications*, 4 (Spring 2018): 49.

6 Terry Thompson, 'Countering Russian disinformation the Baltic nations' way', PRI (10 January 2019) https://www.pri.org/stories/2019-01-10/countering-russian-disinformation-baltic-nations-way.

7 Mark Galeotti, 'We Can't Blame Putin For Brexit, But Leaving The EU Suits His War On The West', *Huffington Post* (21 February 2019) https://www.huffingtonpost.co.uk/entry/vladimir-putin-brexit_uk_5c6559e8e4b0233af97224f3?

8 Raj M. Desai and Itzhak Goldberg, 'Enhancing Russia's Competitiveness and Innovative Capacity', *The World Bank* (2007): 4.

9 Välisluureamet, 'International Security and Estonia 2019', Välisluureamet (2019): 14.

10 Galeotti, 'We Can't Blame Putin For Brexit, But Leaving The EU Suits His War On The West'.

11 The Electoral Commission, 'Report on investigation into payments made to Better for the Country and Leave.EU', The Electoral Commission (1 November 2018) https://www.electoralcommission.org.uk/our-work/roles-and-responsibilities/our-role-as-regulator-of-political-party-finances/sanctions/report-on-investigation-into-payments-made-to-better-for-the-country-and-leave.eu.

12 Institute for Public Policy Research, 'England and its two Unions: The Anatomy of a Nation and its Discontents', IPPR (July 2013): 27 https://www.ippr.org/files/images/media/files/publication/2013/07/england-two-unions_Jul2013_11003.pdf.

13 https://www.theguardian.com/media/2018/apr/24/daily-express-editor-gary-jones-calls-its-front-pages-downright-offensive.

14 Jack Moore, 'Lindsey Graham: We must 'punish Russia' for election interference', *Newsweek* (14 May 2017) https://www.newsweek.com/lindsey-graham-we-must-punish-russia-election-meddling-608900.

15 Paul Waldman, 'Why did Trump win? In part because voter turnout plunged', *Washington Post* (10 November 2016) https://www.washingtonpost.com/blogs/plum-line/wp/2016/11/10/why-did-trump-win-in-part-because-voter-turnout-plunged.

16 Ibid.

17 Lyubov Chizhova, "'Россия не помойка'. Акции против мусоросжигательных заводов', Radio Svoboda (3 February 2019) https://www.svoboda.org/a/29746132.html.

18 https://www.politico.eu/article/how-do-you-solve-a-problem-like-dmitry-medvedev-vladimir-putin-russia/https://www.bloomberg.com/news/articles/2019-01-14/most-russians-want-medvedev-s-government-to-resign-poll-shows.

19 https://www.themoscowtimes.com/2016/09/15/even-the-ducks-in-the-pond-live-like-kings-at-russian-pms-summer-getaway.

BIBLIOGRAPHY

Adler, Katya. 'Baltic States Shiver as Russia Flexes Muscles', 6 March 2015, sec. Europe. https://www.bbc.com/news/world-europe-31759558.

AFP. 'Russia Slams US Approval of Montenegro's NATO Accession'. NDTV. com, 13 April 2017. https://www.ndtv.com/world-news/russia-slams-us-approval-of-montenegros-nato-accession-1680990.

Alexievich, Svetlana. *Second-Hand Time: The Last of the Soviets*. London: Fitzcarraldo Editions, 2016.

Ālīte, Barbara. 'Pētījums: Mediju telpas Latvijā ir nošķirtas'. LA.LV, 18 July 2017. http://www.la.lv/petijums-mediju-telpas-latvija-ir-noskirtas/.

Allen, Dan. 'Bold Art Helps Move the Needle on LGBTQ Acceptance in the Baltics'. NBC News, 29 September 2016. https://www.nbcnews.com/feature/nbc-out/bold-art-helps-move-needle-lgbtq-acceptance-baltics-n654456.

Amnesty International, 'Estonia. Linguistic minorities in Estonia: Discrimination must end'. https://www.amnesty.org/download/Documents/76000/eur510022006en.pdf.

Annus, Epp. 'Layers of Colonial Rule in the Baltics: Nation-Building, the Soviet Rule and the Affectivity of a Nation', 2013. http://www.eki.ee/km/annus/2013%20Bremen%20Layers%20of%20Colonial%20Rule%20in%20the%20Baltics%20Feb11.pdf.

Antelava, Natalia. 'On the Frontiers of the "Russian World"'. Coda Story (blog), 17 January 2016. https://codastory.com/lgbt-crisis/frontiers-of-the-russian-world/.

Antonenko, Oxana. 'Refugees Frustrated in Chilly Baltic States', 4 July 2017, sec. Europe. https://www.bbc.com/news/world-europe-40479224.

Archdeacon, Talis Saule. 'Intrigue Surrounding Missing Businessman Deepens'. *The Baltic Times*, 3 April 2008. https://www.baltictimes.com/news/articles/20131/.

Arkhangelsky, Andrei. 'Роднее Некуда'. Colta.ru, 15 April 2015. https://www.colta.ru/articles/media/7020-rodnee-nekuda.

Arnold, Chloe. 'Victory's Ambiguous Legacy'. RadioFreeEurope/RadioLiberty, 8 May 2017. https://www.rferl.org/a/1076345.html.

Arnold, Chloe. 'Russia: Estonia Row Clouds Victory Day Ceremonies'. RadioFreeEurope/RadioLiberty. Accessed 11 May 2019. https://www.rferl.org/a/1076345.html.

Ashbourne, Alexandra. *Lithuania: The Rebirth of a Nation, 1991–1994*. Lanham: Lexington Books, 1999.

Ashmore, William. 'Impact of Alleged Russian Cyber Attacks'. *Baltic Security & Defence Review* 11 (2009).

Associated Press. 'Putin: Soviet Collapse a "Genuine Tragedy"'. msnbc.com, 25 April 2005. http://www.nbcnews.com/id/7632057/ns/world_news/t/putin-soviet-collapse-genuine-tragedy/.

Associated Press. 'Russia's Leading Environmentalist Flees to Estonia'. *The Guardian*, 20 April 2015, sec. Environment. https://www.theguardian.com/environment/2015/apr/20/russias-leading-environmentalist-flees-to-estonia.

Astakhova, Olesya, and Vera Eckert. 'Nord Stream 2 Pipeline on Track despite Sanctions Risk, Operator Says'. Reuters, 31 August 2018. https://uk.reuters.com/article/uk-russia-gazprom-nordstream-idUKKCN1LG178.

Austruma, Aija. 'Zinību pilni meži: Pokaiņu gadatirgus fotomirkļos'. delfi.lv, 18 September 2017. https://www.delfi.lv/a/49249359.

Balcere, Ilze. 'Comparing Populist Political Parties in the Baltic States and Western Europe', Paper prepared for the 6th ECPR General Conference in Reykjavik, 25–7 August 2011. https://pdfs.semanticscholar.org/8c70/f438122a78d309246930593d40d6ee017053.pdf.

Baločkaitė, Rasa. 'Post-Soviet Transitions of the Planned Socialist Towns: Visaginas, Lithuania'. Vytautas Magnus University, n.d. https://iweb.cerge-ei.cz/pdf/gdn/IRP-cities-post-soviet-transitions-visaginas-balockaite.pdf.

Baltic News Service. 'Lithuanian President Supports Removal of Soviet Sculptures in Vilnius'. DELFI.LT, 24 July 2015. https://en.delfi.lt/culture/lithuanian-president-supports-removal-of-soviet-sculptures-in-vilnius.d?id=68567598.

Barath, Julius and Marcel Harakal. 'Test Bed for Cyber-Attacks Mitigation'. Brasov, Romania: Academiei Fortelor Aeriene (AFASES), 2011. www.afahc.ro/ro/afases/2011/math/BARATH_Harakal.pdf.

Barnes, Julian E. and Anton Troianovski. 'NATO Allies Preparing to Put Four Battalions at Eastern Border With Russia'. *The Wall Street Journal*, 29 April 2016, sec. World. https://www.wsj.com/articles/nato-allies-preparing-to-put-four-battalions-at-eastern-border-with-russia-1461943315.

Barry, Ellen. 'Tens of Thousands Protest in Moscow, Russia, in Defiance of Putin'. *The New York Times*, 10 December 2011, sec. Europe. https://www.nytimes.com/2011/12/11/world/europe/thousands-protest-in-moscow-russia-in-defiance-of-putin.html.

Batchelor, Tom. 'The Map That Shows How Many Nato Troops Are Deployed along Russia's Border'. *The Independent*, 5 February 2017. http://www.independent.co.uk/news/world/europe/russia-nato-border-forces-map-where-are-they-positioned-a7562391.html.\\.

Baryshnikov, Robert and Valentin Coalson, 'Just How Fraudulent Were Russia's Elections?' *The Atlantic*, 21 September 2016. http://www.rferl.org/content/statistics-point-to-massive-fraud-russia-state-duma-elections/28002750.html.

BBC. 'Chernobyl's Continuing Hazards', 25 April 2006. http://news.bbc.co.uk/2/hi/europe/4942828.stm.

BBC. 'Tallinn Tense after Deadly Riots', 28 April 2007. http://news.bbc.co.uk/2/hi/europe/6602171.stm.

BBC. 'Crimea "Votes for Russia Union"', 16 March 2014, sec. Europe. https://www.bbc.com/news/world-europe-26606097.

BBC. 'A Guided Tour of the Cybercrime Underground', 23 February 2017, sec. Technology. https://www.bbc.com/news/technology-38755584.

Bennetts, Marc. I'm Going to Ruin Their Lives. Extended edition. London: Oneworld, 2016.

Bershidsky, Leonid. 'Why NATO Wants Montenegro (Not for Its Military Might)'. Bloomberg, 1 May 2017. https://www.bloomberg.com/opinion/articles/2017-05-01/why-nato-wants-montenegro-not-for-its-military-might.

Birnbaum, Michael. 'How to Understand Putin's Jaw-Droppingly High Approval Ratings'. The Washington Post, 6 March 2016. https://www.washingtonpost.com/world/europe/how-to-understand-putins-jaw-droppingly-high-approval-ratings/2016/03/05/17f5d8f2-d5ba-11e5-a65b-587e721fb231_story.html?utm_term=.8dff48ac71be.

Biziuleviciute, Raminta. 'Gendered Aspects of the Soviet Deportations from Lithuania with the Case Study of the Operation "Vesna", May 22–23, 1948'. MA, Central European University, 2012. http://www.etd.ceu.hu/2012/biziuleviciute_raminta.pdf.

Blank, Stephen J. NATO Enlargement and the Baltic States: What Can the Great Powers Do? Collingdale, PA: Diane Publishing, 1997.

Bleiere, Daina and Rolands Henins. 'The Eastern Latvian Border: Potential for TransFrontier Co-Operation with Russia'. Latvian Institute of Internal Affairs, January 2004. http://liia.lv/site/attachments/17/01/2012/LatvianBorderfinal.pdf.

Blomfield, Adrian, and Mike Smith. 'Gorbachev: US Could Start New Cold War', The Telegraph, 6 May 2008, sec. World. https://www.telegraph.co.uk/news/worldnews/europe/russia/1933223/Gorbachev-US-could-start-new-Cold-War.html.

Blum, Alain, and Amandine Regamey. 'The Hero, the Martyr, and the Erased Rape (Lithuania 1944–2000)'. Clio, no. 39 (10 April 2015). https://doi.org/10.4000/cliowgh.492.

Blumenthal, Ralph. 'Some Suspected of Nazi War Crimes Are Known as Model Citizens'. The New York Times, 18 October 1976, sec. Archives. https://www.nytimes.com/1976/10/18/archives/some-suspected-of-nazi-war-crimes-are-known-as-model-citizens.html.

BNN. 'EC Finances Synchronization of Baltic and European Power Grids'. Baltic News Network – News from Latvia, Lithuania, Estonia, 24 January 2019. https://bnn-news.com/ec-finances-synchronization-of-baltic-and-european-power-grids-196468.

BNS. 'Survey: Less than Half of Estonian Residents Fear Military Conflict'. ERR, 4 July 2017. https://news.err.ee/605662/survey-less-than-half-of-estonian-residents-fear-military-conflict.

Bohlen, Celestine. 'Russia Cuts Gas Supply to Estonia in a Protest'. The New York Times, 26 June 1993, sec. World. https://www.nytimes.com/1993/06/26/world/russia-cuts-gas-supply-to-estonia-in-a-protest.html.

Borogan, Irina, and Andrei Soldatov. 'The Kremlin and the Hackers: Partners in Crime?' openDemocracy, 25 April 2012. https://www.opendemocracy.net/en/odr/kremlin-and-hackers-partners-in-crime/.

Boulègue, Mathieu. 'Five Things to Know About the Zapad-2017 Military Exercise'. Chatham House, 25 September 2017. https://www.chathamhouse.org/expert/comment/five-things-know-about-zapad-2017-military-exercise.

Bovt, Georgy. 'After Surkov'. *The Moscow Times*, 14 May 2013. https://www.themoscowtimes.com/2013/05/14/after-surkov-a24031.

Boša, Anda. 'Izstādē aplūkojami barikāžu laikā izmantotie sakaru līdzekļi', Latvijas Sabiedriskie Mediji (LSM.LV) (14 May 2019). https://www.lsm.lv/raksts/dzive--stils/vesture/izstade-aplukojami-barikazu-laika-izmantotie-sakaru-lidzekli.a318990/.

Bremmer, Ian. 'The Only 5 Countries That Meet NATO's Defense Spending Requirements'. *Time*, 24 February 2017. http://time.com/4680885/nato-defense-spending-budget-trump/.

Broekmeyer, M.J. *Stalin, the Russians, and Their War*. Madison: University of Wisconsin Press, 2004.

Bröning, Michael. 'The Rise of Populism in Europe', 3 June 2016. https://www.foreignaffairs.com/articles/europe/2016-06-03/rise-populism-europe.

Brown, Chris. 'Anti-Canada Propaganda Greets Troops in Latvia'. CBC, 16 June 2017. https://www.cbc.ca/news/world/latvia-propaganda-1.4162612.

Burgess, Matt. 'Exposed: How One of Russia's Most Sophisticated Hacking Groups Operates'. *Wired UK*, 11 January 2017. https://www.wired.co.uk/article/how-russian-hackers-work.

Capon, Felicity. 'Baltic States Say Norway, UK and Finland Have Stolen Their Children'. *Newsweek*, 23 April 2015. https://www.newsweek.com/2015/05/01/baltic-states-say-norway-uk-and-finland-have-stolen-their-children-324031.html.

Carroll, Lauren. 'Obama: US Spends More on Military than next 8 Nations Combined'. Politifact (Poynter Institute), 13 January 2016. https://www.politifact.com/truth-o-meter/statements/2016/jan/13/barack-obama/obama-us-spends-more-military-next-8-nations-combi/.

Center for European Policy Analysis (CEPA). 'Lithuania's Lonely Gambit'. Center for European Policy Analysis (CEPA), 15 May 2008.

Cepītis, Janis and Lilija Jakubenoka. 'Mythical Creatures, The Making of Wearing Apparel and the Landscape'. *Archaeologia Baltica* 15:1, 12 June 2013. https://doi.org/10.15181/ab.v15i1.17.

Černovaitè, Olga. 'Butterfly City: Short Trailer', Vidopress (2016). https://videopress.com/v/WNAZ9B5w.

Chausovsky, Eugene. 'Russian Influence Fades in the Baltics'. Stratfor, 10 June 2016, https://worldview.stratfor.com/article/russian-influence-fades-baltics.

Cheskin, Ammon. 'The Discursive Construction of "Russian-speakers": The Russian-Language Media and Demarcated Political Identities in Latvia', in

M. Golubeva and R. Gould (eds.), *Shrinking Citizenship: Discursive Practices that Limit Democratic Participation in Latvian Politics*. Amsterdam: Rodopi, (2010).

Cheskin, Ammon. 'Identity and Integration of Russian Speakers in the Baltic States: A Framework for Analysis'. *Ethnopolitics* 14:1 (January 2015): 72–93. https://doi.org/10.1080/17449057.2014.933051.

CISCO. 'Cisco 2017 Midyear Cybersecurity Report', July 2017. https://www. cisco.com/c/dam/m/digital/elq-cmcglobal/witb/1456403/Cisco_2017_ Midyear_Cybersecurity_Report.pdf.

Coalson, Robert. 'How Kremlin Gets The "Right" Results'. RadioFreeEurope/ RadioLiberty, 7 March 2008. https://www.rferl.org/a/1079601.html.

'Communism and Crimes against Humanity in the Baltic States'. presented at the Report to the Jarl Hjalmarson Foundation, Stockholm, Sweden, 13 April 1999. https://web.archive.org/web/20010301223347/http://www.rel.ee/eng/ communism_crimes.htm.

'Contentious Politics in the Baltics: The "New" Wave of Right-Wing Populism in Estonia'. openDemocracy, 28 April 2016. https://www.opendemocracy.net/ en/can-europe-make-it/contentious-politics-in-baltics-new-wave-of-right- wing-populism/.

Coynash, Hayla. 'Putin's New Bridge to Crimea Is Doomed to Collapse'. *Newsweek*, 13 January 2017. https://www.newsweek.com/putin-bridge- crimea-doomed-collapse-541578.

Crawford, Angus. 'The Town in Belrus Whose Cigarettes Are Smuggled to the UK', 1 December 2016, sec. UK. https://www.bbc.com/news/uk- 38170754.

Crouch, David. 'Russian buyers have deserted Latvia's high-end property market', *The Financial Times*, 13 April 2015. https://www.ft.com/content/6b06883c- d932-11e4-a8f1-00144feab7de.

Daniels, Jeff. 'Russian Rogue Cell Sites, Spy Drones Target NATO Troop Smartphones, Says Report'. CNBC, 4 October 2017. https://www.cnbc. com/2017/10/04/russian-rogue-cell-sites-drones-target-nato-troop- smartphones.html.

Davidson, Hilary and Ieva Pīgozne. Archaeological Dress and Textiles in Latvia from the Seventh to Thirteenth Centuries: Research, Results, and Reconstructions. *Medieval Clothing and Textiles*, 2010.

Davis, Mark. 'How World War II Shaped Modern Russia'. Euronews, 4 May 2015. https://www.euronews.com/2015/05/04/how-world-war-ii-shaped-modern- russia.

defense-aerospace.com. 'Booz, Allen Escapes Spending Cuts on Consultants'. defense-aerospace.com, 14 May 2010. http://www.defense-aerospace.com/ articles-view/release/3/114842/booz,-allen-escapes-spending-cuts-on- consultants.html.

Delany, Max. 'Latvia Police Say Blood Is Rozhetskin's'. *The Moscow Times*, 26 March 2008. http://www.themoscowtimes.com/sitemap/free/2008/3/article/ latvia-police-say-blood-is-rozhetskins/361426.html.

DELFI. 'Исследование: Почти Половина Жителей Эстонии Опасается Военного Конфликта На Территории Страны'. RUS Delfi, 4 July 2017. https://www.delfi.ee/a/78771916.

Denisenko, Viktor. 'The Basic Concepts of the Baltic States Image in the Russian Periodical Press after the Collapse of the Soviet Union (1991–2009)'. *Journalism Research* 8, 7 December 2015.

Deutsche Welle. 'Man Found Guilty of Abusing Russian-German Teenager Who Fabricated Rape Story | DW | 20.06.2017'. DW.COM, 20 June 2017. https://www.dw.com/en/man-found-guilty-of-abusing-russian-german-teenager-who-fabricated-rape-story/a-39328894.

Deutsche Welle. 'Nord Stream 2: German Environmentalists Sue to Halt Construction of Controversial Gas Pipeline | DW | 03.07.2018'. DW.COM, 3 July 2018. https://www.dw.com/en/nord-stream-2-german-environmentalists-sue-to-halt-construction-of-controversial-gas-pipeline/a-44507377.

Duffy, Jill. 'Toggl', *PC Mag UK* (7 February 2018). http://uk.pcmag.com/software/93243/review/toggl.

Dykman, J.T. 'The Soviet Experience in World War Two'. Eisenhower Institute at Gettysburg College. Eisenhower Institute. https://web.archive.org/web/20181114212650/http://www.eisenhowerinstitute.org/about/living_history/wwii_soviet_experience.dot.

Dzyubenko, Olga. '"Mission Accomplished" for U.S. Air Base in pro-Moscow Kyrgyzstan'. Reuters, 6 March 2014. https://www.reuters.com/article/us-kyrgyzstan-usa-base-idUSBREA251SA20140306.

EAD. 'By Denying Visa-Free Entry to Baltic Non-Citizens, Russia Is Narrowing the Russian World'. EurAsia Daily, 1 September 2016. https://eadaily.com/en/news/2016/09/01/by-denying-visa-free-entry-to-baltic-non-citizens-russia-is-narrowing-the-russian-world.

Easter, Gerald M. 'Preference for Presidentialism: Postcommunist Regime Change in Russia and the NIS', *World Politics*, 49:2, January 1997. http://www.jstor.org/stable/pdf/25053997.pdf.

Editors and staff. 'Дорогим Читателям От Дорогой Редакции (Group Statement)'. Lenta.ru, 12 March 2014. https://lenta.ru/info/posts/statement/.

Museum of Estonian Architecture. 'Kopli Sonata. The Russo-Baltic Shipyard'. Arhitektuurimuuseum, 6 May 2017. https://www.arhitektuurimuuseum.ee/en/naitus/kopli-sonata-the-russo-baltic-shipyard/.

Eesti Statistika. ' '. Statistical Database, n.d. http://pub.stat.ee/.

Efimova, Polina and Katerina Patin. 'Who Were the 27,000 Victims of Russia's Worst Holocaust-Era Crime?' Coda Story (blog), 25 January 2019. https://codastory.com/disinformation/who-victims-russia-worst-holocaust/.

Ellis, Mark S. 'Purging the Past: The Current State of Lustration Laws in the Former Communist Bloc'. *Law and Contemporary Problems* 59, no. 4 (1996): 181. https://doi.org/10.2307/1192198.

Emmott, Robin and Sabine Sebold. 'NATO Split on Message to Send Georgia on Membership Hopes'. Reuters, 27 November 2015. https://www.reuters.com/article/us-nato-georgia/nato-split-on-message-to-send-georgia-on-membership-hopes-idUSKBN0TG1HP20151127.

Enikolopov, Ruben, Vasily Korovkin, Maria Petrova, Konstantin Sonin and Alexei Zakharov. 'Field Experiment Estimate of Electoral Fraud in Russian Parliamentary Elections'. Proceedings of the National Academy of Sciences 110, no. 2, 8 January 2013. https://doi.org/10.1073/pnas.1206770110.

Eror, Aleks. 'Is Post-Soviet Fashion Ethically Problematic?', HighSnobiety, 1 February 2017. https://www.highsnobiety.com/2017/02/01/post-soviet-fashion-trend/.

ERR. 'Kopli €60 Million Development Finally On'. Err.com, 26 August 2015. https://news.err.ee/116583/kopli-60-million-development-finally-on.

ERR. 'Enemies of the People: How the USSR Had 90,000 Deported in Four Days'. ERR, 25 March 2016. https://news.err.ee/117888/enemies-of-the-people-how-the-ussr-had-90-000-deported-in-four-days.

ERR. 'Gazprom Sells Eesti Gaas Stake to Infortar Subsidiary'. ERR, 16 May 2016. https://news.err.ee/118163/gazprom-sells-eesti-gaas-stake-to-infortar-subsidiary.

ERR. 'ERR: Usefulness of Direct Interpretation into Estonian of ETV+ Live Broadcasts Questionable'. ERR, 10 January 2017. https://news.err.ee/120299/err-usefulness-of-direct-interpretation-into-estonian-of-etv-live-broadcasts-questionable.

ERR. 'Ansip, Laaneots: Russian Agents Present during Bronze Night Riots'. ERR, 26 April 2017. https://news.err.ee/592127/ansip-laaneots-russian-agents-present-during-bronze-night-riots.

EER. 'Patarei Fortress Could House Planned Center Investigating Communist Crimes'. ERR, 6 June 2017. https://news.err.ee/600404/patarei-fortress-could-house-planned-center-investigating-communist-crimes.

EER. 'Security Guards Severely Injured in Shooting in Tallinn's Kopli District'. ERR, 3 July 2017. https://news.err.ee/605421/security-guards-severely-injured-in-shooting-in-tallinn-s-kopli-district.

'ESPOO REPORT: Nord Stream 2'. ESPOO, April 2017. https://www.nord-stream2.com/media/documents/pdf/en/2018/07/espoo-report-en.pdf.

Estonian World. 'Estonian Beliefs and Rituals Carried on by Jaanipäev'. Estonian World, 22 June 2017. https://estonianworld.com/life/it-is-this-time-of-the-year-again-jaanipaev/.

Estonian World, 'Estonian drinks maker stands up for LGBTQ rights', Estonian World, 6 October 2017. http://estonianworld.com/business/estonian-drinks-maker-stands-lgbtq-rights/.

Estonian World, 'The UN Classifies Estonia as Northern European country'. Estonian World, 8 January 2018.

European Endowment for Democracy (EED). 'Bringing Plurality and Balance to Russian Language Media – Final Recommendations – European Endowment for Democracy: EED', n.d. https://eedweblb-286123115.eu-central-1.elb.amazonaws.com/news/bringing-plurality-1/.

European Commission. Member States' Support to Emergency Relocation Mechanism, 2018. https://ec.europa.eu/home-affairs/sites/homeaffairs/files/what-we-do/policies/european-agenda-migration/press-material/docs/state_of_play_-_relocation_en.pdf.

European Court of Human Rights (ECHR). 'Kolk and Kislyiy v. Estonia', Reports of Judgments and Decisions 2006:1, 17 January 2006. http://hudoc.echr.coe. int/eng#{"itemid":["001-72404"]}.

Europol, 'European Migrant Smuggling Centre (EMSC): 3rd Annual Activity Report – 2018'. EMSC, 2019. www.europol.europa.eu/sites/default/ documents/emsc_report_final_2019_2final.pdf

Eurostat. 'Household Spending on Alcohol Close to €130 Billion'. Accessed 13 May 2019. https://ec.europa.eu/eurostat/web/products-eurostat-news/-/ DDN-20171204-1.

EWR. 'The Tõnismäe Second World War Memorial'. Estonian World Review, 26 April 2007. https://www.eesti.ca/the-tonismae-second-world-war-memorial/ article16027.

EWR. 'Remediation of Sillamäe's Radioactive Tailings Pond Completed'. Estonian World Review, 11 November 2008. https://www.eesti.ca/ remediation-of-sillamaes-radioactive-tailings-pond-completed/article21671.

Farand, Chloe. 'Swedish Teenagers Claim Russian TV Crew Offered to Bribe Them to Cause Trouble'. The Independent, 7 March 2017. http://www. independent.co.uk/news/world/europe/wedish-teenagers-russian-tv-name- of-channel-crew-money-action-camera-donald-trump-refugee- rape-a7615406.html.

Feder, J. Lester. 'Estonia Becomes First Former Soviet Country to Recognize Same-Sex Partnerships'. BuzzFeed News, 9 October 2015. https://www. buzzfeednews.com/article/lesterfeder/estonia-poised-to-become-first- former-soviet-country-to-reco.

Field, Matthew and Mike Wright. 'Russian Trolls Sent Thousands of Pro-Leave Messages on Day of Brexit Referendum, Twitter Data Reveals'. The Telegraph, 17 October 2018. https://www.telegraph.co.uk/technology/2018/10/17/ russian-iranian-twitter-trolls-sent-10-million-tweets-fake-news/.

Filipov, David. 'Putin Says Russia Planning "Countermeasures" to NATO Expansion'. The Washington Post, 21 November 2016. https://www. washingtonpost.com/world/putin-says-russia-planning-countermeasuresto- nato-expansion/2016/11/21/83f5673c-afe1-11e6-ab37-1b3940a0d30a_story. html?

Flores, Reena. 'Newt Gingrich: NATO Countries "Ought to Worry" about US Commitment'. CBS, 21 July 2016. https://www.cbsnews.com/news/newt- gingrich-trump-would-reconsider-his-obligation-to-nato/.

Foti, Silvia. 'My Grandfather Wasn't a Nazi-Fighting War Hero – He Was a Brutal Collaborator'. Salon, 14 July 2018. https://www.salon.com/2018/07/14/ my-grandfather-didnt-fight-the-nazis-as-family-lore-told-it-he-was-a- brutal-collaborator/.

Fraunhofer-Gesellschaft. 'Hazardous Contaminated Sites in the North and the Baltic Sea'. Phys.Org, 1 August 2018. https://phys.org/news/2018-08- hazardous-contaminated-sites-north-baltic.html.

Freedom House. 'Latvia', 1 March 2012. https://freedomhouse.org/report/ nations-transit/2006/latvia.

Friedman, Uri. 'Can America and Russia Both Be Great Again?' *The Atlantic*, 20 November 2016. https://www.theatlantic.com/international/archive/2016/11/trump-russia-policy/507587/.

Frye, Timothy, Ora John Reuter and David Szakonyi. 'Hitting Them with Carrots: Voter Intimidation and Vote Buying in Russia'. *British Journal of Political Science*, 5 February 2018. https://doi.org/10.1017/S0007123416000752.

Galeotti, Mark. 'Putin's Hydra: Inside Russia's Intelligence Services'. European Council on Foreign Relations (ECFR), 2016.

Galeotti, Mark. 'Crimintern: How the Kremlin Uses Russia's Criminal Networks in Europe', ECR Policy Brief, 2017. https://www.ecfr.eu/publications/summary/crimintern_how_the_kremlin_uses_russias_criminal_networks_in_europe.

Galeotti, Mark and the European Council on Foreign Relations. 'Putin's Hydra: Inside Russia's Intelligence Services', May 2016.

Galetski, Kirill. 'Russian-American Media Investor Missing'. *The Hollywood Reporter*. AP, 27 March 2008. https://www.hollywoodreporter.com/news/russian-american-media-investor-missing-108022.

Garner, Dwight. 'Review: In "Secondhand Time," Voices from a Lost Russia'. *The New York Times*, 24 May 2016, sec. Books. https://www.nytimes.com/2016/05/25/books/review-in-secondhand-time-voices-from-a-lost-russia.html.

Gera, Vanessa. 'Lithuanians Are Preparing for a "Russian Invasion" in the Most Extreme Way Imaginable'. *The Independent*, 1 December 2016. http://www.independent.co.uk/news/world/europe/russia-eastern-europe-lithuania-vladimir-putin-estonia-latvia-a7449961.html.

GINI. Country Report for the Baltic States Estonia, Latvia, Lithuania. Growing inequalities and its impact in the Baltics, 2012. http://www.gini-research.org/system/uploads/606/original/CR-Baltics-v2.pdf?1400771099.

Goettig, Marcin and Lidia Kelly. 'U.S. Says Planned Russian Pipeline Would Threaten European Energy Security', Reuters, 27 January 2018. https://uk.reuters.com/article/uk-europe-nordstream-usa-idUKKBN1FG0ST.

Goldthau, Andreas. 'Assessing Nord Stream 2: Regulation, Geopolitics and Energy Security in the EU, Central Eastern Europe and the UK', July 2016.

Goncharenko, Roman. 'Zapad-2017: "Normal Military Business"'. DW.COM, 27 September 2017. https://www.dw.com/en/zapad-2017-normal-military-business/a-40710010.

Gorenburg, Dmitry. 'Russia's State Armaments Program 2020'. PONARS Eurasia Policy Memo No. 125, 2010. http://www.ponarseurasia.org/sites/default/files/policy-memos-pdf/pepm_125.pdf.

Gorst, Isabel, and Nina Poussenkova. 'Unlocking the assets: energy and the future of central Asia and the Caucasus', Center for International Political Economy and the James A. Baker III Institute for Public Policy Rice University, April 1998. https://www.bakerinstitute.org/media/files/Research/44988762/petroleum-ambassadors-of-russia-state-versus-corporate-policy-in-the-caspian-region.pdf.

GOV.UK. 'Overseas Business Risk – Lithuania'. GOV.UK, 28 March 2017. https://www.gov.uk/government/publications/overseas-business-risk-lithuania/overseas-business-risk-lithuania.

Grebenkin, Alexander and Tatiana Kalinovskaya. 'Belarus Nuclear Power Plant Stirs Fears in Lithuania'. AFP via Kyiv Post, 26 November 2017. https://www.kyivpost.com/world/afp-belarus-nuclear-power-plant-stirs-fears-lithuania.html.

Grigaitė Ugnė and Mažvydas Karalius. 'Intymaus partnerio smurtavimo apraiškos Lietuvoje – moterų perspektyva', Žmogaus teisių stebėjimo institutas, 2018. https://hrmi.lt/wp-content/uploads/2018/10/Intymaus-partnerio-smurtavimo-aprai%C5%A1kos_%C5%BDTSI.pdf.

Grimes, David Robert. 'Russian Fake News Is Not New: Soviet Aids Propaganda Cost Countless Lives'. The Guardian, 14 June 2017, sec. Science. https://www.theguardian.com/science/blog/2017/jun/14/russian-fake-news-is-not-new-soviet-aids-propaganda-cost-countless-lives.

Grove, Thomas, Julian E. Barnes and Drew Hinshaw. 'Russia Targets NATO Soldier Smartphones, Western Officials Say'. The Wall Street Journal, 4 October 2017, sec. World. https://www.wsj.com/articles/russia-targets-soldier-smartphones-western-officials-say-1507109402.

Gruyter, Caroline de. 'Waarom Brexit tot meer cohesie leidt'. NRC, 26 December 2018. https://www.nrc.nl/nieuws/2018/12/26/waarom-brexit-tot-meer-cohesie-leidt-a3127047.

Gusev, Alexey. 'Историк: стать независимой Литве подсказали в Москве'. RuBaltic.Ru, 12 March 2018. https://www.rubaltic.ru/article/politika-i-obshchestvo/12032018-istorik-za-postsovetskoe-vremya-u-litvy-ne-bylo-printsipialnogo-ryvka/.

Hains, Tim. 'BBC's Adam Curtis On The "Contradictory Vaudeville" of Post-Modern Politics'. RealClear Politics, 31 December 2014. http://www.realclearpolitics.com/video/2016/10/12/bbcs_adam_curtis_how_propaganda_turned_russian_politics_into_a_circus.html.

Hanley, Monika. 'Baltic Diaspora and the Rise of Neo-Paganism', The Baltic Times, 28 October 2010. https://www.baltictimes.com/news/articles/27265/.

Harding, Luke. 'Latvia: Russia's Playground for Business, Politics – and Crime'. The Guardian, 23 January 2013, sec. World news. https://www.theguardian.com/world/2013/jan/23/latvia-russian-playground.

Higgins, Andrew. 'In Estonia, Caution but Surprising Cheers for Trump's Victory'. The New York Times, 17 November 2016, sec. World. https://www.nytimes.com/2016/11/18/world/europe/estonia-trump-baltics-putin.html.

Higgins, Andrew. 'Foot Soldiers in a Shadowy Battle Between Russia and the West'. The New York Times, 28 May 2017, sec. World. https://www.nytimes.com/2017/05/28/world/europe/slovakia-czech-republic-hungary-poland-russia-agitation.html.

Higgins, Andrew. 'Nazi Collaborator or National Hero? A Test for Lithuania'. The New York Times, 10 September 2018, sec. World. https://www.nytimes.com/2018/09/10/world/europe/nazi-general-storm-lithuania.html.

Highsnobiety. 'Is Post-Soviet Fashion Ethically Problematic?' Highsnobiety, 1 February 2017. https://www.highsnobiety.com/2017/02/01/post-soviet-fashion-trend/.

Horn, Knut-Sverre. 'Støy fra Russland slo ut GPS-signaler for norske fly'. NRK, 5 October 2017. https://www.nrk.no/finnmark/stoy-fra-russland-slo-ut-gps-signaler-for-norske-fly-1.13720305.

Hounshell, Blake. 'Putin Uses Dog to Intimidate Merkel'. Foreign Policy (blog), 14 June 2007. https://foreignpolicy.com/2007/06/14/putin-uses-dog-to-intimidate-merkel/.

Human Rights Watch. 'Reports: Soviet Union'. Human Rights Watch, 1992. https://www.hrw.org/reports/1992/WR92/HSW-05.htm.

Husa, Anders. 'Meet the Future of Estonian Cooking – Chef Orm Oja'. Andershusa (blog), 13 October 2017. https://andershusa.com/chef-orm-oja-noa-chefs-hall-tallinn-estonia-meet-the-future-of-estonian-cooking.

Hussain, Tharik. 'The Amazing Survival of the Baltic Muslims', 1 January 2016, sec. Magazine. https://www.bbc.com/news/magazine-35170834.

Huseynov, Rusif. 'Baltic States are no longer ex-Soviet', Modern Diplomacy, 20 January 2017.

Interfax.ru. 'Генпрокуратура РФ проверит законность признания независимости республик Прибалтики'. Interfax.ru, 30 June 2015. https://www.interfax.ru/russia/450574.

International Centre for Defence and Security. Estonia's 'Virtual Russian World': The Influence of Russian Media on Estonia's Russian Speakers. Vol. Eesti, 2015.

Invest Lithuania. 'Lithuania Clocks 35 New Fintech Companies in 2017'. Invest Lithuania (blog), 2018. https://investlithuania.com/news/lithuania-clocks-35-new-fintech-companies-in-2017/.

Ivanov, Maxim. 'Телевидение Выходит Из Поля Зрения'. Коммерсантъ, 16 December 2015. https://www.kommersant.ru/doc/2878258.

Jegelevičius, Linas. 'Lithuanian-Russian school teachers say their schools are not vehicles for Moscow propaganda', LT Daily, DELFI, 18 December 2015. http://www.lrt.lt/en/news-in-english/29/122970/lithuanian-russian-school-teachers-say-their-schools-are-not-vehicles-for-moscow-propaganda.

Jewkes, Stephen and Oleg Vukmanovic. 'Suspected Russia-Backed Hackers Target Baltic Energy Networks'. Reuters, 11 May 2017. https://www.reuters.com/article/us-baltics-cyber-insight-idUSKBN1871W5.

Jirušek, Martin and Tomáš Vlček. Energy Security in Central and Eastern Europe and the Operations of Russian State-Owned Energy Enterprises. Brno: Masaryk University, 2015.

Jočienė, Aldona. 'Scandinavian Bank Subsidiaries in the Baltics: Have They All Behaved in a Similar Way?' Intellectual Economics 9:1, April 2015. https://doi.org/10.1016/j.intele.2015.09.002.

Johnson, Jenna. 'Trump on NATO: "I Said It Was Obsolete. It's No Longer Obsolete"'. The Washington Post, 12 April 2017. https://www.washingtonpost.com/news/post-politics/wp/2017/04/12/trump-on-nato-i-said-it-was-obsolete-its-no-longer-obsolete.

Kapersky. *Kapersky Lab Security Bulletin*, 2008. http://kasperskycontenthub.com/
wp-content/uploads/sites/43/vlpdfs/kaspersky_security_bulletin_part_2_
statistics_en.pdf.

Kaitsepolitseiamet (KAPO). 'Estonian Internal Security Service Annual Reviews',
KAPO, 2017. https://www.kapo.ee/en/content/annual-reviews.html.

Kara-Murza, Vladimir. 'Putin's Russia Is Becoming More Soviet by the Day'. *The
Washington Post*, 26 February 2018. https://www.washingtonpost.com/news/
democracy-post/wp/2018/02/26/putins-russia-is-becoming-more-soviet-by-
the-day.

Kasekamp, Andres. *A History of the Baltic States*. Palgrave Essential Histories.
Basingstoke, New York: Palgrave Macmillan, 2010.

Kauffmann, Sylvie. 'Le divorce Europe-Etats-Unis : la famille occidentale sous
tension'. *Le Monde*, 9 November 2018. https://www.lemonde.fr/long-format/
article/2018/11/09/europe-etats-unis-la-famille-occidentale-sous-
tension_5380997_5345421.html.

Kaukule, Aija. 'Mārtiņš Rītiņš: 'Joprojām neesmu piepildījis visu, ko vēlējos, kad
atbraucu uz Latviju!', LA.LV, 15 November 2018. http://kokteilis.la.lv/
martins-ritins-joprojam-neesmu-piepildijis-visu-ko-velejos-kad-atbraucu-
uz-latviju.

Kauno diena. '"Chorų karus" laimėjo Lietuvos aklųjų choras'. *Kauno diena*, 3 May
2015. http://kauno.diena.lt/naujienos/laisvalaikis-ir-kultura/zvaigzdes-ir-
pramogos/choru-karus-laimejo-lietuvos-akluju-choras-688912.

Kaziliūnaitė, Aušra. 'Holiday makeup', in *The Moon is a Pill* (translated by Rimas
Uzgiris), Swansea: Parthian Books, 2018.

Kirss, Tiina and R. Hinrikus (eds.). *Estonian Life Stories*. Budapest; New York:
Central European University Press, 2009.

Kivirähk, Andrus and Christopher Moseley. *The Man Who Spoke Snakish*. First
edition. London: Grove Press UK, 2015.

Knight, Ben. 'Teenage Girl Admits Making up Migrant Rape Claim That
Outraged Germany'. *The Guardian*, 31 January 2016, sec. World news. https://
www.theguardian.com/world/2016/jan/31/teenage-girl-made-up-migrant-
claim-that-caused-uproar-in-germany.

Kobuszynska, Mira. 'Wood Sector in Estonia'. USDA Global Agricultural
Information Network, 20 December 2016. https://gain.fas.usda.gov/
Recent%20GAIN%20Publications/Wood%20Sector%20in%20Estonia_
Warsaw_Estonia_12-20-2016.pdf.

Kojala, Linas. '"Brexit Earthquake" and "Stunning Trump Win": The Baltic
Perspective'. Political State of the Region. Baltic Development Forum, 2017.
http://www.bdforum.org/wp-content/uploads/2017/06/2017_PoliticalRep_
LAPAS-web.pdf.

Kommersant. 'Избирателей Зазывают На Выборы Квартирами и
Машинами'. Коммерсантъ, 8 September 2017. https://www.kommersant.ru/
doc/3404345?tw.

Kórshunov, Maxim. 'Mikhail Gorbachev: I Am against All Walls'. RBTH, 16
October 2014. https://www.rbth.com/international/2014/10/16/mikhail_
gorbachev_i_am_against_all_walls_40673.html.

Kragh, Martin and Sebastian Åsberg. 'Russia's Strategy for Influence through Public Diplomacy and Active Measures: The Swedish Case'. *Journal of Strategic Studies* 40, 6, 19 September 2017. https://doi.org/10.1080/01402390. 2016.1273830.

Kramer, Andrew E. 'Spooked by Russia, Tiny Estonia Trains a Nation of Insurgents'. *The New York Times*, 31 October 2016, sec. World. https://www. nytimes.com/2016/11/01/world/europe/spooked-by-russia-tiny-estonia-trains-a-nation-of-insurgents.html.

Kramer, Mark. 'The Myth of a No-NATO-Enlargement Pledge to Russia'. *The Washington Quarterly*, Center for Strategic and International Studies, 32, no. 2, April 2009.

Kund, Oliver. 'Tartu ettevõtja teenis aastaid Vene sõjaväeluuret'. Postimees: Tänane leht, 12 April 2018. https://leht.postimees.ee/4469203/tartu-ettevotja-teenis-aastaid-vene-sojavaeluuret.

Kurvet-Käosaar, Leena. 'The Traumatic Impact of the Penal Frameworks of the Soviet Regime: Pathways of Female Remembering', in Mary Clancy and Andrea Pető (eds.), *Teaching Empires. Gender and Transnational Citizenship in Europe*. Teaching with Gender: European Women's Studies in International and Interdisciplinary Classrooms 6. Utrecht: Utrecht University, 2009.

Kuusi, Hanna. 'Prison Experiences and Socialist Sculptures – Tourism and the Soviet Past in the Baltic States'. The Finnish University Network for Tourism Studies (FUNTS), 2008. http://hdl.handle.net/10138/28227.

Lamberty, Lydia. 'Explaining Baltic Migration After EU Accession: Determinants and Consequences'. University of Trier, 2015.

Lanoszka, Alexander. 'Strategic Enabler or Point of Vulnerability: What Role for Belarus in Russia's Military Plans?' Modern War Institute (blog), 21 March 2018. https://mwi.usma.edu/strategic-enabler-point-vulnerability-role-belarus-russias-military-plans/.

Laris, Michael. 'Driverless delivery robots could be hitting D.C. sidewalks soon', *The Washington Post*, 23 March 2016. https://www.washingtonpost.com/news/dr-gridlock/wp/2016/03/23/driverless-delivery-robots-could-be-hitting-d-c-sidewalks-soon.

Latvian Ministry of Finance, *Tax System in Latvia*, 17 January 2018. http://www. fm.gov.lv/en/s/taxes/.

Latvian Public Broadcasting. 'Riga Speaks More Russian than Latvian'. LSM.LV, n.d. https://eng.lsm.lv/article/society/society/riga-speaks-more-russian-than-latvian.a129764/.

Ledeneva, Alena V. *Can Russia Modernise? Sistema, Power Networks and Informal Governance*. Cambridge; New York: Cambridge University Press, 2013.

LETA. 'Jakobsons Is Cleared of All Charges in Criminal Case about Ushakov's e-Mail Correspondence'. Baltic News Network – News from Latvia, Lithuania, Estonia, 20 September 2016. https://bnn-news.com/jakobsons-is-cleared-of-all-charges-in-criminal-case-about-ushakov-s-e-mail-correspondence-151485.

LETA/TBT Staff. 'Lithuania to Rename Museum of Genocide Victims after Lengthy Discussions'. *The Baltic Times*, 8 September 2017. https://www.

baltictimes.com/lithuania_to_rename_museum_of_genocide_victims_after_
lengthy_discussions/.

LETA/TBT Staff. 'Ambassadors of Baltic States Ask French *Le Monde* Paper to
Stop Calling Them "Former Soviet Republics"'. *The Baltic Times*, 10
September 2017. https://www.baltictimes.com/ambassadors_of_baltic_
states_ask_french_le_monde_paper_to_stop_calling_them__former_soviet_
republics_/.

LETA/TBT Staff. '17 Refugees Sent Back to Lithuania from Other EU
Countries', *The Baltic Times*, 5 March 2018. https://www.baltictimes.
com/17_refugees_sent_back_to_lithuania_from_other_eu_countries/.

Leung, Iris. 'This Tech Company Uses Remote Work to Win The War For Talent'.
Forbes, 20 July 2017. https://www.forbes.com/sites/irisleung/2017/07/20/
this-tech-company-uses-remote-work-to-win-the-war-for-talent/.

Levada. 'Левада-центр: президентский рейтинг Путина составляет 37%, за
месяц изменился в рамках погрешности', 25 January 2012. https://www.
levada.ru/2012/01/25/levada-tsentr-prezidentskij-rejting-putina-sostavlyaet-
37-za-mesyats-izmenilsya-v-ramkah-pogreshnosti/.

Levada. 'Более половины россиян не видят альтернативы Путину', 10
October 2017. https://www.levada.ru/2017/10/10/bolee-poloviny-rossiyan-
ne-vidyat-alternativy-putinu/.

Levada. 'Сталин в общественном мнении', 10 April 2018. https://www.levada.
ru/2018/04/10/17896/.

Levin, Dov. 'On the relations between the Baltic peoples and their Jewish
neighbours before, during and after World War II'. *Holocaust and Genocide
Studies* 5:1 (1990): 53–66. https://doi.org/10.1093/hgs/5.1.53.

Like a Local, Tallinn City Guide (2017).

Li Ping Luo, 'Demographic Divergence', RFE/RL, 2016. https://www.rferl.
org/a/27927989.html#tabs-migration-2.

Lipman, Masha. 'Constrained or Irrelevant: The Media in Putin's Russia', *Current
History*, October 2005. http://carnegieendowment.org/files/CurHistLipman.
pdf.

Lippus, Urve. 'Transformation of an Institution – the First Soviet Estonian Song
Festival'. *Musik in Diktaturen Des 20.* Jahrhunderts, 2006.

Lithuania MoD. 'National Security Threat Assessment'. Second Investigation
Department under the Ministry of National Defence, 2017.

Lithuania's Ignalina nuclear power plant passes decommissioning milestone, n.d.
https://www.finchannel.com/business/60005-lithuania-s-ignalina-nuclear-
power-plant-passes-decommissioning-milestone.

Loescher, Gil. *Calculated Kindness*. London: Collier Macmillan, 1986.

Lofgren, Mike. 'Trump, Putin, and the Alt-Right International'. *The Atlantic*, 31
October 2016. https://www.theatlantic.com/international/archive/2016/10/
trump-putin-alt-right-comintern/506015/.

Louis Straus, Ira. 'The Myth That Ukraine Cannot Join NATO While Russia
Occupies Some of Its Territory'. Atlantic Community, 3 September 2014.
http://www.atlantic-community.org/-/the-myth-that-ukraine-cannot-join-
nato-while-russia-occupies-some-of-its-territo-1.

Lowe, Christian. 'Kremlin Loyalist Says Launched Estonia Cyber-Attack'. Reuters, 13 March 2009. https://www.reuters.com/article/us-russia-estonia-cyberspace-idUSTRE52B4D820090313.

LRT. 'Lithuanian-Russian School Teachers Say Their Schools Are Not Vehicles for Moscow Propaganda'. lrt.lt, 18 December 2015. https://www.lrt.lt/naujienos/news-in-english/19/122970/lithuanian-russian-school-teachers-say-their-schools-are-not-vehicles-for-moscow-propaganda.

LSM.LV. 'Latvian Television the Most Watched TV Channel in June', 5 July 2016. https://eng.lsm.lv/article/society/society/latvian-television-the-most-watched-tv-channel-in-june.a190668/.

LSM.LV, 'Baltics among 7 NATO countries that hit defense spending target in 2018', LSM.LV, 14 March 2019. https://eng.lsm.lv/article/society/defense/baltics-among-7-nato-countries-that-hit-defense-spending-target-in-2018.a312737/.

Lukin, Alexander. *Pivot to Asia: Russia's Foreign Policy Enters the 21st Century*. New Delhi (India): Vij Books India Pvt Ltd, 2017.

Luxmoore, Matthew. 'Letter from Stalingrad: Volgograd Goes Back in Time as It Remembers Its Darkest Hour'. *The Calvert Journal*. https://www.calvertjournal.com/features/show/9624/letter-from-stalingrad-volgograd-second-world-war.

MacFarquhar, Neil. 'A Russian Master of the "Dark Side" in Film'. *The New York Times*, 23 February 2018, sec. World. https://www.nytimes.com/2018/02/23/world/europe/andrey-zvyagintsev-russia-loveless.html.

Maheshwari, Vijai. 'In the Baltics, Waiting for History to Start up Again'. Politico Europe, 27 January 2017. https://www.politico.eu/article/lithuania-russia-tension-baltics-waiting-for-history-to-start-again/.

Manson, Katrina. 'Why Does Donald Trump Treat Iran Differently to North Korea?' *The Financial Times*, 14 June 2018 https://www.ft.com/content/dac14fb4-6f47-11e8-92d3-6c13e5c92914.

Mardiste, David and Andrius Sytas. 'VP Pence, in the Baltics, Voices Support for Mutual Defense in NATO'. Reuters, 31 July 2017. https://www.reuters.com/article/us-usa-pence-estonia-idUSKBN1AG1G0.

Martin, Margus. 'Aburis raiuti püha his', *Postimees* (Virumaa Teataja), 13 June 2019. https://virumaateataja.postimees.ee/6706070/aburis-raiuti-puha-hiis.

Martyn-Hemphill, Richard. 'Russia's Dissident Poets Society'. Politic Europe, 26 December 2015. https://www.politico.eu/article/russias-dissident-poets-society-latvia-russian-culture/.

Marzouk, Zach. 'Ex-Estonian president: Other countries staying silent over digital ID flaws', *ITPRO*, 14 November 2017. http://www.itpro.co.uk/security/29898/ex-estonian-president-other-countries-staying-silent-over-digital-id-flaws.

Masso, Jaan, Kerly Espenberg, Anu Masso and Inta Mierina. *Country Report for the Baltic States Estonia, Latvia, Lithuania* (GINI), 2012. http://gini-research.org/system/uploads/437/original/Baltics.pdf?1370077200.

Masso, Jaan, Kerly Espenberg, Anu Masso, Inta Mierina and Kaia Philips. 'Country Report for the Baltic States: Estonia, Latvia, Lithuania'. Growing

Inequalities' Impacts (GINI), 2012. http://gini-research.org/system/ uploads/437/original/Baltics.pdf?1370077200.

Matsnev, Oleg. 'Aides to Russian Opposition Leader Sentenced to Jail'. *The New York Times*, 31 January 2018, sec. World. https://www.nytimes. com/2018/01/31/world/europe/navalny-russia-aides-jail.html.

McFaul, Michael, Stephen Sestanovich and John J. Mearsheimer. 'Faulty Powers', *Foreign Affairs*, 28 October 2014. https://www.foreignaffairs.com/articles/ eastern-europe-caucasus/2014-10-17/faulty-powers.

McGuinness, Damien. 'How a Cyber Attack Transformed Estonia', 27 April 2017, sec. Europe. https://www.bbc.com/news/39655415.

Mearsheimer, John J. 'Why the Ukraine Crisis Is the West's Fault', *Foreign Affairs*, October 2014. https://www.foreignaffairs.com/articles/russia-fsu/2014-08-18/why-ukraine-crisis-west-s-fault.

Meduza. 'Welcome to Meduza Russia's Top News and Reporting, in English'. Meduza, 2 February 2015. https://meduza.io/en/feature/2015/02/02/ welcome-to-meduza.

Meduza. 'Riga Mayor Is Fined for Using Russian on Social Media'. Meduza, 27 July 2016. https://meduza.io/en/news/2016/07/27/latvian-mayor-is-fined-for-using-russian-on-social-media.

Meister, Stefan. 'The "Lisa Case": Germany as a Target of Russian Disinformation'. *NATO Review*, 2016. http://www.nato.int/docu/ review/2016/Also-in-2016/lisa-case-germany-target-russian-disinformation/ EN/index.htm.

Meri, Lennart. 'President of the Republic at the XXIII All-Estonian Song Festival on July 3, 1999', n.d. https://vp1992-2001.president.ee/eng/k6ned/ K6ne.asp?ID=4285.

Ministry of Foreign Affairs of Denmark, 'Baltic Sea Cooperation', Ministry of Foreign Affairs of Denmark http://um.dk/en/foreign-policy/baltic-sea-cooperation/.

Milne, Richard. 'Baltics Fear for Any US Policy Changes to Nato'. *The Financial Times*, 12 November 2016. https://www.ft.com/content/0036b09a-a825-11e6-8898-79a99e2a4de6.

Milne, Richard and Henry Foy. 'Russian-built nuclear plant revives Chernobyl fears', *The Financial Times*, 18 September 2017. https://www.ft.com/content/ a98322de-96f7-11e7-b83c-9588e51488a0.

Minorities at Risk Project. 'Assessment for Russians in Lithuania'. University of Maryland, 31 December 2006. http://www.mar.umd.edu/assessment. asp?groupId=36802.

Mirsky, Jonathan. 'The Full Horror of the Siege of Leningrad Is Finally Revealed'. *The Spectator*, 31 December 2016. https://www.spectator.co.uk/2016/12/ the-full-horror-of-the-siege-of-leningrad-is-finally-revealed/.

Molis, Arunas. 'Towards a Regional Gas Market in the Baltic States: Political, Economic and Legal Aspects'. *Humanities and Social Sciences Latvia* 24:1, Spring–Summer 2016.

Moody, Oliver. 'Merkel and Macron Sign Aachen Treaty to Protect Ideals of Europe', *The Times*, 22 January 2019. https://www.thetimes.co.uk/edition/

news/merkel-and-macron-sign-aachen-treaty-to-protect-ideals-of-europe-md902t2kq.

Morello, Carol. 'Top Diplomat for European Affairs Resigns from State Department'. *The Washington Post*, 22 January 2019. https://www. washingtonpost.com/world/national-security/top-diplomat-for-european-affairs-resigns-from-state-department/2019/01/22/ada80048-1e3f-11e9-8b59-0a28f2191131_story.html.

Muiznieks, Nils, Juris Rozenvalds and Ieva Birka. 'Ethnicity and Social Cohesion in the Post-Soviet Baltic States'. *Patterns of Prejudice* 47, no. 3. 1 July 2013. https://doi.org/10.1080/0031322X.2013.812349.

Nardelli, Alberto, Jennifer Rankin, and George Arnett. 'Vladimir Putin's Approval Rating at Record Levels'. *The Guardian*, 23 July 2015, sec. World news. https://www.theguardian.com/world/datablog/2015/jul/23/vladimir-putins-approval-rating-at-record-levels.

National Public Radio (NPR). 'If You Think Wealth Disparity Is Bad Here, Look at Russia'. NPR.org, 10 October 2013. https://www.npr.org/sections/parallels/2013/10/10/231446353/if-you-think-wealth-disparity-is-bad-here-look-at-russia.

NATO. 'Official Text: Bucharest Summit Declaration'. North Atlantic Treaty Organization, 3 April 2008.

Naylor, Aliide. 'Estonian Foreign Minister Cautious but Calm on Relations with Russia'. *The Moscow Times*, 18 October 2015. https://www.themoscowtimes. com/2015/10/18/estonian-foreign-minister-cautious-but-calm-on-relations-with-russia-a50332.

Naylor, Aliide. 'Trump, Russia and the New Geopolitics of the Baltics'. *New Eastern Europe*, 30 January 2017. http://neweasterneurope.eu/2017/01/30/trump-russia-and-the-new-geopolitics-of-the-baltics/.

Naylor, Aliide. 'Russian Media Paint Dark Picture of Montenegro'. Balkan Insight (blog), 19 April 2017. https://balkaninsight.com/2017/04/19/russian-media-turn-hostile-gaze-on-montenegro-04-13-2017/.

Naylor, Aliide. 'All Quiet on the Eastern Front'. Politico Europe, 12 September 2017. https://www.politico.eu/article/eastern-front-zapad-military-exercises-russia-lithuania-belarus/.

Naylor, Aliide. 'Russia's Reaction to The Death of Stalin Shows Its Changing Attitudes towards Him'. *New Statesman*, 23 October 2017. https://www. newstatesman.com/culture/film/2017/10/russia-s-reaction-death-stalin-shows-its-changing-attitudes-towards-him.

Naylor, Aliide. 'Latvia's Kuš! Comics Turns Ten'. *New Eastern Europe*, 12 December 2017. http://neweasterneurope.eu/2017/12/12/latvias-kus-comics-turns-ten/.

Naylor, Aliide. 'Soviet power gone, Baltic countries' historic pagan past re-emerges', Religion News Service, 31 May 2019. https://religionnews. com/2019/05/31/with-soviet-power-gone-baltic-countries-historic-pagan-past-re-emerges/.

Nayyem, Mustafa and Svitlana Zalishchuk. 'Statement of Mustafa Nayyem and Svitlana Zalishchuk, Members of the Parliament of Ukraine before the Subcommittee on Department of State, Foreign Operations, and Related

Programs of the Senate Committee on Appropriations', 2017. https://www.appropriations.senate.gov/imo/media/doc/032917-Nayyem-Zalishchuk-Outside-Witness-Testimony.pdf.

NBC News. 'Baltic States Fear Putin Amid Escalation in Ukraine'. NBC News, 2 September 2014. https://www.nbcnews.com/storyline/ukraine-crisis/baltic-states-fear-putin-amid-escalation-ukraine-n193326.

Nesaule, Agate. *A Woman in Amber: Healing the Trauma of War and Exile*. New York: Penguin, 1997.

Nestor, Madis. 'Uus Eesti Biit: Tommy Cash'. Müürileht, 6 June 2013. https://www.muurileht.ee/uus-eesti-biit-tommy-cash/.

Nikolai, Mezhevich. 'Russia and the Baltic States: Some Results and a Few Perspectives'. *Baltic Region*, 2:24, 2015. https://cyberleninka.ru/article/n/russia-and-the-baltic-states-some-results-and-a-few-perspectives.

Noll, Andreas and Ralf Bosen. 'Merkel and Macron Sign Treaty of Aachen to Revive EU | DW | 22.01.2019'. DW.COM, 22 January 2019. https://www.dw.com/en/merkel-and-macron-sign-treaty-of-aachen-to-revive-eu/a-47172186.

Nollendorfs, Valters, and Uldis Neiburgs. 'The Holocaust in German-Occupied Latvia', Ministry of Foreign Affairs of the Republic of Latvia: Briefing papers of the Museum of the Occupation of Latvia, 16 August 2004. https://www.mfa.gov.lv/en/policy/development-co-operation/789-briefing-papers/5259-the-holocaust-in-german-occupied-latvia.

NPR. 'Estonian President Says Russia's Show of Force Raises Issues Of "Transparency, Trust"'. NPR.org, 22 September 2017. https://www.npr.org/2017/09/22/552986956/estonian-president-says-russias-show-of-force-raises-issues-of-transparency-trus.

Oberländer, Erwin. 'Soviet Genocide in Latvia? Conflicting Cultures of Remembrance of Stalin's Policy, 1940–1953', in Martyn Housden and David J. Smith (eds.), *Forgotten Pages in Baltic History: Diversity and Inclusion*. Amsterdam: Rodopi B.V., 2011.

OCCRP. 'Latvian Bank Was Laundering Tool'. https://www.reportingproject.net/therussianlaundromat/latvian-bank-was-laundering-tool.php.

O'Connor, Kevin. *Culture and Customs of the Baltic States (Culture and Customs of Europe)*. Westport, Conn: Greenwood Press, 2006.

Oliphant, Roland. 'Photos Show Dramatic Near Miss of Russian and US Jets in "Dangerous" Interception Over Baltic Sea'. *The Telegraph*, 23 June 2017. https://www.telegraph.co.uk/news/2017/06/23/photos-show-dramatic-near-miss-russian-us-jets-dangerous-interception/.

Oliphant, Roland. 'Viktor Yanukovych Leaves behind Palace Monument to Greed and Corruption', *The Telegraph*, 23 February 2014, sec. World. https://www.telegraph.co.uk/news/worldnews/europe/ukraine/10657109/Viktor-Yanukovych-leaves-behind-palace-monument-to-greed-and-corruption.html.

Oneworld. 'I'm Going to Ruin Their Lives: Inside Putin's war on Russia's Opposition', Oneworld (25 February 2016).

O'Neill, Sean. 'Putin Crony Arkady Rotenberg Loses Right to Secrecy in Britain'. The Times, 24 February 2018, sec. News. https://www.thetimes.co.uk/article/putin-crony-arkady-rotenberg-loses-right-to-secrecy-in-britain-9gbl8x8rg.

Palveleva, Lilya. 'Russian Museum Celebrating Stalin Slated to Open for Victory Day'. RadioFreeEurope/RadioLiberty, 18 March 2015. https://www.rferl. org/a/russia-stalin-museum/26907807.html.

Pavlenko, Aneta (ed), *Multilingualism in Post-Soviet Countries*, Bristol: Multilingual Matters, 2008.

Passport Magazine. 'Baltic Seeing: Estonia, Latvia, Lithuania', *Passport Magazine*, n.d. https://passportmagazine.com/baltic-seeing-estonia-latvia-lithuania/.

PC Mag. 'Toggl'. *PC Mag UK*, 7 February 2018. https://uk.pcmag.com/ productivity-2/93243/toggl.

Peleschuk, Dan. 'The Migrant Leading Lithuania's Fintech Sector'. OZY, 24 November 2017. http://www.ozy.com/the-migrant-leading-lithuanias-fintech-sector/81467.

Peterson, Nolan. 'Russia Field-Tested Hybrid Warfare in Ukraine. Why That Matters for US'. *The Daily Signal*, 27 October 2017. https://www.dailysignal. com/2017/10/27/russia-field-tested-hybrid-warfare-ukraine-cyberthreat-matters-us/.

Petsinis, Vassilis and Stefano Braghiroli. 'Estonia's Populist and Radical Right: How Radical Are They?' openDemocracy, 18 December 2018. https://www. opendemocracy.net/en/can-europe-make-it/estonia-s-populist-and-radical-right-how-rad/.

Pettai, Vello. 'The Baltic States: Still a Single Political Model?' unpublished conference paper for 'The Fall of Communism: Ten Years On', Mayrock Center, Hebrew University Jerusalem, Israel, 2001.

Pew Research. 'Eastern and Western Europeans Differ on Importance of Religion, Views of Minorities, and Key Social Issues | Pew Research Center', 29 October 2018. https://www.pewforum.org/2018/10/29/eastern-and-western-europeans-differ-on-importance-of-religion-views-of-minorities-and-key-social-issues/.

Phillips, Leigh. 'EU Rejects Eastern States' Call to Outlaw Denial of Crimes by Communist Regimes'. *The Guardian*, 21 December 2010. https://www. theguardian.com/world/2010/dec/21/european-commission-communist-crimes-nazism.

Piirsalu, Jaanus. 'Russian Warplanes Cannot Switch on Transponders'. *Postimees*, 6 September 2016. https://news.postimees.ee/3826371/russian-warplanes-cannot-switch-on-transponders.

Plakans, Andrejs. 'From a Regional Vernacular to the Language of a State: The Case of Latvian', *International Journal of the Sociology of Language*, 100:101, 1993. http://home.lu.lv/~pva/Sociolingvistika/Plakans_From%20a%20 regional%20vernacular_1993.pdf.

Plakans, Andrejs. *A Concise History of the Baltic States*. Cambridge Concise Histories. Cambridge: Cambridge University Press, 2011.

Poissonnier, Aurélien. 'The Baltics: Three Countries, One Economy?' In European Commission: Economic Brief 024, 2017.

Politkovskaïa, Anna. *A Small Corner of Hell: Dispatches from Chechnya.* Chicago: University of Chicago Press, 2003.

Pomerantsev, Peter. 'Inside the Kremlin's Hall of Mirrors'. *The Guardian*, 9 April 2015, sec. News. https://www.theguardian.com/news/2015/apr/09/kremlin-hall-of-mirrors-military-information-psychology.

Pommereau, Isabelle de. 'Estonia reaches out to its very own Russians at long last'. Deutsche Welle, 24 February 2018. http://www.dw.com/en/estonia-reaches-out-to-its-very-own-russians-at-long-last/a-42680725.

Pörzgen, Yvonne. 'Siege Memory – Besieged Memory? Heroism and Suffering in St Petersburg Museums Dedicated to the Siege of Leningrad'. *Museum and Society* 14, no. 3, 9 June 2017. https://doi.org/10.29311/mas.v14i3.654.

Prilenska, Viktorija and Roode Liias. 'Challenges of Recent Participatory Urban Design Practices in Riga'. *Procedia Economics and Finance*, 8th Nordic Conference on Construction Economics and Organization, 21, 1 January 2015. https://doi.org/10.1016/S2212-5671(15)00154-9.

Propastop. 'A Child Removed from Her Family Is Used for Propaganda Accusations'. Propastop, 25 July 2017. https://www.propastop.org/eng/2017/07/25/a-child-removed-from-her-family-is-used-for-propaganda-accusations/.

Putin Knew What to Do! His First Interview, 2000, 2000. https://www.youtube.com/watch?v=EjU8Fg3NFmo.

Radcheva, Elena and Viktoria Odissonova. 'Обиды ненайденных дедов'. Новая газета – Novayagazeta.ru, 17 May 2017. https://www.novayagazeta.ru/articles/2017/05/17/72469-obidy-nenaydennyh-dedov.

Raik, Kristi. 'The Rise of Estonia's Radical Right: To Engage or Not to Engage?' ECFR, 15 October 2018. https://www.ecfr.eu/article/commentary_the_rise_of_estonias_radical_right_to_engage_or_not_to_engage.

Ramm, Aleksey. 'Боевые дайверы Росгвардии защитят мост в Крым', *Izvestia*, 9 September 2016, https://iz.ru/news/631455.

RAND. 'Reinforcing Deterrence on NATO's Eastern Flank: Wargaming the Defense of the Baltics'. S.l.: RAND Corporation., 2016.

Rannut, Mart. 'Estonianization Efforts Post-Independence', in Aneta Pavlenko (ed), *Multilingualism in Post-Soviet Countries*. Bristol: Multilingual Matters, 2008.

Rasulov, Vladimir. 'Расходы На Оборону Вырастут'. Коммерсантъ, 8 October 2017. https://www.kommersant.ru/doc/3433783.

Raun, Toivo. 'Baltic Independence, 1917–1920 and 1988–1994: Comparative perspectives'. The National Council for Soviet and East European Research. Indiana University, 30 June 1994. https://www.ucis.pitt.edu/nceeer/1994-808-12-Raun.pdf.

Razaq, Rashid. 'Pussy Riot Member to Bring Horror of Siberian Prisons to King's Road'. *Evening Standard*, 29 September 2017. https://www.standard.co.uk/go/london/arts/pussy-riot-cofounder-nadya-tolokonnikova-to-recreate-siberian-prison-camp-at-the-saatchi-gallery-a3646631.html.

Re:Baltica. 'Who Has a Second Base in Latvia? | Re:Baltica', 22 February 2015. https://en.rebaltica.lv/2015/02/who-has-a-second-base-in-latvia/.

Reid, Anna. 'Myth and Tragedy at the Siege of Leningrad – Gallery'. *The Guardian*, 15 September 2011, sec. Books. https://www.theguardian.com/books/gallery/2011/sep/15/siege-leningrad-history-anna-reid.

Reuters. 'Chef Martins Ritins Brings Top Cuisine to Small Latvia'. Reuters, 9 December 2008. https://uk.reuters.com/article/us-food-chefs-ritins-idUKTRE4B82BY20081209.

Reuters. 'Disquiet in Baltics over Sympathies of Russian Speakers'. Reuters, 24 March 2014. https://www.reuters.com/article/us-ukraine-crisis-russia-insight-idUSBREA2K07S20140324.

Reuters. 'Phantom Voters, Smuggled Ballots Hint at Foul Play in Russian Vote'. Reuters, 20 September 2016. https://www.reuters.com/article/us-russia-election-fraud-idUSKCN11Q1RI.

Reuters. 'Resettled in the Baltics, Refugees Flee for Wealthier Lands'. Reuters, 28 November 2016. https://www.reuters.com/article/us-europe-migrants-baltics-idUSKBN13N0RY.

Reuters. 'Lithuania Looking for Source of False Accusation of Rape by German Troops'. Reuters, 17 February 2017. https://www.reuters.com/article/us-lithuania-nato-idUSKBN15W1JO.

Reuters. 'Baltic States Agree to Link Their Power Grids to EU Via Poland'. VOA, 8 May 2017. https://www.voanews.com/a/baltic-states-to-link-power-grids-to-eu-via-poland/3843362.html.

Reuters. 'Lithuania Receives First LNG from the United States'. Reuters, 21 August 2017. https://www.reuters.com/article/us-lithuania-lng-idUSKCN1B11BW.

Reuters. 'Russia May Have Tested Cyber Warfare on Latvia, Western Officials Say'. Reuters, 5 October 2017. https://uk.reuters.com/article/us-russia-nato-idUKKBN1CA142.

RFE/RL. 'Latvian Singers, Conductors Stealing Global Spotlight, Thanks To Soviet Legacy'. RadioFreeEurope/RadioLiberty, 16 August 2015. https://www.rferl.org/a/latvia-music-education-spotlight-singers-conductors/27191520.html.

RFE/RL. 'Diverging Demographics'. RadioFreeEurope/RadioLiberty, 2016. https://www.rferl.org/a/27927989.html.

Righton, Natalie. 'Sie Dhian Ho: "Rutte heeft meer nodig dan de zeven dwergen"', de Volkskrant, 7 September 2018. https://www.volkskrant.nl/nieuws-achtergrond/sie-dhian-ho-rutte-heeft-meer-nodig-dan-de-zeven-dwergen-~bea8ddb3/.

Romanova, Tatiana. 'LNG in the Baltic Sea Region in the Context of EU-Russian Relations'. BSR Policy Briefing 1, 2015.

Roonemaa, Holger. 'These Cigarette Smugglers Are on the Frontlines of Russia's Spy Wars'. BuzzFeed News, 13 September 2017. https://www.buzzfeednews.com/article/holgerroonemaa/these-cigarette-smugglers-are-on-the-frontlines-of-russias.

Rospopina, Sasha. 'How Space Travel Replaced Religion in USSR'. The Guardian, 17 September 2015, sec. World. https://www.theguardian.com/world/2015/sep/17/ussr-space-exploration-religion-russia.

Rouillard, Rémy. 'Between East and West Is North: The Loyalties and Allegiances of Russian Authors and Painters Living in EU Estonia'. Journal of Multilingual and Multicultural Development 26:5, 2005.

Rountree, Kathryn, ed. *Contemporary Pagan and Native Faith Movements in Europe: Colonialist and Nationalist Impulses*. EASA Series, vol. 26. New York: Berghahn, 2015.

RT. '"Medieval Barbarism": Riga Mayor Decries Fine for Use of Russian on Official Facebook Account'. RT International, 27 February 2017. https://www.rt.com/news/378811-riga-mayor-russian-language-facebook/.

Rummel, R.J. *Lethal Politics: Soviet Genocide and Mass Murder Since 1917*. New York: Routledge, [1990] 2017.

Russell, Alison Lawlor. *Cyber Blockades*. Washington DC: Georgetown University Press, 2014.

Rybakovsky, Leonid and Sergey Ryazantsev. 'International Migration in the Russian Federation'. United Nations Expert Group Meeting on International Migration and Development, 5 July 2005.

Sander, Gordon F. 'Latvia, a Disappearing Nation'. Politico, 5 January 2018. https://www.politico.eu/article/latvia-a-disappearing-nation-migration-population-decline/.

Salzen, Claudia von. 'Estonia Urges Caution on Nord Stream 2 Pipeline'. Euractiv.Com (blog), 18 July 2017. https://www.euractiv.com/section/energy/news/estonia-urges-caution-on-nord-stream-2-pipeline/.

Sargs.lv. 'Drošības Un Stratēģiskās Pētniecības Centrs: Krievijas Ietekme Latvijā Ir Ierobežota'. Sargs.lv, 20 June 2016. http://www.sargs.lv/Viedokli/2016/06/20-01.

Satversmes Aizsardzības Birojs (SAB). 'SAB 2015: Gada Darbības Pārskats', 2015. http://www.sab.gov.lv/files/2015_parskats.pdf.

Saunders, Paul. 'Sergey Lavrov: The Interview'. Text. *The National Interest*, 29 March 2017. https://nationalinterest.org/feature/sergey-lavrov-the-interview-19940.

Savranskaya, Svetlana and Tom Blanton. 'NATO Expansion: What Gorbachev Heard', 12 December 2017. https://nsarchive.gwu.edu/briefing-book/russia-programs/2017-12-12/nato-expansion-what-gorbachev-heard-western-leaders-early.

Schaack, Beth van. 'The Crime of Political Genocide: Repairing the Genocide Convention's Blind Spot'. *The Yale Law Journal* 106, no. 7, May 1997. https://doi.org/10.2307/797169.

Shlapak, David A. and Michael W. Johnson. 'Reinforcing Deterrence on NATO's Eastern Flank'. RAND Corporation, 2016. https://www.rand.org/content/dam/rand/pubs/research_reports/RR1200/RR1253/RAND_RR1253.pdf.

Schultz, Teri. 'NATO Says More Russian Buzzing of Baltic Airspace a Risk for Deadly Mistakes | DW | 27.06.2017'. DW.COM, 27 June 2017. https://www.dw.com/en/nato-says-more-russian-buzzing-of-baltic-airspace-a-risk-for-deadly-mistakes/a-39440788.

Schultz, Teri. 'Stealthy Sleuths: Lithuania Calls for "Cyber Schengen" Zone'. Deutsche Welle, 28 February 2018. https://www.dw.com/en/stealthy-sleuths-lithuania-calls-for-cyber-schengen-zone/a-42769925.

Schwab, Katharine. 'A Country Created Through Music'. *The Atlantic*, 12 November 2015. https://www.theatlantic.com/international/archive/2015/11/estonia-music-singing-revolution/415464/.

Senn, Alfred Erich. 'The Sovietization of the Baltic States'. *The Annals of the American Academy of Political and Social Science*, 317, no. 1, May 1958. https://doi.org/10.1177/000271625831700116.

Sepp, Kalev. The Estonian Green Belt. Tallinn: The Estonian University of Life Sciences, 2011. http://citeseerx.ist.psu.edu/viewdoc/download?doi=10.1.1.46 5.5277&rep=rep1&type=pdf.

Sherr, James. 'The Baltic States in Russian Military Strategy'. Security in the Baltic Sea Region: Realities and Prospects. *The Rīga Conference Papers 2017*, September 2017.

Shipman, Tim. *Fall Out: A Year of Political Mayhem*. London: William Collins, 2017.

Shtromas, Aleksandras. 'The Baltic States as Soviet Republics: Tensions and Contradictions', in Graham Smith (ed), *The Baltic States: The National Self-Determination of Estonia, Latvia and Lithuania*. Basingstoke: Macmillan Press Ltd., 1996.

Shtromas, Alexander, Robert K. Faulkner and Daniel J. Mahoney. *Totalitarianism and the Prospects for World Order: Closing the Door on the Twentieth Century. Applications of Political Theory*. Lanham, Md: Lexington Books, 2003.

Simon, Matt. 'San Francisco Tries to Ban Delivery Robots Before They Flatten Someone's Toes'. *Wired*, 17 May 2017. https://www.wired.com/2017/05/san-francisco-wants-ban-delivery-robots-squash-someones-toes/.

Sköns, Elisabeth. 'Russian Military Expenditure, Reform and Restructuring | SIPRI'. Stockholm International Peace Research Institute (SIPRI). Oxford University Press, July 2013. https://www.sipri.org/yearbook/2013/03.

Smith, Rowena. 'Tabula Rasa Review – Ambitious Staged Work Suffused with Arvo Pärt's Mystical Music'. *The Guardian*, 10 November 2017, sec. Music. https://www.theguardian.com/music/2017/nov/10/tabula-rasa-review-arvo-part-traverse-theatre.

Smogorzewski, Casimir. 'The Russification of the Baltic States'. *World Affairs*, 4 (1950).

Snyder, Timothy and Simas Čelutka. 'Taking Bad Ideas Seriously'. *Eurozine*, 28 August 2017. https://www.eurozine.com/taking-bad-ideas-seriously/.

Sperling, Valerie. *Sex, Politics, and Putin: Political Legitimacy in Russia (Oxford Studies in Culture and Politics)*. Oxford: Oxford University Press, 2015.

Spiegel Online. 'Spiegel Interview with Estonian President Toomas Hendrik Ilves: "We Want to Re-Write History"'. Spiegel Online, 26 June 2007, sec. International. https://www.spiegel.de/international/europe/spiegel-interview-with-estonian-president-toomas-hendrik-ilves-we-want-to-re-write-history-a-490811-2.html.

Spokesperson. 'Inclusion of the Levada Centre in the "Foreign Agents Registry" of the Russian Federation'. European External Action Service, 6 September 2016. https://eeas.europa.eu/headquarters/headquarters-homepage_en/9497.

Springe, Inga and Sanita Jemberga. 'Russians Moving to Latvia: Dream or Nightmare?' OCCRP, 12 March 2015. https://www.occrp.org/en/investigations/3754-russians-moving-to-latvia-dream-or-nightmare.

Sputnik. 'Посольство РФ: В Ситуации с Беллой Михайловой Держим Руку На Пульсе'. Sputnik, 17 July 2017. https://ee.sputniknews.ru/

society/20170717/6481491/posoljstvo-eref-situatsija-bela-mihailova-derzhim-ruka-puljs.html.

State Chancellery of Latvia. 'Towards the State of Latvia: Barricades of January 1991 and their role in restoring Latvia's independence', LV100, 2018. https://www.mk.gov.lv/sites/default/files/editor/barikades_eng.pdf.

Statista. 'TV Audience Market Share – Estonia 2013'. Statista. Accessed 11 May 2019. https://www.statista.com/statistics/482903/tv-audience-market-share-in-estonia/.

Statistics Latvia. http://data.csb.gov.lv.

Šteinfelde, Ilze. 'Saldā cukura rūgtā cena – ko maksājusi mums ES cukura reforma?' nra.lv, 4 October 2017. https://nra.lv/latvija/224383-salda-cukura-rugta-cena-ko-maksajusi-mums-es-cukura-reforma.htm.

Stepanov, Sergei. 'Krenholm Plans More Layoffs'. *The Baltic Times*, 12 February 2004. https://www.baltictimes.com/news/articles/9459/.

Stratfor, 'Despite Looming U.S. Sanctions, the Nord Stream 2 Pipeline Will Likely Proceed', Stratfor, 17 July 2019. https://worldview.stratfor.com/article/despite-looming-us-sanctions-nord-stream-2-pipeline-will-likely-proceed.

Strmiska, Michael. 'The Music of the Past in Modern Baltic Paganism'. Nova Religio: *The Journal of Alternative and Emergent Religions* 8:3, March 2005. https://doi.org/10.1525/nr.2005.8.3.39.

'Subscribe to Read'. *Financial Times*. Accessed 13 April 2019. https://www.ft.com/content/0036b09a-a825-11e6-8898-79a99e2a4de6?mhq5j=e7.

Svetova, Zoya. 'Политтехнолог Всея Руси. Владислав Сурков – Человек с Тысячью Лиц'. *The New Times*, 7 March 2011. https://newtimes.ru/articles/detail/35589.

Swedish Agency for Economic and Regional Growth, 'The Baltic Sea Region Strategy for Beginners', Swedish Agency for Economic and Regional Growth, 2016. https://www.balticsea-region-strategy.eu/news-room/documents-materials?task=document.viewdoc&id=26.

Sytas, Andrius. 'Baltic States Agree to Link Their Power Grids to EU Via Poland', VOA, 8 May 2017. https://af.reuters.com/article/worldNews/idAFKBN1841T4.

Sytas, Andrius and Gederts Gelzis. 'Baltics Keep Fingers Crossed That Trump Won't Keep His Campaign Pledges', Reuters, 9 November 2016. https://www.reuters.com/article/usa-election-baltics-idUSL8N1DA597.

Sytas, Andrius and Gederts Gelzis. 'Resettled in the Baltics, refugees flee for wealthier lands', Reuters, 28 November 2016. https://www.reuters.com/article/us-europe-migrants-baltics/resettled-in-the-baltics-refugees-flee-for-wealthier-lands-idUSKBN13N0RY.

Tammaru, Tiit, Kadri Leetmaa and Rein Ahas. 'Temporal and Spatial Dynamics of the New Residential Areas around Tallinn'. *European Planning Studies* 17:3 (n.d.).

Tamm, Marek, Henry of Livonia, Linda Kaljundi and Carsten Selch Jensen (eds.). *Crusading and Chronicle Writing on the Medieval Baltic Frontier: A Companion to the Chronicle of Henry of Livonia*. Farnham, Surrey: Ashgate, 2011.

Tamtik, Merli and Soon Young Jang. 'Administering Higher Education Policies in the Baltic States: Balancing the Language Demands in Multilingual Society'. *Journal of Multilingual and Multicultural Development*, 2018.

Tarasiewicz, Stanisław. 'Rosjanie Kłajpedy Również Chcą Podwójnych Nazw Ulic'. *Kurier Wileński*, 30 January 2013. https://kurierwilenski.lt/2013/01/30/rosjanie-klajpedy-rowniez-chca-podwojnych-nazw-ulic/.

TASS. 'Shell May Invest in Nord Stream-2 to Improve Europe's Energy Security'. TASS, 2 February 2017. http://tass.com/economy/928641.

TASS. 'Latvian Government Endorses Reform of Russian-language Schools'. TASS, 23 January 2018. http://tass.com/society/986468.

TASS. 'СМИ: У Семьи Грудинина Имеется Недвижимость в Латвии'. TASS, 20 February 2018. https://tass.ru/politika/4974577.

TASS. 'About 1,000 in Central Riga Rally Against Reform of Russian-language Schools'. TASS, 24 February 2018. http://tass.com/society/991446.

TASS. 'Putin Confesses He Would Have Liked to Prevent USSR Breakup If He Could'. TASS, 3 March 2018. http://tass.com/politics/992609.

TASS. 'Bill Against Russian Language in Latvian Schools Passed in Second Reading'. TASS, 9 March 2018. http://tass.com/society/993327.

Teabeamet. 'International Security and Estonia'. Estonian Information Board (Teabeamet), 2016. https://www.valisluureamet.ee/pdf/2016-en.pdf.

Tharoor, Ishaan. 'Don't Forget How the Soviet Union Saved the World from Hitler'. *The Washington Post*, 8 May 2015. https://www.washingtonpost.com/news/worldviews/wp/2015/05/08/dont-forget-how-the-soviet-union-saved-the-world-from-hitler.

The Baltic Course-Балтийский курс. 'In Latvia TV3 Remains Most Popular TV Channel'. The Baltic Course | Baltic States news & analytics, 5 August 2014. http://www.baltic-course.com/eng/good_for_business/?doc=94707.

The Baltic Course. 'In Latvia TV3 Remains Most Popular TV Channel'. The Baltic Course | Baltic States news & analytics. Accessed 11 May 2019. http://www.baltic-course.com/eng/good_for_business/?doc=94707.

The Baltic Course-Балтийский курс. 'PBK TV Channel Appeals EUR 10,000 Fine Imposed by Latvia's Broadcasting Watchdog'. The Baltic Course | Baltic States news & analytics, 23 February 2016. http://www.baltic-course.com/eng/markets_and_companies/?doc=117096.

The Baltic Course, 'Cheaper business opportunities probably lead to Barclays' decision in Lithuania', The Baltic Course. 23 April 2018. http://www.baltic-course.com/eng/Technology/?doc=139500.

The Baltic Times. 'Incumbent Reform Party Wins Estonian Parliamentary Elections', 2 March 2015. https://www.baltictimes.com/incumbent_reform_party_wins_estonian_parliamentary_elections/.

The Baltic Times. 'Russian-Language First Baltic Channel Most Fined TV Station in Latvia Last Year', 27 April 2015. https://www.baltictimes.com/russian-language_first_baltic_channel_most_fined_tv_station_in_latvia_last_year/.

The Economist. 'A Cyber-Riot'. *The Economist*, 10 May 2007. https://www.economist.com/europe/2007/05/10/a-cyber-riot.

The Economist. 'A Minister Comes Out'. *The Economist*, 12 November 2014. https://www.economist.com/ eastern-approaches/2014/11/12/a-minister-comes-out.

The Economist. 'Putin's War on the West'. *The Economist*, 12 February 2015. https://www.economist.com/leaders/2015/02/12/putins-war-on-the-west.

The Economist. 'How the Baltic States Resist Russia'. *The Economist*, 31 January 2019.

The Mercury News. 'Sidewalk Robots Smacked down in S.F. Coming to San Jose'. *The Mercury News* (blog), 16 April 2018. https://www.mercurynews. com/2018/04/16/sidewalk-robots-smacked-down-in-s-f-coming-to-san-jose-company/.

The Moscow Times. 'Highest Average Salary in Russia Is in Gas-Rich Siberian Town'. *The Moscow Times*, 13 April 2015. https://www.themoscowtimes. com/2015/04/13/highest-average-salary-in-russia-is-in-gas-rich-siberian-town-a45713.

The Moscow Times, 'Russia's Skeptical Youth is Getting a Kremlin News Site', 8 November 2017, https://themoscowtimes.com/news/the-kremlin-is-launching-a-news-site-for-teenagers-59508.

The Moscow Times. 'Generation P'. *The Moscow Times*, 2018. https://generationp. themoscowtimes.com/.

The New York Times. 'Transcript: Donald Trump on NATO, Turkey's Coup Attempt and the World'. *The New York Times*, 21 July 2016, sec. U.S. https:// www.nytimes.com/2016/07/22/us/politics/donald-trump-foreign-policy-interview.html.

The White Guide. 'There Is No Better Time than NOW to Visit Baltic Restaurants | White Guide', 29 November 2017. http://whiteguide-nordic. com/nyheter/there-is-no-better-time-than-now-to-visit-baltic-restaurants.

Tomkinson, Martin and Cole Moreton. 'The Missing Multi-Millionaire: A Cut-Throat Mystery for the New Cold'. *The Independent*, 11 May 2008. http:// www.independent.co.uk/news/world/europe/the-missing-multi-millionaire-a-cut-throat-mystery-for-the-new-cold-war-825920.html.

Traynor, Ian. 'Patriots or Nazi Collaborators? Latvians March to Commemorate SS Veterans'. *The Guardian*, 16 March 2010, sec. World news. https://www. theguardian.com/world/2010/mar/16/latvians-march-commemorate-ss-veterans.

Treisman, Daniel. 'Why Putin Took Crimea: The Gambler in the Kremlin'. *Foreign Affairs* 95, 2016.

Trenin, Dmitri. 'The Revival of the Russian Military: How Moscow Reloaded'. *Foreign Affairs* 95, 2016.

Troianovski, Anton. 'The Putin Generation.' *The Washington Post*, 9 March 2018. https://www.washingtonpost.com/news/world/wp/2018/03/09/feature/ russias-young-people-are-putins-biggest-fans/.

UNESCO. 'The Baltic Way'. 2008. http://www.balticway.net/uploads/ Booklet%20BALTIC%20WAY%20en%20fr%20ru.pdf.

United Nations, Department of Economic and Social Affairs (2015). 'Trends in International Migrant Stock: Migrants by Destination and Origin', United Nations database, POP/DB/MIG/Stock/Rev.2015.

UN Security Council (UNSC). 'Topic B: Cyberterrorism'. *Cleveland Council on World Affairs*, March 2014. https://www.ccwa.org/wp-content/uploads/2014/03/UNSC_Topic-B.docx.

UNIAN. 'Lavrov Blames NATO for Russian Aggression in Ukraine'. Ukrainian Independent Information Agency (UNIAN), 19 February 2018. https://www.unian.info/politics/10012331-lavrov-blames-nato-for-russian-aggression-in-ukraine.html.

Urtāns, Juris and Guntis Eniņš. 'Latvian Sandstone Caves as Cultural Phenomena'. *Journal of Baltic Studies* 32:1, March 2001. https://doi.org/10.1080/01629770000000251.

US-CERT. 'Russian Government Cyber Activity Targeting Energy and Other Critical Infrastructure Sectors', United States Computer Emergency Readiness Team. https://www.us-cert.gov/ncas/alerts/TA18-074A.

Utekhin, Ilia. 'Memories of Leningrad's Blockade: Testimonies from Two Generations'. Forum for Anthropology and Culture: Generations in Europe 4 (n.d.). http://anthropologie.kunstkamera.ru/files/pdf/eng004/eng4_utekhin.pdf.

Varlamov, Ilya. 'Ивангород – Нарва: Евросоюз На Том Берегу'. Varlamov.ru, 21 June 2017. https://varlamov.ru/2434012.html.

Västrik, Ergo-Hart, 'In Search of Genuine Religion: The Contemporary Estonian Maausulised Movement and Nationalist Discourse' in Kathryn Rountree (ed), *Contemporary Pagan and Native Faith Movements in Europe: Colonialist and Nationalist Impulses*. EASA Series, vol. 26. New York: Berghahn, 2015.

Velsker, Liis. 'Venemaa heaks luuranud Romanov juhtis salakaubaveo grupeeringut', *Postimees*, 23 February 2016. www.postimees.ee/3594319/venemaa-heaks-luuranud-romanov-juhtis-salakaubaveo-grupeeringut

Vero, Tacita. 'Many Ethnic Russians in Estonia Are Still Living in Post-Soviet Limbo'. *Slate Magazine*, 13 March 2017. https://slate.com/news_and_politics/2017/03/many_ethnic_russians_in_estonia_have_gray_passports_live_in_legal_limbo.html.

VOA. 'Opposition to Russia's Nord Stream Pipeline Growing in Eastern Europe'. RadioFreeEurope/RadioLiberty, 9 March 2018. https://www.rferl.org/a/opposition-growth-eastern-europe-russia-nord-stream-2-pipeline-germany-baltic-sea-lithuania-estonia-latvia/29087938.html.

Walker, Shaun. 'Ukraine's EU Trade Deal Will Be Catastrophic, Says Russia'. *The Guardian*, 22 September 2013, sec. World news. https://www.theguardian.com/world/2013/sep/22/ukraine-european-union-trade-russia.

WBUR. 'Latvian President Raimonds Vējonis On Security And Russia Tensions'. *Here & Now*. WBUR, 21 September 2017. https://www.wbur.org/hereandnow/2017/09/21/latvia-raimonds-vejonis-russia.

Webers, Harry. 'Van Hanzepaper naar Hanzepep[p]er', *Die Evolutie Gids* (n.d.) https://www.evolutiegids.nl.

Wei, Whitney. 'Meet "Kanye East," the Estonian Rapper Who Spoofs American Pop Culture', *Vogue* (24 January 2018). https://www.vogue.com/article/tommy-cash-kanye-east-west-estonia-rapper-pussy-money-weed-merch-yeezy-off-white-virgil-abloh-vetements-life-of-pablo-pavel.

Weiss, Michael. 'Back in the USSR'. Foreign Policy (blog). https://foreignpolicy.
com/2013/12/11/back-in-the-ussr/.

World Nuclear News. 'Ignalina 2 Free of Used Fuel', 27 February 2018. http://
www.world-nuclear-news.org/WR-Ignalina-2-free-of-used-fuel-27021802.
html.

World Population Review. 'Lithuania Population 2019 (Demographics, Maps,
Graphs)'. *World Population Review,* 2018. http://worldpopulationreview.com/
countries/lithuania-population/.

Wright, Helen. 'Narva Is Aiming to Become European Capital of Culture in
2024'. *Estonian World,* 1 February 2018. https://estonianworld.com/culture/
narva-aiming-become-european-capital-culture-2024/.

Zadeh, Joe. '"Is This for Real?" Meet Tommy Cash, the Surreal, Post-Soviet Rap
Sensation'. *The Guardian,* 19 June 2017, sec. Music. https://www.theguardian.
com/music/2017/jun/19/tommy-cash-surreal-post-soviet-rap-sensation.

Zake, Ieva. 'Politicians Versus Intellectuals in the Lustration Debates in
Transitional Latvia'. *Journal of Communist Studies and Transition Politics* 26,
no. 3, September 2010. https://doi.org/10.1080/13523279.2010.496327.

Zake, Ieva. '"The Secret Nazi Network" and Post-World War II Latvian Émigrés
in the United States'. *Journal of Baltic Studies* 41:1, March 2010. https://doi.
org/10.1080/01629770903525340.

Zerkal, Olena. 'NordStream 2 and Ukraine's and Europe's Interests', 15th YES
Annual Meeting, 15 September 2018.

ZNAK. 'Источник: Московских Студентов Сгоняют На Митинг-Концерт в
«Лужниках» в Поддержку Путина'. ZNAK, 26 February 2018. https://www.
znak.com/2018-02-26/istochnik_moskovskih_studentov_sgonyayut_na_
miting_koncert_v_luzhnikah_v_podderzhku_putina.

Zublin, Fiona. 'Why Folk Religions Are Booming in Lithuania'. OZY, 14
February 2018. http://www.ozy.com/fast-forward/in-lithuania-an-imagined-
link-to-india-is-strengthening/83397.

Вольтская, Татьяна. 'В Санкт-Петербурге журналиста Романа Захарова не
отключат от "прослушки"'. Радио Свобода, 19 August 2016. https://www.
svoboda.org/a/27933969.html.

Гузенкова, Тамара et al. 'Политика Евросоюза в Отношении Стран
Постсоветского Пространства в Контексте Евразийской Интеграции –
Перспективы'. Perspektivy, 8 July 2015. http://www.perspektivy.info/rus/
desk/politika_jevrosojuza_v_otnoshenii_stran_postsovetskogo_
prostranstva_v_kontekste_jevrazijskoj_integracii_2015-07-08.htm.

Дергачев, Владимир. 'Россияне Стали Лучше Относиться к ВЧК и КГБ'.
РБК, 21 February 2018. https://www.rbc.ru/politics/21/02/2018/5a8d59f49a
79471a70e186ba.

Захаров, Андрей, and Полина Русяева. '«Фабрика Троллей» Потратила На
Работу в США Около $2,3 Млн'. РБК, 17 October 2017. https://www.rbc.
ru/technology_and_media/17/10/2017/59e4eb7a9a79472577375776.

'Иван Лаврентьев – Михкелю Муттю: разговоры об автономии Нарвы
опасны'. Rus.Postimees.ee, 29 June 2017. https://rus.postimees.ee/4162273/
ivan-lavrentev-mihkelyu-muttyu-razgovory-ob-avtonomii-narvy-opasny.

Иванов, Вячеслав. 'Почему русские не хотят уезжать из Эстонии'. Новая газета, 6 February 2015. https://www.novayagazeta.ru/articles/2015/02/06/62945-chemodan-151-vokzal-133-i-obratno.

Миронова, Анастасия. '«Они Постоянно Говорят о Еде»'. Газета.Ru, 8 September 2017. https://www.gazeta.ru/comments/column/mironova/10874966.shtml.

Наргиз, Асадова. 'Интервью / Жизнь русских в Литве / Наргиз Асадова'. Эхо Москвы, 20 August 2013. https://echo.msk.ru/programs/linguafranca/1139146-echo/.

Носович, Александр. 'Директор ВЦИОМ: в странах Балтии боятся говорить о советском прошлом'. RuBaltic.Ru, 28 January 2014. https://www.rubaltic.ru/article/obrazovanie-i-nayka/direktor-vtsiom-v-stranakh-baltii-boyatsya-govorit-o-sovetskom-proshlom28012014/.

Носович, Александр. 'Литва вмешивается в российские выборы'. RuBaltic.Ru, 5 February 2018. https://www.rubaltic.ru/article/politika-i-obshchestvo/05022018-litva-vmeshivaetsya-v-rossiyskie-vybory/.

Рамм, Алексей. 'Боевые Дайверы Росгвардии Защитят Мост в Крым'. Известия, 9 September 2016. https://iz.ru/news/631455.

РБК. 'В Лондоне Исчезла Жена Леонида Рожецкина'. РБК, 23 September 2008. https://www.rbc.ru/society/23/09/2008/5703cf1c9a79473dc814923c.

Россия 24. 'Russian Forecaster Says Weather Is "excellent" for Bombing Syria – Video'. The Guardian, 5 October 2015, sec. World news. https://www.theguardian.com/world/video/2015/oct/05/russian-forecaster-says-weather-is-excellent-for-bombing-syria-video.

Туровский, Даниил. 'Грузить по полной программе Зачем госкорпорации понадобилась система для организации DDoS-атак. Репортаж Даниила Туровского'. Meduza, 3 September 2015. https://meduza.io/feature/2015/09/03/gruzit-po-polnoy-programme.

Фон Эггерт, Константин. 'Провидец Из Вильнюса'. The New Times, 17 October 2016. https://newtimes.ru/articles/detail/116605.

Эхо Москвы. 'Москвичам предложили поучаствовать в митинге-концерте в поддержку Владимира Путина за деньги'. Эхо Москвы, 28 February 2018. https://echo.msk.ru/news/2156366-echo.html.

INDEX